TRADING
BEYOND UNDERSTANDING

CURRENCIES

New Thinking for Financial Times

STEFAN EICH AND MARTIJN KONINGS, EDITORS

Trading
Beyond
Understanding

Machine Learning, Risk, and Markets

CHRISTIAN BORCH

STANFORD UNIVERSITY PRESS

Stanford, California

Stanford University Press
Stanford, California

Library of Congress Cataloging-in-Publication Data
Names: Borch, Christian, author.
Title: Trading beyond understanding : machine learning, risk, and markets / Christian
    Borch.
Other titles: Currencies (Series)
Description: Stanford, California : Stanford University Press, 2026. | Series: Currencies :
    new thinking for financial times | Includes bibliographical references and index.
Identifiers: LCCN 2025039505 (print) | LCCN 2025039506 (ebook) |
    ISBN 9781503636804 (cloth) | ISBN 9781503645523 (paperback) |
    ISBN 9781503645530 (ebook)
Subjects: LCSH: Artificial intelligence—Financial applications. | Artificial
    intelligence—Social aspects. | Machine learning—Social aspects.
Classification: LCC HG4515.5 .B675 2026 (print) | LCC HG4515.5 (ebook)
LC record available at https://lccn.loc.gov/2025039505
LC ebook record available at https://lccn.loc.gov/2025039506

Cover design: George Kirkpatrick

The authorized representative in the EU for product safety and compliance is: Mare
Nostrum Group B.V. | Mauritskade 21D | 1091 GC Amsterdam | The Netherlands | Email
address: gpsr@mare-nostrum.co.uk | KVK chamber of commerce number: 96249943

For Martha, Albert, and Susanne

Contents

ONE

Two Tales of the City

FRANK USED TO THRIVE IN the crowded, noisy grain pit at the Chicago Board of Trade, where he shouted out his orders to buy or sell grain, vying for his peers' attention and the chance to close profitable trades. Today, such pit trading, where traders physically jostle for space, has nearly vanished. Most financial exchanges in the US and Europe are now electronic, with the majority of buy and sell orders executed by fully automated computer systems. Some systems try to predict market movements months ahead, but many operate on far shorter timescales, hunting for profitable opportunities at speeds beyond human perception. This shift from pit to algorithm has fundamentally upended financial markets, transforming the skills and traits traders need. According to Frank, "The skill set you needed for being on the floor was more being an ex-football player, or a cop, or a fireman—kind of being big and willing to push people around and be loud." In contrast, automated trading demands mathematical acumen and a deep understanding of computer systems. While some math skills were useful on the trading floor—"My ability to multiply fractions in my head was useful on the floor, but that was about it," Frank recalls— math is now indispensable.

Despite these changes, unlike many of his former colleagues, Frank successfully transitioned from pit to automated trading. When I met him in 2018, he had traded the Windy City for another global financial hub, the City of London. There, he served as the head of trading at a smaller proprietary trading firm, or "prop shop"—a firm trading its own capital rather than clients'. As head of trading, Frank's job is to devise new strategies that can be automated through the firm's software and hardware infrastructure and to fine-tune the strategies already in place. Essentially, along with the rest of the trading team, Frank is the mastermind behind the trading decisions that the firm's computers execute in the markets: barring any technical glitches, whatever the firm's algorithms do is essentially decided by Frank and his colleagues, a direct extension of their financial expertise. At least, this is the ideal.

Meanwhile, across the City of London, just half a mile from Frank's office, Simon works in another prop shop that also specializes in automated trading. Simon's background is a study in contrasts: he graduated with a degree in computer science in 2007, focusing on machine learning (ML)—a field that was still a niche at the time. ML, the use of machines to identify patterns in large datasets and to provide actionable predictions on that basis, is at the heart of Simon's current role. Together with other ML experts at his firm, he is developing an automated trading system that can identify and capitalize on trading opportunities in the markets while continuously learning from its own trading behaviors. Unlike at Frank's firm, where humans dictate the trading strategies, Simon and his colleagues are designing a machine capable of devising and executing its own strategies. In other words, they essentially seek to create a *trading automaton*—a machine endowed with the autonomy to decide how and when to trade financial assets.

The types of automated trading that Frank and Simon engage in share certain similarities. They are part of the sweeping transformation of financial markets already hinted at, where, over the past couple of decades, the buying and selling of financial assets has become increasingly computer generated. With automated trading, the decision to place an order—such as buying a certain number of shares at a particular price—is executed through a complex assemblage of software and hardware, without direct human intervention. Instead of trades being made among individual human traders, they are now largely executed among anonymous automated trading systems housed within exchange data centers, which must cool the heat from the rows upon rows of computer servers that now constitute the engine room of markets.

Numbers support the claim about markets transforming in light of automation. Although exact figures are difficult to obtain, estimates suggest that so-called high-frequency trading (HFT)—a form of low-latency (that is, high-speed) automated trading—accounts for approximately 55 percent of the trading volume in the US equities markets, 80 percent in currency futures, and 66 percent in treasury markets (Foucault and Moinas 2018, 2; MacKenzie 2018b, 1638). As HFT is only a subset of automated trading, albeit an important and widely discussed one, the actual overall presence of automated trading systems in markets is therefore much larger than these figures suggest. In fact, in some markets, automated trading is reportedly behind as much as 99.6 percent of all trading messages (Yadav 2018, 234). The orders that Frank's and Simon's systems spit out contribute to this massive flow.

Another similarity between the systems Frank and Simon deploy is that, despite their design differences, they are exceptionally complex to develop, and many attempts go awry despite years of persistence. Furthermore, given their extreme attention to software and hardware dimensions, firms focusing on automated trading resemble highly specialized technology firms more than traditional financial services firms. Illustratively, PhD degrees in disciplines such as computer science and physics are common among people specializing in automated trading (Borch and Lange 2017). While men remain vastly overrepresented, the offices they work in lack the brash atmosphere popularized in *Wolf of Wall Street* (Belfort 2007) and similar accounts. Instead, these are generally quiet spaces, conducive to intellectual absorption.

Despite such similarities, I argue in this book that Frank's and Simon's approaches to automated trading differ significantly. These distinct approaches essentially narrate two tales of the City of London—and of financial markets more generally—that is, two fundamentally different ways of doing automated trading. To clarify these differences, I refer to them as first- and second-generation automated trading, respectively (Borch and Min 2023). *First-generation systems* are designed end-to-end by humans, implementing trading decisions based on human-conceived rules. In contrast, *second-generation systems* center on ML techniques. While they also demand extensive human curation, their trading decisions are machine generated. The use of ML is what transforms these second-generation systems into true trading automatons.

Pursuing ML-based automated trading has profound consequences for trading firms, financial markets, and the sociological understanding of these realms. For example, the two generations present different risk profiles. First-generation systems' key risks involve growing so complex that they suddenly act differently than their human designers intended, necessitating comprehensive system testing and effective real-time monitoring. Such risk-mitigating procedures are also needed for second-generation systems, but they face a qualitatively different risk: their human designers might not fully understand why their systems make specific trading decisions, raising significant questions about their market behaviors. Simon acknowledged this, saying, "We have no clue" when discussing why the ML-based system he helped develop makes the decisions it does. This lack of insight into the decision-making process is fraught with risk. Despite rigorous testing and surveillance, might the system suddenly veer off course? Might it engage in illegal market behaviors? Could unforeseen market actions trigger wider disruptions? As more firms transition from first- to second-generation automated trading, the urgency of addressing these questions only increases.

I explore risk and potential risk mitigation extensively in this book. But its aim is broader—understanding how, why, and with what implications ML-based systems are trading financial assets in today's markets. To this end, I compare and contrast first- and second-generation automated trading. This allows me to highlight overlaps and stress distinct consequences of adopting ML for risk and beyond. By doing so, I provide a lens through which to envision the future of markets increasingly shaped by ML technologies.

My focus lies on the modus operandi of these trading forms. I provide a ground-level account, attending to the considerations, concerns, practices, and reflections of market professionals active in automated trading. I pay close attention to how these professionals describe their work and challenges: What is automated trading about? What motivates it? How is it organized in practice? What types of expertise are at play? What kinds of human-machine interaction does it involve? What risks does it entail and what forms of risk mitigation exist? Addressing these questions helps me piece together the broader landscape of automated trading, encompassing financial exchanges and regulation.

Inquiring into the motivations behind and practical implementations of first- and second-generation automated trading systems allows me to tell a broader story about how new technologies revolutionize financial markets. In the constant quest for an advantage, or "edge," market participants have always turned to novel technologies. Whether analog or digital, new technologies attract market participants' attention because they promise better or faster access to market data, exploitable for trading. I elaborate further on this below, but a key point I make is that, while the adoption of ML marks the latest technological fad, it also fundamentally changes the relationship between humans and markets. Earlier technologies primarily enabled human market participants to access and respond to market information faster or more reliably; to assess data better or more comprehensively; or to implement multiple human-conceived strategies at once. ML might assist in these areas too, but when deployed at firms like Simon's, the technology transcends mere assistance to or extension of human decision-making; it replaces humans as the primary actors directing market trades. While ML use always involves human curation—and as I discuss in later chapters, such curation is complex and extensive—the central shift this technology introduces is one where human decision-making recedes and machine action (and machine-machine interaction) assumes a pivotal role.

Taking that shift seriously has important implications for sociology. Sociology has always revolved around humans and their actions and interactions. Although sociologists have different views on understanding human action, there is widespread (and, admittedly, fairly understandable) agreement that humans are central to sociological inquiry. This applies even to theoretical traditions that argue for including nonhumans in the analytical mix—humans still play a key role in these (Cerulo 2009; Latour 2005). However, when firms design ML-based automated trading systems to identify their own strategies, the role of humans is redefined, and semi-independent machines, or trading automatons, take center stage in understanding market action. Therefore, in addition to detailing the shift from first- to second-generation automated trading and the workings and risks associated with these systems, this book aims to explore the implications for sociology and its understanding of markets and machines.[1] I hint at where this journey takes me below.

Trading Automatons

When characterizing second-generation automated trading systems as automatons, I evoke a notion steeped in a long and complex history, largely divorced from the realm of finance. Indeed, *automaton* is a polysemous term that, as Minsoo Kang (2011) has illustrated in a sweeping intellectual history, has captivated the European imagination for over two millennia. In ancient Greek, the term referred to a "self-moving" entity—a concept that retained its allure during the Renaissance and the seventeenth century. This notion later evolved to include a life-imitating dimension. Under this expanded understanding, an automaton is "a self-moving machine built for the specific purpose of mimicking a living creature" (2011, 7). Famous examples of such automatons include drum- and flute-playing machines as well as mechanical ducks. The idea of a life-imitating machine is also central to Adrienne Mayor's (2018, 1) exploration of what she terms *biotechne*, or "life through craft": an automaton is "made, not born," crafted with the intent of "imitating, augmenting, and surpassing natural life."

Both Kang (2011, 297–309) and Mayor (2018, 213–18 et passim) trace the lineage from ancient automatons to present-day robotics and ML. I build on this foundation by viewing second-generation automated trading systems as modern-day automatons: human-made entities designed to make independent market decisions and to learn, in a self-moving manner, from their market actions, ultimately surpassing the trading decisions that human traders can achieve.[2]

I reserve the term *trading automatons* for second-generation automated trading systems, although one might argue that first-generation systems also qualify as automatons: they, too, are made, not born—crafted to mimic and enhance the decision-making capacities of their human creators through greater speed and consistency. However, their inability to independently identify strategies and learn from their actions and interactions is a critical distinction. First-generation systems are not designed to be truly self-moving; they remain tethered to the financial imagination of their inventors' trading strategies. In contrast, second-generation systems are designed to cultivate their own financial imagination, as it were, refining it through continuous learning. (Note that throughout this book, I use *second-generation automated trading systems* and *trading automatons* interchangeably. But since the former is admittedly unwieldy, I primarily use it when making implicit or explicit comparisons with first-generation automated trading systems. Additionally, I often refer to these systems using the shorthand *first-* and *second-generation systems*.)

My definition of trading automatons as machines endowed with the autonomy to decide how and when to trade financial assets can now be further specified: these are ML-powered automated trading systems that learn, semi-independently, to identify trading strategies and continuously adapt based on their past market actions. Their underlying software and hardware architectures are designed by humans, just as humans feed them the data needed for their initial training. These critical human aspects are the reason why trading automatons remain only semi-independent—the human curation is the push the automaton needs to become self-moving.[3]

I attend to both sides of trading automatons—their semi-*independent* and *semi*-independent dimensions—and argue that emphasizing one over the other has important theoretical implications. Depending on which dimension is highlighted, well-known sociological concepts encounter either centrifugal or centripetal forces: some are pushed to the periphery, becoming less relevant for understanding markets. This includes the otherwise important sociological notion about economic action being embedded in ongoing social relations (Granovetter 1985). While this notion has occupied a central place in sociological understandings of markets during the past four decades, it fails to account for the semi-*independent* market actions of trading automatons, irreducible as these are to human action and inter-action. In contrast, when the *semi*-independent aspects of trading automatons are emphasized, sociological concepts and traditions best known from nonmachine contexts are drawn into focus. This includes theories of role taking (Mead 1934) and how to explain social action (Martin 2011), both of which, as I discuss in chapter 5, are useful for exploring how humans are trying to understand why complex trading automatons make the decisions they do.

Studying Automated Trading

This book stems from a decade of fieldwork in the automated trading industry. As in many fieldwork stories, my entry was serendipitous. In the summer of 2013, I secured funding from the Independent Research Fund Denmark to lead a research project exploring crowd and herding dynamics in financial markets. The core re-search team consisted of Ann-Christina Lange, Kristian Bondo Hansen, and myself. Though automated trading was gaining attention back then, I (mistakenly) thought it a niche activity, so our focus was on crowd dynamics among traders in nonautomated electronic trading. Specifically, we aimed to understand crowding among traders glued to their screens, fingers poised over mice and keyboards, ready to pounce on profitable opportunities (what I call the "electronic screen-trading" market arrangement below).

Before applying for funding, I had arranged for ethnographic access at an in-vestment bank where the head of trading had welcomed us to follow their electronic screen traders. However, after securing the funds, the head of trading ran our agree-ment through the bank's compliance department, which promptly shut us down. Compliance officers insisted that traders notify all clients of our presence, a demand the head of trading understandably resisted. With that door closed, we approached other firms, only to hit similar walls, largely due to compliance issues. Despite these setbacks, we began interviewing finance industry professionals, including those in automated trading, although early interviews reinforced the notion that automated trading was not widespread.

Then, in early 2014, Michael Lewis published *Flash Boys,* a searing journalis-tic inquiry into HFT and its numerous alleged negative consequences. The central accusation in Lewis's book was that firms engaging in this form of trading were essentially rigging markets. *Flash Boys* not only highlighted my underestimation of automated trading's role but also prompted some HFT specialists to defend themselves against the uproar sparked by the book. This created an unexpected, brief window of opportunity: Lange managed to secure access for ethnographic observations at a New York–based HFT firm. She initially immersed herself in the firm's operations for four weeks, observing and conversing with traders developing automated trading algorithms. She later revisited the firm for an additional two weeks and subsequently returned for a shorter visit, during which I joined her. Beyond observational work, Lange expanded her interviews within the automated trading industry. I collaborated with Lange on some of these interviews and also conducted my own to complement her findings. This ongoing work dovetailed with a broader concurrent effort by a group of sociologists—including Marc Lenglet, Donald MacKenzie, Juan Pablo Pardo-Guerra, Robert Seyfert, and anthropologist Alexandre Laumonier—to understand the mechanics and impacts of automated asset trading through fieldwork within the industry.

In 2016, I was fortunate to receive a grant from the European Research Council, enabling me to assemble and lead a research team to significantly expand the examination of automated trading. This new project, titled "Algorithmic Finance," or "AlgoFinance," included five full-time researchers working alongside me: although Lange had temporarily left academia for another career path, Hansen remained, and we were joined by Bo Hee Min, Nicholas Skar-Gislinge, Pankaj Kumar, and Daniel Souleles. Zachary David, a former Chicago-based automated trader, was hired as a consultant, bringing essential industry expertise to the project. While David, Kumar, and Skar-Gislinge explored automated trading from an agent-based modeling perspective, the rest of us embarked on a comprehensive mapping of the industry, resulting in 195 interviews with professionals involved in or connected to automated trading. Including the interviews I conducted in the previous research project, this book is based on a total of 223 interviews, conducted from October 2013 to April 2025, of which I carried out 80 individually or jointly. Our informants included traders, quantitative analysts, software developers, risk and compliance officers, HR staff, and executives from prop shops, hedge funds, and banks, as well as brokers, data analytics providers, technological infrastructure staff, regulators, exchange personnel, central bankers, asset and investment managers, and others deploying, servicing, or being affected by the rise of automation in financial trading. In essence, we aimed to map all crucial aspects of the landscape—at least as it appears in the US and Europe.

In addition to the interview data, we managed to secure access for limited ethnographic observations at select trading firms. For instance, Min and I observed operations at a London-based trading firm specializing in second-generation automated trading. Some firms also shared internal documents with us, detailing organizational procedures and various aspects of their technological systems. I delve deeper into the data and methods in the Appendix.

Though we amassed an archive of more than two hundred interviews, gaining access to conduct qualitative fieldwork in the automated trading industry is widely known to be challenging—an obstacle encountered by other sociologists in this field (MacKenzie 2021; Seyfert 2016). As one of my informants, Charles, candidly remarked, "Trading firms are notoriously closed mouth." (I address aspects of this secrecy in chapter 2 when discussing first-generation systems, though it applies equally to firms operating second-generation systems.) This pervasive secrecy has several implications, chief among them being the lack of a reliable overview of the firms engaged in automated trading and related activities. Some major players in the industry are known, largely through press coverage. These include Citadel Securities, a leading US market maker—providing liquidity to other market actors and profiting from this role—with over 1,700 employees, responsible for nearly a quarter of US equity market volume;[4] Renaissance, a major US investment management firm with around three hundred employees (G. Zuckerman 2019); Two Sigma, a key US quantitative hedge fund with more than two thousand employees; Virtu Financial, a prominent US-based market maker with nearly one thousand employees (Virtu Financial 2022); and Optiver, an Amsterdam-based market maker employing close to two thousand people.[5] Beyond these and similar high-profile firms, the industry is populated by a multitude of smaller, lesser-known companies. Identifying these firms often requires diligent probing, as they typically maintain minimally informative websites.

In my experience, the level of secrecy increases with the size and prominence of trading firms. The interview data underpinning this book reflect this pattern. Although we spoke with individuals who either had previously held roles in the aforementioned echelon of large firms or currently worked in them or their peers, the data are skewed toward smaller proprietary trading firms and hedge funds (similarly, Seyfert 2016). Some of the firms where our interviewees worked had only a handful of employees—some even fewer—while others employed between fifty and one hundred staff. That said, firm size is not an unambiguous measure of significance. As MacKenzie (2021, 5) observed, "In particular niches, even firms with only a handful of employees can be important."

This observation was corroborated several times during my fieldwork. One of the most extreme examples is Jack, who said that, at its peak, the three-person automated trading firm he cofounded—comprising himself, a cofounder, and an assistant—was trading "0.5–1.0 percent of the daily volume on the New York Stock Exchange." Similarly, Jonathan, an algorithmic trader at a Chicago firm that at its peak consisted of twenty-one people, mentioned that in the specific futures markets in which they were active, they accounted for 1 to 2 percent of the volume on average. However, "During the night sessions [when the market] is much less liquid, . . . sometimes we're 5–10 percent of it in certain products." Another informant claimed that their firm, with approximately sixty employees, was responsible for 20–40 percent of the volume in one of the world's significant multi-trillion-dollar markets. While I cannot validate these numbers, the point remains: many informants from smaller firms insisted that the number of employees does not necessarily correlate with market significance. Many small firms seem to punch above their weight.

While our primary focus was on conducting interviews within hedge funds, proprietary trading firms, exchanges, and brokers, we also extended our conversations to individuals at various banks, ranging from global giants to smaller regional institutions. Although some banks have a long-standing history with automation, they are generally not considered leaders in automated trading. On the contrary, because of their relatively unsophisticated algorithmic capabilities, the slower systems they operate, and the heightened regulation they face, banks have long been vulnerable to faster, automated market participants. Illustratively, the main narrative of Lewis's *Flash Boys* centers on how the protagonist, Brad Katsuyama, then an employee at the Royal Bank of Canada, discovered that the orders he sent to the market were being exploited by HFT firms (Lewis 2014). This state of affairs is commented on by MacKenzie (2021, 5), who drily notes that, in relation to HFT, "the rapid development of the fast, highly specialized software systems that are needed can be difficult in a large, bureaucratic organization" such as a big bank.[6]

The interviews we conducted in banks revealed several examples of teams tasked with either running automated trading systems or exploring the potential for new investments in, for example, ML-based approaches. Nonetheless, in line with existing research (Lange 2016; MacKenzie 2018b, 2021), my data suggest that the full-scale turn to automation is much more of a hedge fund or prop shop specialty. This book's analyses reflect that.

A Brief History of Financial Market Arrangements

Before delving into second-generation automated trading and its distinctions from and similarities to first-generation systems, it is crucial to place automated trading within the broader historical context of financial markets and their trading activities. I draw inspiration from Mitchel Abolafia's (1996) now-classic sociological study of Wall Street. On the basis of fieldwork from the late 1970s to the early 1990s, Abolafia (1996, 8) aimed to examine the "trading floor and its market arrangements," which he defined as "the set of rules and relationships that determine who trades with whom and under what conditions." Pursuing an institutionalist approach, Abolafia sought to understand the formal rules and informal norms of trading floors, while recognizing that these were partly shaped by "the political, economic, and regulatory environments of the market" (1996, 9). Besides detailing these rules and norms, Abolafia argued that more powerful market actors could mold market arrangements to their own advantage. Indeed, one of the central contributions of his study was highlighting the forms of opportunism inherent to financial markets.

Despite its many insightful analyses, Abolafia's investigation fell short of capturing the role of technology in markets.[7] This oversight includes not considering that markets evolve not only through the influence of powerful human actors but also through actors' access to technological advancements. Moreover, new technological innovations can swiftly disrupt existing power structures in markets, with incumbents losing ground to more tech-savvy newcomers. Inspired by extensive literature emphasizing the material co-constitution of markets (e.g., Beunza, Hardie, and MacKenzie 2006; Callon and Muniesa 2005; MacKenzie 2009, 2018b), I propose supplementing Abolafia's institutional conception of market arrangements with a material-technological dimension. This includes considering the role of the "contact technology" of markets (Baker 1984b, 807), which refers to the technological setup mediating market participants at trading venues; the material infrastructures enabling and supporting trading activities (MacKenzie 2018b); and the technological tools deployed by trading firms (Beunza and Stark 2004; MacKenzie 2017; Svetlova 2012, 2018). When I refer to market arrangements in this book, the notion therefore encompasses a material-technological component in addition to Abolafia's institutionalist framing. Although the term *material market arrangements* would capture this point better, it is also more cumbersome.

Market arrangements are not static. Their evolution is due to various factors, such as regulatory pressure, technological developments, and shifting power balances among actors. Moreover, at any given moment, market arrangements might manifest differently across types of markets, asset classes, and countries. Although a brief sketch of the evolution of market arrangements will necessarily overlook much of this complexity, I will nonetheless attempt a rough overview to provide a backdrop for understanding the nature and emergence of automated trading.

Specifically, I find it useful to distinguish between four market arrangements. These are (1) *interhuman trading*, where humans trade directly with one another with little or no technological mediation, such as on an exchange trading floor (Abolafia 1996; Baker 1984b; Zaloom 2006); (2) *electronic screen trading*, where human traders interact electronically with the market as it manifests on their computer screens and send orders to buy and sell assets by clicking their mouse (Knorr Cetina and Bruegger 2002a, 2002b; Wansleben 2015; Zaloom 2006); and two separate forms of *automated trading*, or intermachine trading, where fully automated algorithms send orders to the markets: (3) first-generation automated trading, where trading strategies are conceived end-to-end by humans, and (4) second-generation automated trading, where ML-based systems—trading automatons—develop the trading rules semi-independently.

Two caveats are important. The first is that, although I describe the history of financial markets as a gradual replacement of one dominant market arrangement by another, all four market arrangements may be considered analytical ideal types that, despite portraying distinct features, often coexist in practice. For instance, the New York Stock Exchange (NYSE), once an epitome of interhuman trading, later largely, and resistantly, followed the trend of most other stock exchanges in the US and Europe, moving toward electronic trading in the 1990s and 2000s. It nonetheless retains traditional interhuman trading floors of some importance to this day. Similarly, the London Metal Exchange—the world's most important exchange for the trading of metals (lithium, copper, zinc, and so on)—allows for electronic trading but has maintained its interhuman trading floor, the Ring, despite much discussion of whether to give it up.

These two examples underscore a second caveat: the scope of my discussion below, and throughout this book, is predominantly confined to US and European developments. Granted, several informants operated within US and European firms that maintain offices in other regions, including Japan, Hong Kong, and Singapore, facilitating the circulation of ideas and practices among them. Many informants also had experience working in other geographies or had moved across regions during the years my fieldwork took place. Nevertheless, the transformations

I describe, along with market participants' experiences and their strategies for navigating these changes, may not fully capture the nuances of how financial markets function beyond the US and Europe. I revisit this limitation in chapter 6.

INTERHUMAN TRADING

Interhuman trading is the oldest and longest-existing market arrangement. In its modern formalized form, it is closely tied to the rise of stock and commodity exchanges, which replaced trading at coffee shops. Prime examples include the New York Stock and Exchange Board (precursor to the NYSE), established in 1817, and the Chicago Board of Trade, founded in 1848. Both exchanges set up specific contact technologies to organize the interaction of human market participants. In New York, brokers were initially seated in chairs and, sitting down, shouted out their bids to buy and offers to sell. Later, the chairs were replaced with a trading floor containing designated locations for the trading of specific stocks. Members of the exchange would then move around the floor as they saw fit and place their orders where relevant. In Chicago, trading was soon organized around its to-become-famous "pits"—octagonally shaped structures with steps descending into the middle, each dedicated to trading specific assets.[8]

The interhuman trading arrangement has attracted considerable attention in classic economic sociology examinations. Important studies include Max Weber's (2000b) late nineteenth-century portrayal of stock and commodity exchanges; Wayne Baker's (1984a, 1984b) seminal work on the pits of the Chicago Board Options Exchange (CBOE), based on fieldwork conducted in the late 1970s; and Abolafia's analysis of Wall Street trading floors. None of these analyses focused heavily on technology. Instead, they emphasized how trading floors constituted spaces where orders were placed and trades consummated before being cleared and settled (activities done outside the floors), and where market participants interacted directly, face-to-face, under the influence of formal and informal rules.

I began this chapter by briefly relating Frank's account of the trading floor's face-to-face—or body-to-body—environment and the importance of physical stature in it. This physical-bodily dimension receives extensive analysis in Caitlin Zaloom's (2006) rich ethnographic study of the Chicago pits. For example, Zaloom (2006, 144) notes that, in the pit, important "information is transmitted through the bodies of traders and received by their colleagues." As per Erving Goffman's (1959, 14) distinction between the expressions a person gives and gives off—respectively, the information conveyed deliberately and involuntarily—traders would carefully monitor each other for any visual and oral cues that might inadvertently add communicative layers to what they expressly cried out. As a pit trader interviewed by Zaloom put it, "You can't be like a panic loud because once the panic comes out of your mouth you're pretty much admitting to whoever wants to assume the other side of the trade with you that that's not a good trade" (Zaloom 2003, 263).

Given the premium on both visibility and audibility, pits were fiercely competitive arenas where traders strained to secure prime positions, using their bodies to gain an edge. While it might seem clichéd to assert that being big and being loud were highly prized attributes in the pits, my informants confirmed that these traits were indeed crucial in the interhuman market arrangement. George, a former pit trader who later transitioned to providing low-latency technology solutions, recounted how his entry into the pits was largely due to his physical stature, though it ultimately proved insufficient for success:

> I was a football player in college, and one of my coaches was a trader on the floor. We called him Coach Commodities. He saw some things in me that would make me a good fit down here [in Chicago], and as soon as I graduated, he was like, "Come on down and check it out, I'll get you a job as a runner."[9] I was a runner for him for about six months and then I got more interested in the trading side, and I went to work for a proprietary trader on the side and I clerked for about a year or two years just learning the business, and then the guys thought, "Well, you're a really good clerk, you'd probably be a really good trader." Well, it turns out I wasn't a very good trader due to my inability to remember numbers short term. I fumbled along, I kind of broke even, which was a miserable life just to break even. . . . I wasn't hired for my technology background, nor because I was a brilliant math person. I initially got my break into the business because I was a bigger, athletic, and competitive guy.

Even if traders' physical stature was attributed great importance, technology was not absent in the interhuman market arrangement. In fact, it was precisely because of the design of the contact technology of this market arrangement—the physical floor or pit—and the crowding of bodies it produced that it was important for traders to stand out physically from their peers. Because traders' physical stature mattered, low-key technologies were used as bodily enhancements. For example, Zaloom (2006, 149) reports that some Chicago traders would affix "extra inches of black foam . . . to the soles of their shoes" to compensate for any lack of height or to gain further advantage. Again, this observation was corroborated by my informants. Chuk, a former pit clerk, recalled: "When I first went to the trading floor when I was eighteen or nineteen, I saw a couple of guys [and] their heels were like this high [showing with his fingers]. I didn't get the concept. Eventually, I learned: because they're taller they can stick out more and people can see them easier in a crowd."[10] This is admittedly an exotic example, but it illustrates how even simple technological adaptations might prove useful in otherwise sophisticated markets. Yet more advanced technologies may obviously also be utilized to gain an edge. For instance, sociologists and historians have detailed how nineteenth-century innovations like the telephone, the telegraph, and the stock ticker were quickly adopted by market participants to obtain fast access to market information, significantly affecting the ways traders and others related to markets, including how orders would eventually arrive on the trading floors (Cronon 1991; Handel 2022; Hochfelder 2006; Preda 2006; Stäheli 2013). This shows that while the interhuman market arrangement's technological mediation is limited compared to other market arrangements, technology certainly played an important role in its market information transmission channels. These were not necessarily external to the trading floors but could form an integral inner part of them. One example came up in an interview with Chuk and George, highlighting the role of printers for floor trading:

> Chuk: My job was to go down to the trading floor and fix people's printers to make sure they could print all data of their trading in the pits. . . . They would make a trade, they'd write it down on a card, flip it to an operations person, and they would punch it into the GMI system [a clearing and accounting system], and then the traders could punch out their statements—print out and see what their statements are and what their positions are in the market. That was my job, to make sure the printers work because if they can't print out their statements they don't know where they stand in the market, they don't know their positions. . . .
> George: Now everyone looks for really fast computers; back then people were looking for really fast printers—like how many pages can it print per minute? The faster they'd get their pricing sheets the better.
> Chuk [echoing this]: There'd be a queue of guys saying, "Give me my statement, give me my statement, give me my statement."

Serving as illustrations of how the interhuman market arrangement was technologically co-constituted, these examples testify to my point that the ambition of turning to technology to obtain an advantage over competitors is part and parcel of the history of financial markets and not unique to automated trading, though obviously manifesting in a highly radicalized form there.

ELECTRONIC SCREEN TRADING

While the interhuman market arrangement long held its ground, the 1960s and '70s brought significant pushes toward a more electronic trading landscape. As my focus is on the eventual replacement of the interhuman market arrangement, I will gloss over much of this complex evolution, highlighting only a few key milestones (for more detailed accounts, see Borch 2020; Buck 1992; Gorham and Singh 2009; MacKenzie 2015b; Pardo-Guerra 2010). One pivotal moment was the launch of Nasdaq in 1971. Nasdaq's groundbreaking innovation was to create an electronic platform for over-the-counter dealer quotations, allowing market participants to look at their computer screens to see market quotes. Initially, the Nasdaq system did not involve electronic order matching. "To actually buy or sell required a phone call," but the quotes for 2,500 stocks were now visible on screens (Gorham and Singh 2009, 72).

Although the over-the-counter setup differed from the traditional exchange-traded markets in New York, Chicago, and elsewhere, the idea of computerized trading gradually permeated these bastions of finance, bolstered by calls for greater automation (Black 1971a, 1971b). By the 1980s, traders increasingly relied on computer technology while interacting on the trading floor. Then, in the 1990s, many exchanges abandoned floor trading entirely, embracing electronic trading (Gorham and Singh 2009, 29–78). This shift enabled trading to be conducted remotely, with orders sent to the market through computers.

This transformation ushered in the era of electronic screen trading, characterized by traders manually placing orders to buy or sell financial assets on their computers. Swapping one contact technology for another had profound implications for trader profiles and methodologies. Perhaps most significantly, the pit's body-to-body trading dynamics gave way to a more disembodied interaction. "On the screen, a trader needs only eyes to read the market and a finger to click" their mouse (Zaloom 2006, 144). Instead of using their entire bodies to gauge the market's pulse, electronic screen trading narrowed the sensory focus to vision—meticulously monitoring market fluctuations as they materialized on the screen.

The shift to electronic trading did not entail lesser consideration of market information. As Karin Knorr Cetina and Urs Bruegger (2000, 2002a, 2002b) have detailed in their examinations of electronic screen trading, for traders active in this market arrangement, the screen represents the market. But contrary to the trading pit, the electronic market conceals the identities of participants: while traders would previously know with whom they traded (though not, as a rule, which clients brokers were acting on behalf of), electronic screen trading is anonymous—though this does not prevent traders from trying to guess who (including which institutions) places which orders in the faceless market (Zaloom 2006).[11]

Furthermore, "Since these markets are exteriorized and concentrated on screen, traders not only participate in these markets, they relate to them as a complex 'other' with which they are strongly, even obsessively, engaged" (Knorr Cetina and Bruegger 2002b, 162). Based on this observation, Knorr Cetina and Bruegger argue that the form of sociality characterizing this market arrangement is fundamentally different from that of interhuman trading. The latter can largely be described as one of interhuman sociality: human market participants interact with other human market participants.[12] In contrast, the electronic screen trading market arrangement captures what Knorr Cetina refers to as "postsocial relationships," where human traders orient themselves primarily not toward other humans but rather toward particular technological objects—their computer screens and the markets visually represented on them. Or, as Knorr Cetina and Bruegger (2002b, 163) prefer to phrase it, the screen serves as a form of market "appresentation": it "brings a geographically dispersed and invisible market close to participants, rendering it interactionally or response-present."

Knorr Cetina's notion of postsocial relations exemplifies how sociology needs to reassess its conceptual apparatus in light of the shift from one market arrangement to another. In her vocabulary, this market transformation manifests as a shift from "a network architecture where social relationships carry much of the burden of specifying market behavior" to what she calls a "flow architecture" of markets (2003, 7). The latter emphasizes that while markets are global, in that the same (and similar) instruments are traded across geographies, they are also microsociologically structured such that individual traders observe and respond to them in front of their local screens. Indeed, it is the *technological* interconnections (rather than interhuman interconnections) among the traders' screens that enable the flow of financial data and decisions on a global scale.

This analysis contrasts sharply with the view advanced by Baker. Commenting on discussions in the early 1980s about replacing interhuman trading with the electronic matching of orders sent by humans on their computers, he insisted that, in the end, the fundamental features of markets would remain the same: "Though orders could be matched by a computer algorithm, the buyers and sellers who place these orders are still subject to bounded rationality and still operate in an environment of uncertainty and complexity. . . . Changing the contact technology of the market would affect the social structure of the market, but it would never escape the fact that markets are socially structured" (1984b, 807). In other words, for Baker, technology might influence how the embeddedness of market action within social relations plays out, but embeddedness nonetheless remains at the core of markets. In contrast, Knorr Cetina's central point is that embeddedness is pushed to the background: while electronic screen traders certainly talk to one another in the firms where they are employed—and interpret the clues they seek from their peers (Wansleben 2015; Zaloom 2006)—their main attention is focused on the market as it appears onscreen. The kinds of market action arising from this have little to do with the social structure of known peers or socially shaped actions as in the interhuman market arrangement. As hinted at, the advent of second-generation automated trading has a centrifugal effect on the analytical purchase of the notion of embeddedness, pushing its relevance even further into the background.

The shift from interhuman to electronic screen trading also has implications for risk. One of the risks of the interhuman market arrangement concerned the extent to which its design features made it susceptible to manipulation or misconduct. An example of this is the risk that NYSE "specialists" might misuse privileges granted them under this market arrangement. A specialist was the NYSE term for a market maker responsible for managing the trading of a specific set of stocks (they are now called "designated market makers"). The specialist was tasked with maintaining a fair and orderly market for these stocks by matching buy and sell orders from other market participants and, when necessary, trading from their own inventory to provide liquidity and stabilize prices. To this end, they oversaw an "order book" (a list of unmatched bids to buy and offers to sell) for specific stocks. However, as this order book was private to them, they were in a position where various forms of market manipulation were possible. This included so-called front running, where upon receiving, say, a new buy order, they could trade ahead of it—buy shares on their own account and sell these again when the incoming order was finally executed and had driven up the price (for a discussion of this and similar tactics, see MacKenzie 2015a). Although exchanges had rules against such behaviors, these rules were not always followed.

Obviously, market participants might also misuse their positions in the electronic screen trading market arrangement. For example, electronic screen traders might make overly risky, unauthorized, or fraudulent trades—whether in the form of fund managers acting against the interests of clients (Arjaliès et al. 2017, 47–48) or rogue traders acting far beyond the risk limits set by management. A famous case is that of Jérôme Kerviel, who produced losses worth billions of euros for Société Générale in 2008. But the more important question is whether, similar to the interhuman market arrangement, certain design features make electronic screen trading particularly susceptible to risk. And indeed, this market arrangement poses risks that are of a more interorganizational, or even systemic, nature. Its heavily technologically inculcated setting couples a larger number of market participants more tightly to one another. The market to which human screen traders feel attached appears simultaneously on-screen for traders around the globe, and market fluctuations are therefore likely to exacerbate faster and more intensely (Knorr Cetina and Bruegger 2002a; Knorr Cetina 2003). This risk may be further intensified if rival firms are deploying the same or similar financial models: if trading decisions are based on overall similar assumptions or expectations, their "resonance" may reinforce sudden ruptures (Beunza and Stark 2012; see also MacKenzie and Spears 2014a, 2014b; Svetlova 2018).

Let me conclude the discussion of electronic screen trading by reiterating a point made earlier: although I distinguish this market arrangement from that of interhuman trading (corresponding to Knorr Cetina's distinction between a network and a flow architecture of financial markets), the two may coexist and have indeed done so in the past. One illustration of this concerns the form of "program trading" that gained traction in the 1980s (Holzer and Millo 2005; Katzenbach 1987). *Program trading* refers to the trading of a basket, or portfolio, of assets simultaneously (rather than of individual assets each at a time) and is usually associated with portfolio insurance or index arbitrage. In the former, a fund manager overseeing a large portfolio of stocks uses futures contracts to mitigate losses in falling markets, effectively establishing a floor under the portfolio's value. In contrast, index arbitrage is about profiting from price misalignments between a stock index and the corresponding index futures. Although in principle the calculations behind program trading could be done manually, in practice they often involved computerization. The popularity of program trading in the 1980s was in large part tied to the NYSE's so-called Designated Order Turnaround system (DOT), introduced in 1976. This system "allowed NYSE member firms to transmit large volumes of buy and sell orders through their own connections to the NYSE common message switch and have them routed to a specialist/trading post. If the specialist did not report execution of the trade within three minutes, the NYSE gave confirmation of execution at a reference price. If the trade was not made with a third party, then the trade was put on the specialist's account" (Carlson 2007, 5). Program trading represents a hybridity of interhuman and early electronic trading. On the one hand, computers would typically be involved in this form of trading, suggesting optimal forms of portfolio insurance or index arbitrage. On the other hand, individuals would usually make the final investment decisions based on those suggestions and implement them in the markets (Furbush 1993). Additionally, once orders were entered into the DOT system, they would need to be printed and handed over to the relevant specialists at their trading posts.

Program trading is an intriguing example, not merely of the interhuman trading market arrangement blending with an early phase of electronic screen trading, but also of how the technological components of these arrangements generated anxieties about risk. For instance, after Black Monday, the massive market crash of October 19, 1987, concerns were voiced that the widespread use of program trading either was partly to blame for the crash or at least exacerbated it.[13] Similar to the idea of resonance (Beunza and Stark 2012), this concern revolved around the notion that investment decisions based on similar models (and responding to similar signals) might further aggravate a crash-prone situation. Indeed, on October 19, 1987, significant sell orders flooded the NYSE's system—then known as SuperDOT, a more advanced iteration of DOT—largely initiated by portfolio insurers and index arbitrageurs. According to one of the key government investigations into the Black Monday crash, the massive sell pressure not only made stock prices spiral downward but also created clogs in the trading system:

> This unprecedented traffic at times overwhelmed the mechanical printers that print DOT orders at certain trading posts, resulting in significant delays in executing market orders and in entering limit orders. These delays meant that market orders were executed at prices often very different from those in effect when the orders were entered. The delays also meant that limit orders may not have been executed because of their limits having been passed by the time the order reached the trading post. (Presidential Task Force on Market Mechanisms 1988, 47)

Given that automated trading is much more technology dependent than previous market arrangements, it is no surprise that the risk of technological mishaps having serious adverse effects on markets increases considerably in it. I discuss this in more detail in chapter 4.

AUTOMATED TRADING

I mentioned that automated trading can be divided into two distinct market arrangements, corresponding to first- and second-generation automated trading, respectively. While I examine the differences between these two generations in detail throughout the book, I will, for now, set aside those distinctions to focus on the origins of automated trading itself. Automated trading has several roots. It is sometimes associated primarily with a narrative about increasing market efficiency—suggesting that automated trading took off because it removes many inefficiencies of previous market arrangements and lowers the costs of trading (Gorham and Singh 2009). While this perspective captures part of the story, it does not tell the whole tale. A more accurate account frames automated trading as a contingent outcome of a complex mélange of interconnected factors. These include computing technology becoming available on a new scale (and at lower cost), providing new opportunities in the quest for competitive advantage; the increasing prominence of quantitative expertise within markets; and regulatory adaptation to a more technology-rich landscape, further accelerating its advance by removing benefits previously granted to humans in the interhuman market arrangement. While full-scale automation was pursued by some firms in the 1990s, it was not until the early 2000s that it became a widespread phenomenon.

A sense of how traders and trading venues came to deepen their reliance on technology—each side prodding the other along—appears in MacKenzie and Millo's (2003) account of the shifting dynamics in the CBOE's trading pits. In 1986, the CBOE introduced a system known as "Autoquote," designed to enable continuous quoting and to automatically generate bid and ask prices. Over time, this system reshaped traders' actions as they took advantage of the opportunities it afforded:

> In 1986, human beings were still at the center of the market, and technical systems were their aids. By 2000, the balance had shifted. . . . Most market makers now [this is based on observations made in November 2000] carry handheld computers. . . . Such is the array of screens, computers, and communication systems on the CBOE's trading floors that other heating is needed only when the Chicago temperature drops below -10°F. Dotted inconspicuously among all this automation are the touch screens used to set Autoquote working. (2003, 127–28)

To be sure, this is not full-blown automation. After all, the touch screens had to be touched to generate a quote, for which reason, at this time, "Human beings remain[ed] in ultimate command" (2003, 128). But the example is nonetheless a useful demonstration of how an amalgamation of interhuman and early electronic screen trading moved in the direction of automation.

This shift was further facilitated by quantitative expertise gaining traction within the finance industry. In his autobiography, *My Life as a Quant* (2004), Emanuel Derman recounts that when he began working as a quantitative researcher, or "quant," at Goldman, Sachs and Co. in 1985, quants were generally looked down upon by the traders whose work they were servicing through expertise in quantitative modeling. However, over the years, "Being a quant has slowly become a more legitimate profession," with traders eventually realizing that "spending money on research and development is not a zero-sum game" (2004, 13, 251). This observation echoes other accounts detailing a growing prominence of quantitative approaches to the trading of financial assets taking off in the 1980s and eventually morphing into fully automated trading (e.g., Patterson 2010, 2012).

However, as Abolafia's institutionalist approach makes plain, external factors such as regulation have also shaped automated trading and its emergence. The role played by regulation in making automated trading possible on a large scale has been analyzed by others (Castelle et al. 2016; Lange 2020; MacKenzie 2021), so I will restrict myself to just a few US highlights. One is the Regulation Alternative Trading Systems (Reg ATS) that the Securities and Exchange Commission (SEC) proposed in 1998 and adopted in 1999. A key aim of Reg ATS was to address the proliferation and increasing prominence of trading venues like so-called electronic communication networks (ECNs). For all practical purposes, ECNs were small electronic exchanges: orders were entered electronically (allowing for automated trading) and anonymously, and a "matching engine" would then automatically pair matching buy and sell orders, doing so at a lower execution cost than the Nasdaq and NYSE could offer. Initially, the main ECNs primarily facilitated trading of Nasdaq-listed stocks that traders found difficult to execute at Nasdaq (MacKenzie 2021, 91). But as Reg ATS gave ECNs regulatory backing, integrating them into the national market system, it effectively broadened their scope and influence (SEC 1998).

The effects of Reg ATS on the market landscape were substantial: the ECNs offered heavy competition to Nasdaq and NYSE. For example, from the point of view of market participants such as institutional investors, one of the key advantages of ECNs was that they were both cheaper and potentially more reliable than Nasdaq and NYSE. Despite the advances provided by Nasdaq's electronic platform for dealer quotations and NYSE's Dot/SuperDot system, both exchanges needed human intermediaries—be it Nasdaq's dealers or NYSE's specialists—to finally match incoming orders. In contrast, placing orders on ECNs was done anonymously (and more cheaply), and this "attracted more institutional traders to ECNs. On the floor of the NYSE and in the Nasdaq dealer community there was always a risk of word leaking out about a large order coming in, which could cause the NYSE floor traders or

Nasdaq dealers to drive up the price. These leaks do not happen on a computer screen of ECNs where buyer and seller orders are matched by the system" (Gorham and Singh 2009, 73–74). Faced with the increasing competition from ECNs, Nasdaq and NYSE—along with other exchanges—were eventually, though hesitatingly, forced to adapt to many of the former's distinct features, including allowing for the automated matching of orders. Getting there took a while, though, for despite increasing competition, incumbent exchanges retained some of their key privileges. Most notably, although attempts had been made since the 1970s to challenge the predominance of the NYSE, a lot of share trading continued to pass through its trading floor, effectively giving its human specialists huge power over the trading process.

One particular regulatory feature, introduced with the so-called Intermarket Trading System (ITS) in 1978, secured this sustained importance of the specialists. The aim of the ITS was to connect all US stock exchanges electronically so that brokers and market makers on each could send a request to trade via the system rather than having to go through the brokers at other exchanges. MacKenzie (2021, 72) notes that one of the advantages many market participants associated with this system was that members of smaller exchanges now had "direct access to the NYSE trading floor, and thus the capacity to strike deals with the NYSE's specialists without having to pay a fee to a NYSE broker."

While this might seem to secure a more dynamic market flow—at least from a conceptual point of view—the ITS had its choke points. In particular, when a request-to-trade message was sent, its recipient "had two minutes (eventually reduced to 30 seconds) to respond" (MacKenzie 2021, 73). So rather than leading to direct electronic order execution, the ITS merely linked nodes of fairly slow human decision-making at the exchanges. More problematically, the system ensured that, all the while trading at ECNs grew, "if they wanted to trade NYSE-listed stock, those venues would have to keep pausing trading to wait for the result of a request-to-trade message" sent to the NYSE specialists (MacKenzie 2021, 95). In other words, the ITS effectively gave priority to the NYSE specialists and thus guaranteed NYSE's enduring significance.

This landscape began to shift dramatically with the Regulation National Market System (Reg NMS) introduced by the SEC in 2005 to modernize the regulation of US equity markets. Recognizing that new technologies demanded a rethinking of existing regulatory frameworks, the SEC (2005, 23) noted that "the ITS provisions... were drafted for a world of floor-based markets and fail to reflect the disparate speed of response between manual and automated quotations." One of the key changes brought by Reg NMS was the "Order Protection Rule," which mandated that trading venues offer investors the best available price. As a part of this, the SEC aimed to eliminate "trade-throughs," situations where a venue executes an order at a worse price than what could have been achieved at another venue. Since the "Order Protection Rule protects only quotations that are immediately accessible through automatic execution" (SEC 2005, 23), the previous privilege of human specialists—that electronic trading would need to adjust to them—was abolished. Indeed, Reg NMS shifted the emphasis decisively from floor trading to automated trading. By creating a regulatory environment where automated execution was paramount, it compelled trading venues, including established exchanges, to embrace and facilitate automated trading.

As this shows, one of the driving forces for regulators and market participants moving toward automated trading was the desire to address certain limitations of the interhuman market arrangement. Front running and information leakage were already mentioned, but there was more. The interhuman market arrangement afforded human floor traders significant discretionary power that could be easily abused. Baker discussed this in relation to the pit's so-called first rule. According to this rule, when a market participant on the floor cried out an offer, the "first person to respond orally to [it] is formally entitled to the entire volume offered or any part thereof" (Baker 1984b, 782). However, market participants would manipulate this rule to sanction peers they perceived as violating the social norms of the pit (if they, say, acted overly opportunistically) by pretending not to have heard the "first" person and trading with others instead. Such tactics were made possible by the fact that pit activity was not properly recorded. One of my informants, Roland, a senior economist at one of the key US regulatory bodies (and a former pit trader), argued that this was precisely one of the benefits of moving to automated trading. The electronic platforms underlying automated trading would record every order sent to the venue, thus limiting certain forms of market misconduct:

> One of the issues of floor trading is there's less of an audit trail. You certainly can't have message data like we do [with automated trading]. Basically, anything you do in electronic trading gets recorded, so if you put in an order—even if it gets canceled—it gets recorded. But if you shout a bid into the pit you're just shouting into the air, and it doesn't get written down. So you do get an imperfect record, and this allowed some space for violations that you don't have in the electronic space.

While it is true that, in principle, automated trading on electronic exchange platforms increases accountability—since all orders are meticulously recorded—it is crucial not to mistake this for genuine transparency. Yes, the electronic registration of orders does enhance transparency to some extent. Venues and regulators can retrospectively scrutinize potential misconduct by accessing detailed order books. Market participants also gain a clearer picture of the market's status when the order book is accessible to all who can afford it, rather than being the exclusive domain of floor specialists. However, a practical issue with automated trading is that each machine can churn out thousands of orders per second, a volume that dwarfs the output possible in interhuman and electronic screen trading. As the number of automated trading systems proliferates, the sheer volume of generated orders is set to explode.

This is indeed what has happened. In 2000, US securities markets saw "on average about 5 million trades and quotes per *day*; in the fall of 2012, at peak times there were up to 5 million trades and quotes per *second*" (Malinova, Park, and Riordan 2013, 1, original emphasis). Later figures confirm this surge in market activity, a direct consequence of automated trading. Referring to 2016 data, Walter Mattli reports that the Financial Industry Regulatory Authority (FINRA)—a US nongovernmental, self-regulatory organization that operates under the SEC's authority and supervision to regulate broker-dealers and brokers—"monitors on average about 50 billion market events (quotes, cancellations, and trades) a day across equities, options, and a few other markets" (2019, 142). These staggering numbers reveal that, while every single order is electronically recorded and can, in theory, be traced and analyzed after the fact, automated trading has unleashed an unprecedented frenzy of activity. Markets are flooded with orders, creating a labyrinthine setting that firms and regulators must navigate. The remainder of this book explores how firms grapple with this complex landscape and how the adoption of ML has become a vital strategy for managing it.

Overview of the Chapters

Chapter 2 explores the complex process by which trading firms strive to develop and implement first-generation automated trading systems—machines designed to execute strategies conceived by human intellect. I illustrate that, just as the evolution of financial markets is partly a saga of new market arrangements addressing specific flaws in their predecessors, so too is this form of trading spurred by a desire to mitigate deficiencies inherent in electronic screen trading. For example, machines are thought to be immune to the cognitive constraints that human screen traders encounter. Moreover, reflecting the tightly woven and intricate com bination of financial and technological aspects inherent in automated trading, this chapter also discusses how firms must establish a complex technological infrastructure before executing any automated trades. Similarly, I show that the production pipeline—from the conception of strategies to their testing, encoding, and ongoing monitoring—hinges on a specialized division of labor among traders, quants, and software developers. While the chapter predominantly details the extensive steps trading firms undertake to achieve first-generation automated trading, along with the cultural and organizational facets of this endeavor, it also scrutinizes the myriad dimensions where failure looms large.

Using the discussion of first-generation systems as a backdrop, chapter 3 delves into the creation of second-generation systems. Focusing on two widely used ML techniques I encountered during my fieldwork—genetic programming and deep learning—I illustrate that a central impetus for developing trading automatons stems from the limitations of first-generation systems: since these systems merely execute human-devised strategies from a distance, they cannot surpass the intellectual capabilities encoded within them. In contrast, the primary goal of designing trading automatons is to craft machines that outshine human traders in detecting tradeable market patterns and that continually learn from, and refine, their actions in the markets.

Additionally, I trace the production pipeline for second-generation systems, covering stages such as data preparation, experimentation, delivery, and deployment, demonstrating the critical role of human curation in creating these trading automatons. I also emphasize that first- and second-generation systems share much of the same technological and data infrastructure, even though the vulnerabilities of second-generation systems differ—a direct result of their design to enable machines to independently detect patterns. Finally, I show that while both generations often rely on the same type of order-book data, the introduction of ML has driven a quest for tradeable patterns in so-called alternative data, such as satellite imagery and social media data, significantly broadening the range of what is deemed relevant in a trading context.

Chapter 4 deepens the comparison between the two generations, concentrating on the distinct risks they each pose and the regulatory frameworks designed to mitigate them. First-generation systems are built to execute the intentions of their human designers, yet they can unintentionally engage in unforeseen risky behaviors. For instance, the algorithmic complexity of these systems tends to grow over time as new strategies are layered on top of existing ones. This accumulation makes such systems susceptible to what Charles Perrow, in his seminal 1984 book *Normal Accidents,* described as "normal accidents"—major, unanticipated failures that emerge from the complex interactions and tightly coupled components of these systems (Perrow 1999).

Trading automatons may also encounter normal accidents, but the primary risks they introduce are of a different kind. Specifically, systems that rely on deep learning techniques grapple with the fundamental problem that, in this type of ML, it is notoriously difficult to explain the rationale behind the decisions they make. As a result, firms deploying these advanced techniques face the daunting possibility that their trading automatons might learn to trade in ways that are either manipulative or excessively risky. While I discuss how this issue might be partially addressed through a focus on organizational reliability, I also consider the broader systemic risk these automatons pose—particularly, the risk of inadvertently converging on similar trading strategies, which could lead to financial herding and contagion.

As mentioned, a significant challenge with deep learning–based trading automatons is the opacity of their inner workings, even to their human designers (K. Hansen and Borch 2021). This issue of explainability extends beyond trading systems and is a fundamental concern in deep learning techniques as a whole. In chapter 5, I delve into this problem. After detailing how computer scientists have attempted, albeit unsuccessfully so far, to address the challenge of explainability, I propose an alternative sociological perspective on the relationship between explainability and trading automatons. Specifically, I examine how the staff at one of the trading firms I studied became deeply engaged in deciphering their deep learning-based automaton's "reasoning"—a task that involved treating the automaton as an entity with which some form of postsocial relationship was both possible and essential. While this approach might be easily dismissed as an uneasy anthropomorphism of machines, I argue for interpreting it as being in line with calls for grounding sociological explanations of action in a more robust first-person perspective (Martin 2011) and for emphasizing the importance of taking the role of the other (Mead 1934)—extending this perspective to include nonhuman entities.

Chapter 6 synthesizes and reflects on my key findings, anchoring this reflection partly through Mark Granovetter's (1985) thesis on the embeddedness of economic action in interpersonal relationships. I examine the extent to which Granovetter's human-centric concept applies to the market arrangement of automated trading, contending that while it retains some analytical relevance, it falls short in instances where (a) market actions are carried out by trading automatons that, because of

their semi-independent nature, are effectively disengaged from interpersonal connections; and (b) market interactions occur solely among automated systems. I
argue for the development of a new "intermachine sociology" to better understand
how trading automatons interact with each other and with other automated systems. I close the book with reflections on areas that extend beyond the study of
trading automatons: the dynamics of finance in the Global South, the emerging
frontier of quantum computing, and the growing presence of automatons in nonfinancial domains.

A few brief observations are warranted based on this overview of the chapters.
First, my scope extends beyond MacKenzie's work on HFT. While I engage with
the material infrastructures MacKenzie has explored in great depth in relation to
HFT, my focus is broader and includes (a) the organizational level of trading firms,
particularly their efforts to establish functioning automated systems—concerns
that go beyond material infrastructures; (b) the risks introduced by the adoption
of ML; and (c) the implications of these developments for the sociology of finance.
Additionally, it is important to note that while MacKenzie's research on HFT
provides limited insight into the uptake of ML, HFT can be pursued using both
first-generation and second-generation systems. Indeed, several of the trading automatons designed by my informants were developed specifically for HFT.

Another observation is that many dimensions of ML's integration into finance
extend beyond the scope of this book. Specifically, since my focus is on automated
asset trading, I do not examine how ML is increasingly utilized for other functions
within the financial sector. A 2019 survey, conducted jointly by the Bank of England and the British Financial Conduct Authority (2019), highlighted that ML
is applied across various areas, including—in addition to asset trading—risk management, compliance, customer engagement, and credit processes, such as credit
scoring (similarly, see Spears and Hansen 2025; World Economic Forum 2018). The
exploration of ML's role in these sectors will be left for future studies.

TWO

Human Action at a Distance

First-Generation Automated Trading Systems

LASALLE STREET IN CHICAGO IS home to the Chicago Board of Trade (CBOT) building. Completed in 1930, this iconic Art Deco skyscraper was the city's tallest for
more than three decades. For an even longer period, it symbolized the essence of
interhuman trading, with its six-story-high trading floor hosting an array of pits
where traders, like Frank introduced in chapter 1, would engage with one another.
Testifying to its importance, the CBOT plays a central role in Zaloom's (2006)
exploration of the shift from interhuman to electronic screen trading, based on her
fieldwork as a runner there in the late 1990s.[1] When I visited the building over a few
days in 2014, my focus was not on the pits. By that time, most pits had been closed,
with only a few options pits still active, reflecting the transformation analyzed by
Zaloom. Instead, I was there to conduct interviews in firms located many stories
above, where the buying and selling of assets had been redefined by sophisticated
automated computer systems. The key characteristic these offices shared with the
floors below was the quiet emanating from the now-empty pits. Beyond that, these
were entirely different environments—in the offices upstairs, people worked in
front of their individual stacks of screens, soda cans littered the desks, and a relaxed
yet focused atmosphere prevailed. Couches and pinball machines stood unused, left
to their own devices.

In this chapter, I explore the inner workings of first-generation automated trading firms like those I visited in the upper echelons of the CBOT building. These

firms aim to translate human-conceived trading strategies into code. My focus is on understanding the organizational and technological factors that shape such firms, including their internal workflow, the material and technological infrastructures they must establish, and some of the primary challenges they encounter. As Souleles (2024, 62) aptly notes, in automated trading, "Before any trade can occur, traders need computer systems to access markets." However, establishing the infrastructure to provide this access is a highly intricate and multidimensional task, fraught with numerous risks if executed incorrectly.

To shed light on these complexities, I ask: How is first-generation automated trading carried out in practice? What endeavors does it involve? What kinds of division of labor, expertise, and collaboration are necessary? And where do attempts at automated trading most commonly go wrong? While much of the chapter addresses the concerns and practices of those working to set up first-generation automated trading systems, I conclude with some reflections on the broader implications of this type of trading—specifically, whether it is embedded in or detached from the real economy. However, the chapter begins by addressing a more fundamental question: Why automate the trading of financial assets in the first place?

I should note that, because automation allows for a range of approaches, much of what I discuss here applies broadly, regardless of the specific strategy or strategies trading firms employ. While my focus in the following sections is not on the particular trading strategies of the firms I interviewed, it is helpful to provide a sense of the diversity of strategies that exist. For example, several of my informants specialized in market making. Similar to a secondhand car dealer, a market maker is someone willing to buy from sellers and sell to buyers. The underlying business model revolves around earning the "spread" between the bid and the ask price, which essentially represents the compensation the market maker receives for providing liquidity to other market participants.[2] Other common automated trading strategies include various forms of arbitrage, which seek to exploit temporary price discrepancies across correlated assets; momentum strategies, which aim to profit from predicting price movements in either direction; mean-reversion strategies, which attempt to capitalize on the idea that prices, after rising or falling for some time, will revert to a historical mean; and combinations of these strategies.

Similarly, brokers executing orders on behalf of clients—such as large institutional investors—frequently rely on "execution algorithms," automated tools designed to execute client orders in an optimal manner. These algorithms are typically engineered for high-speed operation, aiming to minimize their market footprint and reduce price impact. Placing a large order directly into the market can disrupt supply-and-demand dynamics, potentially triggering price fluctuations. Before the order is fully executed, prices may shift unfavorably, leaving the client with a less desirable outcome than intended. To counter this, execution algorithms break down large parent orders into smaller child orders, executing them over an extended period, possibly throughout the entire day. In other words, nearly any conventional trading or execution strategy can be automated.

Why Automate?

Why would a trading firm embrace automation, given the considerable costs and complexities involved? Industry insiders offer four main—often overlapping—reasons for automating asset trading. The first reason has to do with the inherent limitations of electronic screen trading. Central to this is a *cognitive constraint*. While electronic screen trading was initially championed as a rational alternative to the visceral, body-driven dynamics of pit trading—holding the promise of transforming the human trader into "an efficient trading machine" (Zaloom 2006, 83)—this market arrangement is fundamentally restricted by the sheer volume of information a human can process and respond to. No matter how much discipline these traders cultivate in their methodical approach to the task (Zaloom 2006), their actions are still confined by the limits of what they can comprehend from their screens. Adding to this, monitoring the market—hour after hour—is not only physically taxing but also mentally draining. This challenge arises both in periods of rapid market movement, when traders must quickly absorb and react to large amounts of information, and during quieter periods, when traders must resist the temptation "to take a position for the sheer stimulation of being in the game" (Zaloom 2006, 137).

Relatedly, because of the cognitive limitations of electronic screen trading, this form of trading is not scalable. A trader monitoring market developments on three or four screens cannot suddenly expand their attention to include fifteen more, nor can they track a large number of financial instruments with the same degree of focus. Scaling this type of trading would require bringing in additional personnel to monitor new markets in real time. This is where automation offers a solution. Jack, who was introduced in chapter 1 and who led a small first-generation automated trading firm, emphasized how automation enabled his firm to expand its operations: "At the very beginning when we had fifteen positions, it wasn't auto-

mated, and it was extremely difficult to manage. You would spend a whole day star-
ing at the computer. It was exhausting and you'd make all kinds of mistakes, but at
the end we had about maybe four hundred positions long or short at any one time,
and it wouldn't have been humanly possible to do it other than fully automated."
Charles, an experienced CEO of a proprietary trading shop specializing in automation, echoed this sentiment:

> A lot of [electronic screen] traders have this attitude of "I have to watch the screen
> and then I have to process [the information on] it and then I have to make the
> decision based on what I see in the market." I think that limits the scale, because
> how many things can you actually watch? [Electronic screen trading] is tiring. It's
> mistake prone. It's not a scalable approach, . . . but if we can codify what you do as
> a [screen] trader—and maybe we can't codify it to the same degree but if we can
> codify it to *some* degree—we can scale it like thousands of times larger than you
> could do by sitting in front of the screen and watching [it]. . . . So, it's not [about]
> trying to be better than a person but it's [about] recognizing that a person has a very
> limited capacity and not letting that be a limiting factor in the scale of the business.

Charles pointed out that these cognitive and scalability limitations translate directly into practical challenges. Disregarding holidays, the Chicago Mercantile Exchange (CME) operates electronic trading from Sunday at 5:00 p.m. until Friday at
4:00 p.m. CT, with only a single one-hour break each day. During this hour, traders can enter, modify, or cancel orders during a fifteen-minute "preopen" session,
although no matching of orders occurs. Essentially, therefore, markets are active
twenty-three hours a day, from Sunday to Friday, leaving just a forty-five-minute
daily pause.[3] For a human, monitoring and responding to market developments
nonstop is clearly impossible. However, automation is perfectly suited to handle
this continuous activity. As Charles emphasized, the shift to automated trading is
"about trying to create an infrastructure where we can take advantage of all the opportunities around the globe in a way that's low cost and flexible and very scalable."
Once the infrastructure is in place, automated strategies can be deployed across
different markets and time zones without requiring human traders to constantly
monitor screens for new exploitable opportunities.

A second key motivation for automating the trading of financial assets is *speed*.
This, in part, addresses the limitations of electronic screen trading mentioned
earlier. While a human trader might see an opportunity on the screen and click
their mouse to place an order within one or two seconds, automation allows for
a far faster observation-and-response time—well beyond anything a human could

achieve. The drive to exploit machines' speed has sparked intense competition over "latency," the time it takes for market participants to react to changes. As discussed in chapter 1, being faster than competitors has always been a coveted edge in trading, with history offering numerous examples of new technologies being adopted to improve latency. Automation offers a radical solution to the speed race. By entrusting market response to computer algorithms and the infrastructures that support them, automation enables latencies far shorter than anything achievable by human perception.

This is precisely what MacKenzie (2021) highlights in his work on the material political economy of HFT: thanks to automation, latencies have continued to shrink, nearing the speed of light. MacKenzie reports that, using the fastest microwave data transmissions available (as of 2016), it takes only 3.98 milliseconds (thousandths of a second) to transmit data between Chicago's data centers—the hub of derivatives trading—and New Jersey, where the primary US stock exchange servers are located. For comparison, the "Einsteinian limit," as MacKenzie (2021, 146) describes it—"the speed of light in a vacuum"—clocks in at 3.94 milliseconds. For strategies where firms are in direct competition to be the fastest—such as market making, where it is crucial to be "on top of the order book" (see below)—one firm's advantage in latency will drive others to close the gap.[4]

A third major reason for adopting automation is the belief that it provides a *more systematic approach* to trading. This ties into risk management and the cognitive limitations faced by human screen traders, including their difficulty in fully grasping their risk exposure at any given moment. Ken, head of algorithmic trading at a large regional bank, noted that "there are so many trades, thousands per day, that it is almost impossible for a human trader to grasp the actual risk he has," whereas automated systems "continuously keep track of what risk we have."

In addition to allegedly ensuring more prudent risk management, entrusting market entry and exit decisions to computer algorithms is believed to significantly reduce the emotional dimension of trading (Borch and Lange 2017). In preautomated markets, human decision-making was vulnerable to emotional influences. This susceptibility evokes long-standing tropes about traders being swept up in market shifts—whether through sudden panic or by being drawn into a "social avalanche" (Borch 2020)—where individual behavior becomes influenced by the crowd's momentum (Borch 2007; K. Hansen 2015, 2021a; Stäheli 2013; Zimmerman 2006).[5] Such tropes are not confined to interhuman trading, where traders physically share space on the floor. They also apply to electronic screen trading, where traders can become overly attached to the markets they observe (Knorr Cetina and Bruegger 2002b). The danger in such emotional engagement is that it may lead traders to make impulsive decisions—ones they regret in hindsight. Automation, therefore, is presented as an antidote to this risk. One "how to" guide on automated trading, for example, frames automation as the cure for emotion-driven, high-risk market behavior: "An important part of algorithmic trading is that it takes out the human emotional aspect of trading. Trading decisions made by algorithms are based solely on the data analysed and not the whims, fear and greed of an individual human trader" (Vaananen 2015, 210).

Finally, the shift to automated trading is driven by *cost concerns*. This is particularly relevant for market participants such as banks that employ large teams of electronic screen traders. These traders command high salaries, so automating their tasks presents a clear opportunity for cost savings. As Ken pointedly asked, why "should we . . . have twenty traders, who are very, very expensive, to sit and do something that in reality seven people can do" through automation? This reflects a broader, long-standing pursuit in industrialized societies: the replacement of costly human labor with more efficient machine power. Karl Marx's observation in *Grundrisse* (1993, 704) about manual labor applies just as well to the modern trader in the age of automation: "What was the living worker's activity becomes the activity of the machine."

Getting the Infrastructure Right

At first glance, automating the trading of financial assets might seem straightforward. First-generation automated trading is essentially about converting human-conceived strategies into computer code and implementing that code on machine infrastructures, linking individual trading firms to the various venues where they wish to trade. Yet, despite these systems merely being designed to enact the ideas of their human creators—essentially, forming machine-mediated human action at a distance—the efforts required to do this successfully are substantial. In fact, compared to previous market arrangements, automated trading demands a far greater commitment to technological components, where hardware and software are deeply intertwined. This emphasis on technology is reflected in how many automated trading firms now see themselves to be as much technology companies as they are finance companies. As Charles explained, "I would liken us to a tech start-up where you don't have any customers." To succeed, he added, "What's important is that you are building the right foundation." Building the right foundation means crafting a meticulously tailored infrastructure—both software and hardware—where IT and technology are not just afterthoughts but are placed firmly at the core.

A key reason for this focus is that firms specializing in first-generation systems typically design their strategies around the electronic order books of trading venues. As discussed in chapter 1, an electronic order book is a list maintained by a financial exchange or trading venue of unmatched bids to buy or offers to sell particular financial assets.[6] For example, if a firm's automated trading system places an order to buy one thousand Apple shares at a specific price, that bid is added to the venue's electronic order book if it cannot immediately be matched with an offer to sell one thousand shares (or a portion thereof) at the requested price. Figure 2.1 provides an idealized view of an electronic order book.

In this example, the electronic order book operates on a price-time matching principle, which means that (a) orders are prioritized based on their price, with the best prices executed first; and (b) for orders at the same price level, the system uses a "queue" matching principle, where earlier orders are fulfilled first when a counterparty becomes available—akin to a line of people waiting to buy a cup of coffee. This price-time matching model, also referred to as the "first in, first out" (FIFO) principle, is the most widely used approach in electronic trading. However, some

Figure 2.1: Example of an order book, inspired by MacKenzie (2019a, 44).

Bids to buy				Offers to sell			
Most recently added		First added		First added			Most recently added
			$51.21	690	350	100	
			$51.20	250	80		
			$51.19	220			
			$51.18	100	300	500	
			$51.17	350	250		
	220	100	$51.16				
350	400	50	$51.15				
		650	$51.14				
100	350	200	$51.13				
700	600	200	$51.12				

Source: Author.

trading venues adopt an alternative model known as "pro rata," where larger orders are given priority over smaller ones, regardless of their time of entry. Whatever the matching principle, any changes to the electronic order book represent crucial information that automated trading strategies typically observe and respond to. For example, if more bids to buy begin accumulating relative to offers to sell, this signals an impending price increase, and an automated trading system may be designed to exploit that signal (MacKenzie 2021, 18).

In addition to order-book updates, automated trading systems typically consider other relevant market data, such as trade and price data (that is, information about when and at what prices bids and offers are matched, opening and closing prices, and similar). Indeed, order-book and market data form the essential informational universe for automated trading systems. To be more precise, these data *are* the market. There are exceptions and nuances to this pattern. For example, some first-generation systems might combine order-book data with "fundamental data," including company earnings reports, securities analysts' reports (E. Zuckerman 2004), or announcements of key economic figures, such as unemployment rates, inflation numbers, and interest rates. However, firms pursuing low-latency strategies typically focus more on granular order-book and market data.

The electronic order book, along with how it is accessed, is the product of a complex assemblage of hardware and software components. From a trading firm's perspective, establishing a connection to the venue or venues on which it wishes to trade is a crucial task. While this is largely a hardware challenge, as I will discuss shortly, it is also a matter of "speaking the venue's language," which is primarily a software issue. Specifically, a trading firm must establish a communication channel with the trading venue, ensuring that its orders are submitted in a way that the venue can process while also receiving various market data from the venue. Jonathan explained that "each exchange has a protocol language for how you communicate with it." In the United States alone, there are thirteen registered national stock exchanges, over forty alternative trading venues, and the CME, the central hub for futures trading. At first glance, this may suggest a bewildering variety of protocols, reminiscent of a Babylonian language landscape. In practice, however, the situation is simpler because the Financial Information eXchange (FIX) protocol, introduced in 1992 as a messaging format among market participants, has become the industry standard. Many exchanges use FIX as the foundation for their systems. For example, CME Globex, the first electronic trading platform for futures and options contracts, which also launched in 1992, is built on the FIX protocol.[7]

Using the venue-specific protocol, firms can send messages to the venue specifying orders to buy or sell financial assets, as well as messages regarding modifications or cancellations of existing orders. These messages first arrive at the venue's "order gateway"—essentially a computer that "acts as a check that the message is properly formatted" (meaning it follows the venue's messaging protocol) and then "routes it to the correct matching engine," the venue's server responsible for matching incoming bids to buy and offers to sell, provided that a counterparty is available (MacKenzie 2021, 137). I will return later to why it is critically important for trading firms to build their own replica of this matching engine, but for now it is enough to note that if an incoming order can be matched, the venue sends a "fill" or partial fill message to the respective parties (the buyer and seller). If the order cannot be matched, it is added to the electronic order book, in which case the firm submitting the order receives a "confirm" message. Similarly, when a firm submits an order cancellation message, it receives an acknowledgment from the venue (Borch, Skar-Gislinge, and David 2025; MacKenzie 2021, 138–39).

While this describes the direct, back-and-forth messaging between trading firms and venues—and importantly, each venue requires its own distinct messaging system, which, though FIX based, may include venue-specific features—automated trading firms also rely on another type of message from venues: the so-called market data feeds. These feeds include trades, price data, and order-book updates, which detail new orders, modifications, or removals of existing orders. These feeds are essential, as they offer rapid insights into the current state of the market. However, subscribing to them is costly.[8] In addition to the fast data feeds received directly from venues, trading firms operating in the US also subscribe to a slower "consolidated" data feed. This official feed consolidates quotes for shares and options traded on and across US exchanges.

The data received from various feeds are substantial. According to one software developer, Peter, his firm receives "hundreds of gigabytes a day, an awful lot of stuff," from the CME alone. To manage the enormous data-feed input, trading firms develop specialized "feed handlers." These are software applications that receive real-time venue and consolidated feeds, check for errors and inconsistencies (including discrepancies between venue feeds and consolidated feeds), convert the raw data into a format that the firm's algorithms can process, and then forward the data to the automated trading system, which observes and responds to it. The system then decides, on the basis of the latest market data and the firm's risk profile, whether and how to act.

For firms focused on low-latency strategies, the speed at which feed handlers process data is critical. The faster the data feeds are handled and sent to the automated trading system, the quicker it can respond to market movements. Alex, a senior software developer, emphasized that, when "the full life cycle of a trade" is considered, the first priority is how quickly the data "coming out of the exchange—out of a market data feed—[get] to you." He described it as a "firehose of information," stressing that the speed at which these data are processed is a key challenge and that developing efficient feed handlers is crucial. "Then it's how quick can you make a decision and how fast can you get it through risk and back to the exchange as an order."

This is where software and hardware considerations intersect. The speed of the feed handler depends in part on the hardware technology on which it is implemented. In recent years, field-programmable gate arrays (FPGAs) have become more common, as they are among the fastest hardware technologies available in this field (again, see MacKenzie 2021, 169–71). But even with FPGAs, software plays a pivotal role. As Alex put it, "You [could] have the fastest hardware, but you still could write inefficient algorithms, so your software has to be the best. You have to have the best algorithms and the best programmers to implement the fastest algorithms" so as to receive, process, and respond to market data quickly.

FPGAs are just one example of how materiality plays a critical role in automated trading. Another important example is "colocation"—a service offered by trading venues where automated trading firms, particularly those specializing in low-latency trading, purchase access to place their own computer servers in the venue's data center, where the matching engine is hosted. Colocation ensures that the trading firm's server is physically close to the exchange's server, connected via cables through which messages are sent back and forth, and through which the venue transmits its data feeds. The entire rationale behind this service is straightforward: having one's server physically proximate to the venue's server reduces the length of the connecting cables, and shorter cables mean faster data transmission (i.e., lower latency). Large firms typically purchase colocation directly from exchanges, while smaller firms might opt for more affordable alternatives, such as leasing access through technology providers.

To be sure, setting up an infrastructure that supports low-latency trading is not equally relevant for all firms engaged in first-generation automated trading. Firms that specialize in longer-term strategies—those seeking to capitalize on price movements expected over weeks or months—do not need to prioritize speed. However, for firms employing automated market-making strategies, latency is a critical concern for two reasons. First, market makers place passive orders, meaning they submit buy and sell orders that other participants can accept if they choose to, and to earn the spread between bid and ask prices it is vital that these passive orders find counterparties. When order matching follows a FIFO principle, the likelihood of passive orders being executed increases if those orders are positioned "on top of the book." To secure this advantageous position, the system must not only submit orders with competitive prices but also do so more quickly than competing systems. Second, automated market-making strategies require hedging positions to limit risk exposure, which involves placing orders for multiple financial instruments simultaneously. If the price of one instrument shifts, the firm must quickly adjust its orders for the other instruments to avoid being run over. Indeed, having "stale quotes" in the market is considered a significant risk for market-making strategies (MacKenzie 2021). As Charles explained, the central implication is that automated market making is less about the specific strategy itself and more about the latency infrastructure supporting it: "The math behind a market-making trading strategy is actually really simple. It's bid plus offer divided by two and then shaded somehow. [However,] you have to be at the top of the book, but being at the top of the book means it's not about math, it's all about technology."

A final, critical component of the fundamental infrastructure that trading firms must have in place before engaging in any automated trading activity is an internal replica of the matching engine briefly mentioned earlier. Every electronic trading venue has a matching engine responsible for pairing incoming buy and sell orders. This matching engine effectively encapsulates the venue's trading rules, functionalities, and logic. These elements not only vary over time but also differ across venues. For instance, matching engines may use different algorithms to match orders, such as FIFO or pro rata, and they may support different types of orders (which will be discussed later). It is crucial for trading firms to build their own version of the venues' matching engines in order to test their strategies. Once firms have designed this internal replica, they can assess the likelihood that their automated strategies will consistently generate profits. I will return to the intricacies of this process below.

By now, two things should be clear. First, automated trading is not solely about developing software systems—or algorithms. Instead, it involves a sophisticated interplay of layers encompassing hardware, software, data, access, and more. Kristian Bondo Hansen (2024, 4) aptly captures this complexity by describing it as a "stack," defined as "a structure of vertically organized interoperable and thus interdependent layers." Second, setting up the basic infrastructure for first-generation automated trading—getting the stack in place, not to mention maintaining its functionality—is both complex and expensive. The costs extend beyond hardware, colocation, and data; they also include the salaries for the extensive preparatory work needed before a single order to buy or sell assets can be placed. For instance, designing and developing the software platform that connects a firm to trading venues—enabling communication, receiving, processing, and responding to market data—is a formidable coding task. One of my informants, Raymond, a senior software developer who had previously worked at a hedge fund, was part of a four-person team tasked with building the fund's automated trading software infrastructure from scratch. Raymond's specific responsibility was coding the "FIX communication engine." Meanwhile, another person handled the order-matching system, someone else managed the market data collector (the feed handler), and a fourth team member developed the risk management system. Even with each member working full-time on these separate components, it took the team "about a year and a half to develop all the systems."

Beyond building the infrastructure, the strategies to be executed through it need to be developed, adding further time to the overall process. Setting up an entire organization for automated trading can therefore take significantly longer than 1.5 years. For illustration, Charles noted that even three years after launching his firm, "we're probably 75 percent of the way. There there's still a critical 25 percent of stuff that's not automated," referring to the software components that still needed to be implemented on the underlying platform.

Taking Automated Trading from Ideas to Code

Once the basic infrastructure is in place, the process of hunting for and implementing automated trading strategies can begin. This typically involves collaboration between traders, quantitative analysts (or quants), and software developers—commonly referred to in the industry as simply "developers," who are usually proficient in programming languages like Java and C++. The specific roles of traders, analysts, and developers, as well as the tasks they perform and the expertise they bring, vary both historically and depending on the size of the firm (Seyfert 2016). In general, traders are responsible for strategy detection. Drawing on their market knowledge, they identify potential trading opportunities. Quantitative analysts assist with testing these proposed strategies and formalizing them to ensure that they can be more easily translated into code. Developers then take the formalized strategies and convert them into actual code, ensuring that it aligns with the firm's underlying infrastructure so that the strategies can be executed on the company's servers.

In larger firms the roles of trader, analyst, and developer tend to be more distinctly separated, whereas in smaller firms there is often some overlap between them (Seyfert 2016). However, even smaller firms may have clearly defined roles. The firm where Frank serves as head of trading, though consisting of just eleven people, maintains a clear division of labor among traders, analysts, and developers, paired with strong collaboration between them. As Frank explained, the traders "come up with trading ideas, which we can then simplify enough for the algorithms to trade them. . . . We might say, 'We are looking for an algorithm that will exit [its positions] when these parameters are breached.'" The analysts would then assist with the research needed to support those ideas.[9]

What exactly does a "trading strategy" refer to? Broadly, it means seeking to exploit "signals" or statistical patterns in the markets. Traders are generally agnostic about what constitutes a signal, as long as it can be used in a trading strategy. That said, MacKenzie (2018b, 1638) has identified several common classes of signals used in first-generation low-latency automated trading systems. These include order-book dynamics (such as imbalances between offers to sell and bids to buy), "futures lead" (where changes in the share-index futures market tend to precede changes in the market for the underlying shares), correlations across assets (such as stocks within the same industry), and fragmentation across markets (where the same asset may trade at different venues).[10] However, even within these classes, the challenge lies in correctly identifying a true signal. As Jonathan observed, "There really isn't a lot of signal in the markets; it's almost all noise." Further complicating matters, what initially looks like a signal may turn out to be a spurious pattern. "It's possible that the same pattern can happen twice without any meaning," he continued, raising the question "Can we trade that pattern profitably? If the pattern occurs with some regularity, and after that pattern occurs we make money on it however we're trading it, then we assume that that would be a signal."

In their search for signals, traders may draw on their past market experience or attempt to learn from existing strategies, often conducting post-trade analyses to evaluate how already-implemented strategies are performing. Regardless of the source of their ideas, traders typically begin by examining them using programming languages like Matlab, Python, or R. If the initial analysis is promising, traders and quants may then move forward and assess how the prospective strategy performs in a simulated market environment. This ties into the essential infrastructure of automated trading: before any strategy goes live, it must undergo rigorous testing in an artificial market that mirrors actual markets in all important respects. This is why one of Raymond's teammates, mentioned earlier, coded a matching engine—trading firms need to replicate the functionalities of the venues' matching engines to assess how a strategy is likely to perform once executed.

The emphasis on functionalities is intentional, because one trading venue's matching engine may differ significantly from another's, meaning the same strategy could produce varying results depending on where it is executed. Key functionalities include the speed at which orders are processed, the types of orders that can be placed, the messaging protocol used, and the principles by which orders are matched. If two venues are trading the same (or closely related) financial assets but handle incoming orders at different speeds, this could have serious implications for a strategy's success—making it vital to test these variables before deploying the strategy. As Raymond explained to me, the simulation environment needs to account for "how long it would take to fill the order[s]," including "how the fills were handled if you had different order types." This points to the fact that there are countless ways to send orders to buy and sell assets. Perhaps the best known are "market orders" and "limit orders." A market order buys or sells a certain number of assets at the best current price. A limit order, in contrast, aims to buy a certain number of assets at or below a specific price or to sell them at or above a designated price. Different venues and their matching engines may support a vast array of limit orders. Mattli (2019, 123) reports that the NYSE offers eighty different order types, while other exchanges allow for up to "2,000 different combinations of instructions for placing orders." Once again, the viability of a strategy may hinge on the specific order type used, and this is something that can—and should—be tested by replicating a matching engine capable of supporting such functionalities.

As with many other aspects discussed thus far, the idea of setting up a simulation environment to test prospective strategies may sound straightforward, but in practice it involves a great deal of effort, and many thorny questions arise along the way. As Charles put it, when "you build a matching engine for simulation, you can build a lot of bad assumptions into it. So you have this whole model drift, if you will, that's just based on the fact that your matching algorithm is not exactly what the exchange's is." The fundamental problem is that, ideally, the simulation environment should replicate the operations of actual exchanges as closely as possible. But how do you know when this has been achieved? According to Raymond, his team took several steps to ensure that their simulation environment provided a realistic representation of the exchanges where they intended to trade. By placing orders on the exchanges and collecting all market data, including tick data (every trade and order-book event), along with accurate time stamps, they could capture the actual order flow and real order fill latencies. This dataset was then compared to their simulation environment:

> We would try and make sure that the simulation was correct by [saying], "[We] have the market data that was reported; [we] have the orders that [we] placed that day on the exchange . . . and the exact times we sent them." . . . Then you run that through the simulator. If, say, 50 percent of the orders [fill] the way that you experienced on that day, there may be something wrong, so you have to work on it and tweak the simulator. Something like 80 to 90 percent [correct filling] is pretty accurate.

The actual testing of strategies typically involves two steps: historical back-testing and paper trading. First, the strategy is analyzed in light of historical data—the analysts examine how well the strategy would have performed given how the markets evolved over the past five to ten years, for instance. While this is, by design, a hypothetical test, its value lies in the assumption that, given the sheer number of market events over time, testing a strategy's multiyear historical performance offers the best possible evaluation of the scenarios and market conditions under which it is likely to succeed if eventually deployed.

Two things are crucial when it comes to strategies and their back-testing. First, as hinted at earlier, many traders adopt a highly pragmatic approach to the ideas they pursue when searching for new strategies. When asked whether his firm is committed to specific types of strategies, William, a quantitative researcher at a major global investment management firm, said, "No, not at all. Any new idea, if we can back-test it, we will take it," as long as it is "right in 51 percent of the cases." Second, back-testing an automated strategy's performance involves far more than just evaluating its profitability (Borch and Lange 2017). Informants emphasized that back-testing also considers factors such as the strategy's risk profile, including how hedging might be conducted; fill-rate probabilities (the chance that submitted orders will be executed fully or partially); order resting time (the duration for which orders remain in the order book before being filled or canceled—this is significant because higher resting times equate to longer exposure); and the consistency of the strategy's performance across different market scenarios.

If a strategy is found to perform well on historical data—as well as under the stress tests I return to in chapters 3 and 4—the next step in the testing process is to let it "paper-trade." This, too, is a simulation exercise, but instead of relying on historical data, it lets live market data flow through the simulation environment. The goal of this step is to address potential issues arising from the fact that historical data might differ in crucial ways from present-day market conditions. For instance, the overall liquidity or volatility of markets may have shifted, making certain strategies that performed well historically less suited to the current market regime. To account for such differences, the simulation lets the automated strategy place orders in an environment that closely mirrors the real-time market, but without taking actual positions—meaning no money is at risk.

Testing the strategy in simulation often leads to fine-tuning at various stages. Traders and analysts may adjust its parameters—such as the amount of risk it takes, the frequency of order placement, how it responds to different volatility levels, and how and when it enters and exits positions—and explore the expected outcomes of these modifications. This phase of strategy development is a highly collaborative effort between traders and analysts. As Adnan explained: "If the trading [team] wants to find a way to do something better on the hedging side, they might ask me to think about it, or they might come up with a solution, or we can sit and talk about it." As this suggests, preparing a strategy for market deployment often requires multiple back-and-forth iterations between traders and analysts. In some cases, a proposed strategy might even be scrapped if the testing procedures yield negative results. Given that strategies can vary widely in complexity, informants offered different estimates of how long it takes to develop and test a new first-generation strategy. Timothy, a director of investment, said: "It really depends on how complicated they are. I think the longest one we've ever had would have been total about a year. Some of them, you know, just a day, it really depends on how many moving parts there are and how many constraints we have." Jonathan similarly suggested that it occasionally takes "very little time, days," to develop a strategy. However, others, such as Gregor, the head of technology at one of the world's major banks, dismissed the idea of such a quick turnaround: "I consider it to be probably like six months at the minimum. It really depends on if you're starting completely from scratch or you already have ten strategies and you need to deliver the eleventh. It's not really easy to answer the question, but I would say probably three to six months depending on the situation—definitely not a couple of days."

What happens when a strategy is deemed promising enough to go live in the markets? The first step is to incorporate it into the firm's software architecture. This is the developers' domain, as they are responsible for the underlying code base. After receiving the fully tested strategy from the analysts, the developers encode it so that it fits seamlessly into the framework, which includes the messaging protocol system, the risk management system, and the feed handler. At one firm where I conducted interviews, this translation into code involved a division of labor between analysts and developers. If it was a new strategy or a significant modification to an existing one, the developers handled the code implementation, with the analysts reviewing it to ensure that it aligned with the traders' intentions. If the traders and analysts had come up with only a minor improvement to an existing strategy, the analysts would implement the code, while the developer team reviewed it. So the responsibility for final code implementation depended on the extent to which the underlying system infrastructure was affected, with more fundamental changes requiring the developers' specialized coding expertise.

The next step is to begin trading the strategy. Typically, this is done gradually, starting with small orders and progressively adding more capital behind it. The reason for this cautious approach is rooted in the limitations of simulation-based testing: no matter how rigorous the testing, it is always hypothetical and approximative, capturing only parts of the market, since no actual orders are placed. As Peter, the developer, put it, "Testing is very difficult. We can test our algorithms to the nth degree, and we can say under these input conditions, these things will happen. The reality is, you can't simulate an entire market." John, the head of quantitative research at a bank, echoed this sentiment: "You can only simulate so much. At some point you have to put [the strategy] in the wild and see how the markets react to it before you know if it's a good idea or not."

Specifically, the critical issue that testing does not address is the potential impact a strategy's orders might have on the market. In other words, what cannot be tested through historical data and paper trading is how the automated system's orders could move prices and influence order-book dynamics, including how other market participants might respond. The importance of this issue depends largely on the types of strategies being pursued and the liquidity profile of the market. Charles emphasized that the market impact issue is more significant for strategies like market making, which provide liquidity, whereas it is less of a concern for more aggressive strategies that take liquidity. The reason is simple: when orders are posted passively, they are added to the order book, potentially triggering other participants to adjust their orders in response. In contrast, aggressive orders immediately consume liquidity, and while this action does alter the order book, the fact that such orders do not linger means they are far less exposed to strategic reactions from other market participants.

Similarly, market impact is less of a concern in highly liquid markets, where individual orders are unlikely to have much influence unless they are large. But in less liquid markets, this is a much bigger issue. For example, even though orders to buy or sell assets can be placed outside regular "market hours," liquidity typically drops significantly during these "after-hours." The CEO of a firm specializing in automated options trading flagged this as a major challenge. While options markets vary in their liquidity profiles (some options contracts are highly liquid, while others are not), "The liquidity profile of most markets after hours is very different than real time hours, and that [entails] a whole different set of math and behaviors and algos." Jonathan, the Chicago-based algorithmic futures trader mentioned in chapter 1, echoed this point, explaining that since their automated system sometimes traded 5 to 10 percent of the volume of certain futures contracts during after-hours sessions, they had "started to reach that point [where orders make an impact]. So yeah, you have to be kind of conscious of that effect."

Because this impact is difficult to simulate, Peter noted that when their firm encountered situations where their orders left a recognizable market impact, traders had the discretion to "override the algos" and handle the situation manually, relying on their experience. This touches on the issue of monitoring: once an automated trading strategy is deployed and active in the market, it needs to be continuously monitored.

Monitoring Algorithms: Learning through Trading

The monitoring of strategies serves several purposes. The most immediate is ensuring that they perform as expected. No matter how thoroughly strategies have been tested, software bugs may still lurk, potentially triggering unforeseen behaviors. It is also possible that the system does something unexpected because certain interactions between components were not anticipated. As John described: "Suddenly you see there's a trade that's gone through at a wrong price. Then it's everybody on the deck to figure out, where did that wrong price come from? Where in the system did that transpire? Why was it not caught by the various safety valves? So then you're poring through the logs and trying to use your knowledge of how the various components are connected to resolve the issue as quickly as possible."

Moreover, automated systems may not always behave as their designers intended once they begin *interacting* with other systems in the market. While these systems are conceived as extensions of their human creators—ideally executing traders' ideas directly—when they interact via the order book, it can resemble a complex system where unforeseen behaviors occasionally emerge (Borch, Skar-Gislinge, and David 2025). I will return to this specific issue, along with the challenges it poses, in chapter 5. However, monitoring algorithms in the market is also crucial because of external events that could not have been easily anticipated or tested for. For example, sometimes exchanges experience system failures, leaving trading firms temporarily blind to their positions and forcing them to rely on human intervention. This might involve pressing the "kill button," or "kill switch," which instantly withdraws their orders from the markets. Additionally, political, economic, or other events may suddenly and dramatically disrupt markets, fundamentally altering the conditions under which a strategy had performed well during testing. In such cases, traders may need to pull their automated strategies altogether. Raymond described the procedure at his former hedge fund: "We had two people monitoring the system at all times. They [would] look at the risk profile and pull the strategy if a news story was coming out which we didn't know [how it would affect volatility]. Volatility is obviously good, but sometimes it's unpredictable. If your strategy is getting a huge position, that's not good at the moment because the market can move against you." While some aspects of monitoring can be automated—triggering alerts when something seems off—Raymond's point highlights the necessity of real-time human oversight. As Charles noted, "From a regulatory perspective . . . you cannot *not* have someone watching the algo because in case it ever did something crazy, somebody has to hit the [kill] button." Firms that trade around the clock typically staff different teams of traders to oversee the algorithms during their respective shifts.

Another key reason for monitoring automated systems during live trading is the potential for learning—whether to optimize existing strategies, tweak specific features, or gain inspiration for developing new ones. In an ideal world, traders would devise such brilliant strategies that the entire workflow, from idea generation to quant testing to developer implementation, would produce a golden stream of profits needing no future adjustments. However, that image has little resonance with reality. While some informants recounted instances where they had created strategies that were profitable for several years[11]—or shared anecdotal accounts of rival firms reportedly generating consistently lucrative strategies—the prevailing sentiment was that the profitability of any automated strategy tends to have a short lifespan. The reason most often mentioned for this decay was increasing competition: strategies deployed in automated trading are viable for only a brief time before competitors either adopt them or figure out how to trade against them. Opinions varied about how long strategies tend to remain profitable, but many suggested that most automated strategies deteriorate after a few months and certainly need continuous adjustments to stay effective (Borch and Lange 2017; Seyfert 2016, 265). Gregor remarked that depending on the strategy, "either on a daily or weekly basis you need to do some calibration. . . . Probably every six months you need to do some significant tweaking" to retain profitability.

In light of the challenge posed by strategy decay—requiring traders who devise automated strategies to constantly hunt for new exploitable ideas—monitoring live algorithms incorporates an essential "learning from doing" component for first-generation automated trading.[12] As Charles noted, "We wanna trade because we're learning through trading." Elaborating on this, he explained: "We really only have two strategies, we're constantly evolving the strategies. . . . We're always trying to tweak the logic of the algorithm. . . . They're constantly in flux. . . . A lot of what we do is just figuring out, 'Okay, how can we take the next step and improve this [algorithm]?'" This continuous tweaking of first-generation systems was echoed by other informants. Jim, an algorithmic trader, said his algorithms' parameters needed "to change every month," with much of that change driven by monitoring:

> Jim: You have to monitor [the algorithm] . . . but that gives you ideas. I really do
>   think that if you don't look at your trading you won't get ideas. You won't be
>   inspired, and you won't have lines of inquiry for how to improve it at all.
> Christian: So the ideas you generate are coming from monitoring your trading
>   activity?
> Jim: Oh, very much, very much.

Typically, monitoring would fall under the responsibility of the traders, but post-trade analysis—particularly in identifying and addressing any inefficiencies in the automated strategy—often sparks new rounds of collaboration between traders and analysts. For example, Adnan noted, "We have something running, it's working, but something is not quite right when markets move a lot." In such instances, analysts would work together with traders to devise a solution to the problem. In this way, beyond generating new strategies, a significant portion of the work for both traders and analysts involves refining and enhancing existing strategies through continuous learning from live trading. This iterative process can also include ongoing improvements to the simulation environment, which allows for more accurate testing and better assessments of new strategy elements.

What Could Possibly Go Wrong?

Not surprisingly, the design and execution of first-generation systems can fail at every step of the production pipeline. Insufficient attention to hardware infrastructure, software development, data quality, and strategy creation can each negatively affect the effectiveness of these systems. This is often referred to as "model risk," which concerns the possibility that a model, if built on inaccurate assumptions, poorly developed, insufficiently tested, or improperly implemented, may produce orders that result in financial losses (Svetlova 2018, 105–8).

On the hardware side, firms specializing in low-latency automated trading must pay constant attention to seemingly minute technological details. One of the most obvious considerations is data transmission networks, as analyzed by MacKenzie (2021). Firms that operate across several markets, such as derivatives markets in Chicago and equities markets in New York, need to stay informed about the latest, fastest means of transmitting data between correlated markets. As the latency gap steadily narrows toward the speed of light, even a minor latency advantage or disadvantage can have substantial consequences for the profitability of automated strategies. Therefore, keeping pace with this technological frontier is of critical importance.

However, less apparent material factors also require vigilance. For instance, Seyfert (2016, 265–66) notes that even small fluctuations in temperature can affect the speed at which computer servers process data. If the colocated server and the simulation environment operate under different thermal conditions, the simulation's output may fail to reliably mirror the performance dynamics of the production server it is meant to emulate.

This highlights the critical importance of maintaining a simulation environment, including a matching engine, that closely mirrors actual exchanges. Trading venues regularly update their matching engine functionalities, and being unaware of these changes can lead to dire consequences: testing strategies on a simulation framework that does not reflect the current exchange protocol can lead to failed implementations. Conversely, staying up to date with new functionalities can provide a temporary market edge—just as failing to do so can quickly render previously successful strategies unprofitable. One notable case that illustrates this point is the collapse of algorithmic trader Haim Bodek's firm Trading Machines in 2011. Bodek's once-successful automated strategies were undermined by competitors exploiting a new order type introduced by a trading venue—a functionality Bodek was unaware of until learning about it at a social event hosted by the venue (Mattli 2019, 124–25; Patterson 2012). After Bodek filed a complaint with the SEC, his case drew considerable attention, and the exchange ultimately agreed to pay a fine.

Perhaps because of the attention garnered by the Bodek case, the market professionals I interviewed expressed a heightened awareness of the importance of keeping their systems updated with the latest matching engine functionalities and exchange protocols. Jeff, a senior quantitative researcher, and Gregor emphasized this point: "You have to keep your system up to date with the latest modification of the [exchange's] protocol" (Jeff), because if exchanges "make a change to their protocol, my system might stop working" (Gregor). Informants often conveyed a sense of frustration over these updates, given the amount of work they require from trading firms. As Jim noted, "There's a lot of communication that ends up happening" between exchange staff and firms when the latter attempt to integrate exchange protocol changes into their systems.

Software development presents its own distinct challenges. Part of this stems from software bugs and the failure to detect them. But more broadly, the difficulty lies in how developers translate traders' strategies into code—a translation that might not always fully encapsulate the traders' original intentions. This misalignment often reflects the differing "epistemic regimes" (Seyfert 2016) of traders, quants, and developers, shaped by their diverse professional backgrounds. Beyond that, there are deeper issues stemming from the continuous expansion of the code base, as new strategies are constantly developed and existing ones refined. More strategies mean more lines of code, and the addition of new instruments or markets further inflates this code base. As it grows, different problems arise. One is the risk of unintended feedback effects between components that have been incrementally added. Jonathan described how, as the code base for their first-generation system expanded—"It's probably around the million mark at this point"—the system became so intricate that "every time we changed one part, something else could be affected." A chief risk officer at an automated trading firm voiced a similar concern, noting: "What's very common at the biggest prop firms is that they've added a team over the years, and they've added a new culture and a new technology and a new way of thinking. And over time that builds up and those systems don't talk very well to each other."

Another, partially related issue is the rise of "technical debt." This term refers to the long-term costs that result from pushing development too quickly without adequate foresight. As one developer explained:

> If you allow too many problems to come [into the code base], then you get to a point where the only thing you can do is rewrite. And that's obviously very costly for a company. So I think managing that is quite difficult. Ensuring that you've thought about scalability and not painting yourself into a corner. If you don't have an experienced developer architect, you can get to the point where you might have something working, but when you want to, for argument's sake, put it into a different market, it's gonna take you six months. Because whoever wrote this bit here wrote it specifically for, I don't know, FX options only. And now you can't put it to the commodities [markets], because they haven't written it generic enough. So there's a lot of that. . . . If it's not architected properly from the beginning, you can cause yourself headaches down the road.

Barry, the head of a prop shop, affirmed this point, saying that many firms have "a lot of legacy code" that makes them unable to adapt to changing market conditions.

Then there are issues surrounding data: order-book and market data are integral to proper back-testing. If a firm back-tests its strategies on only a few years' worth of data or an incomplete dataset—such as one containing omissions or faults—this is likely to negatively affect the quality of the testing. Similarly, if a firm is paper trading or live trading without its data feed handler receiving full and up-to-date access to data from venues, it essentially trades in a market setting with less information than its competitors. In other words, both the amount and the quality of market data are central in securing that market participants have an accurate representation of the market. However, both the quality and the volume of data are causes for concern. Regarding data quality, Nick, a senior hedge fund researcher, remarked, "If you don't clean [data] properly, you can find a lot of amazingly profitable strategies" that have no real foundation. The sheer volume of market data creates its own challenges. As mentioned earlier, automated trading has led to an explosion of quotes and trades, which is reflected in the large amounts of data that trading venues channel back to firms subscribing to their feeds. Managing such massive amounts of data means that many firms introduce semiautomated processes for data handling and cleaning. However, as Seyfert (2016, 267) points out, these processes may themselves generate data pollution, for instance by removing apparent outliers that could otherwise provide important information about black swan events.

Yet another data issue concerns time stamps. If order-book and market data are recorded incorrectly or with insufficient granularity, it may be impossible to detect real patterns in the data, or the patterns observed might be misleading. For example, if a series of orders received by a trading venue has been time-stamped wrongly, so that the data suggest that the orders that arrived first came after those that actually arrived last, this distorts any real connection between them. Jim complained that detecting issues with improper time stamps is both difficult and potentially frustrating work. Sometimes even understanding the basic formatting of the data received can be a complex exercise:

> You have to really dig a lot to find this stuff out [concerning time-stamp issues] because when you look at [the data] you think, "Oh, this is useful," and you do the back-test and everything looks great. Then you dig around and realize this is not collected the way you thought it was, [so] you have to throw out the whole project. . . . And then there're obviously interpretation problems: What does this column [in the dataset] mean? It's not always obvious. [Exchanges and data providers] give you one hundred columns . . . with obscure-sounding names, and you have to ask them the right questions about "How exactly was it collected [and] who collected it?"

Data from venues might also not arrive in a standardized form, demanding considerable amounts of standardization work for the firms trying to detect patterns across venues. Peter speculated that the trend toward mergers and acquisitions in the space of financial exchanges was partly to blame for this, with the large exchange conglomerates arising from this focusing less on data standardization.[13] Referring to one of the major US exchanges, Peter said: "They're getting better, but their reference data was all over the place to start with. And I think it's probably because they consumed all of these other exchanges. They all had their own individual systems and everything's not quite the same shape. So there is a bit of data massaging that needs to happen [upon receiving the data]."

In addition to challenges revolving around material infrastructure, software development, and data, strategy development can obviously be done with more or less care as well. One developer, Alex, told me the following anecdote: "I saw a guy once, he's a PhD in math and he paper-traded his algorithm for one day. He got one data point and then decided to change the algorithm. I said, 'You're a mathematician, how can you define a trend with one data point? You need two data points to even draw a line!'" This is an extreme example, and I did not come across other similarly extreme accounts in my fieldwork. However, the example does point to an issue that other informants stressed—namely, that there is an imminent risk of shortcutting the testing of strategies once a tradeable pattern seems to have been detected. As Jonathan put it, "There are always multiple causes that can get to the same effect, so we have to be careful not to just pick the cause that we think we want," especially highlighting the concern that statistical tests may churn out spurious patterns. In spite of the care needed in this domain, some informants suggested that sometimes the ideal production process from strategy development, to systematic testing, to deployment is replaced by a more pragmatic approach. For example, Peter described instances where testing might not be conducted as rigorously as desired before strategies are deployed in markets:

> A lot of stuff just gets tried and if it's not successful it doesn't stick around for long. (Laughs) And that does cut out an awful lot of the process. However, it's not the way we want to work. We work like that, because it's just faster to market. Sometimes we don't have the tooling [in the test environment] and you know, are we gonna wait two months for the tooling to test this idea, or are we gonna test it [on what we have] and move on? So we end up doing more of the second. Any of us would love to say that we do the first thing, but we do the second.

But Alex's anecdote also relates to an oft-reported challenge that, while automated trading is partly motivated by its allegedly more systematic, nonemotional approach (vis-à-vis electronic screen trading), emotions do frequently creep in, distorting traders' assessment of their strategies. In one of my interviews with him, Alex said he felt that traders are sometimes overconfident about their algorithms, so much so that they do not take unexpected behaviors and losses seriously enough:

> The mistake I've seen traders make is they don't have an exit strategy or a failsafe. They'll let human judgment—the ego—say, "Well, it's losing money, but it's a really good algorithm, so [let's] keep it running." It's losing more money, "Well, it's a really good algorithm, it's going to come back." They let their greed and their ego [rule]—"I know it's right, it's going to work"—so finally they lose so much money that a finance or risk officer will come in and say, "Enough!"

The likely reason for this is that traders see their algorithms as extensions of themselves, as entities that enact their decisions at a distance (Borch and Lange 2017). Given that they conceived the strategies, and the back-tests went fine, traders might grow overly confident that the ideas they generated must be working well and that any indications of the opposite can be dismissed as negligible mishaps (on the role of confidence within automated trading, see also Min and Hansen 2024). Not only may they become too confident in the algorithmic strategies, but traders may also become so attached to them that they pay insufficient heed to poor or irregular performance. Several algorithmic traders interviewed by Lange and quoted in Borch and Lange (2017) testified to this, suggesting that the kinds of emotional attachment electronic screen traders develop toward the market-on-screen (Knorr Cetina and Bruegger 2002b) find an equivalent in the automated market arrangement. As indicated in the quote by Alex, attachment to an algorithmic strategy can turn into a peril if it is not matched with sufficient concern with associated risk and care for losses.[14]

Expertise and Recruitment

In the remainder of this chapter, I want to step back from the central workflow of first-generation automated trading to examine the broader culture that shapes firms specializing in this market arrangement, as well as the significant implications this type of trading holds for markets and their sociological interpretation. I start by analyzing the various forms of expertise embedded in the production pipeline, comparing them to other sectors within the financial industry.

A useful reference here is Karen Ho's ethnographic study of Wall Street investment banking. Ho (2009, 78–79) notes that in this area of finance, "front office" personnel—those directly engaged in investment banking, trading, and asset management—are viewed as the "most valuable employees," largely because they are seen as revenue generators. By contrast, the "back office" serves as a support function, viewed strictly as a "cost center." This division is not merely economic but carries social significance as well. According to Ho (2009, 78–79), while front-office employees are "extravagantly recruited" and participate in a wide array of training programs, social events, and retreats, back-office staff typically do not receive such treatment: back-office personnel are usually "not considered 'officers' of the bank," and they miss out on the "elaborate orientations and training sessions, cocktails and presentations, fancy dinners and retreats" that front-office employees enjoy.

Traditionally, the distinction between front and back office was also a gendered one. As Melissa Fisher (2012) notes in her historical study *Wall Street Women*, women initially entered Wall Street as analysts positioned in the back office, while the front office remained predominantly male. Over time, women analysts gradually transitioned into front-office roles (Fisher 2012; Ho 2009); however, in trading, male traders generally retained the upper hand, especially in terms of compensation. Reflecting this, Leon Wansleben (2015) observes that in interactions between electronic screen traders and analysts, the latter often struggle to gain recognition as market experts, illustrating a clear social hierarchy between the two (similarly, Lépinay 2011).

Considering the critical role of software and hardware infrastructure in first-generation automated trading, this market arrangement demands a far greater recognition of functions that traditionally remained in the back office. Effective automation hinges on meticulous attention to technological nuances, thereby increasing the value of expertise in these areas. Reflecting on this, Charles remarked that at his firm, "technology is on par with the trading. They are equal partners here," emphasizing that developers and IT professionals are not viewed as "second-class citizens." Nonetheless, especially when it comes to software development, traditional distinctions between front- and back-office roles often persist in automated trading environments, as the specific forms of software expertise required tend to differ across these functions.

For instance, Gregor emphasized that while software development is now integral to the front office, the required skills vary significantly between front- and back-office functions. He differentiated between "writing algorithms" and "writing [code] for market data." In the context of automated trading, the latter embodies the core of what I described as "getting the infrastructure right." This involves handling market data—ensuring proper access, cleaning, processing, and maintaining efficient data transmission to trading venues. Such tasks remain anchored in the back office. As Gregor explained, "For technically complicated or advanced systems, [this involves] a very unique skill set which requires knowledge of how a low-latency system is built." In other words, this kind of software development is deeply tied to technical concerns. On the other hand, writing trading algorithms—translating traders' ideas into code—is less immediately focused on technical infrastructure and more on domain expertise, specifically an in-depth understanding of market microstructure.

The observation that algorithmic traders need to possess a reasonable level of software proficiency ties back to a point I made at the outset of this book: automated trading requires a type of trader fundamentally different from those of earlier market arrangements. The shift from interhuman to electronic screen trading transformed recruitment practices, with a growing emphasis on hiring university graduates (Lépinay 2011; Zaloom 2006). The rise of automated trading has further altered the profile of those who now fill trader roles, along with the skills that are deemed essential for the job. This shift, however, does not preclude cases like Frank's, where individuals successfully transition from pit to automated trading. Indeed, several leading firms in the automated trading industry—such as DRW, Interactive Brokers, and Jump Trading—were founded by individuals with experience in floor trading.

Still, the advanced level of mathematical literacy required for developing first-generation automated trading strategies means that the backgrounds of algorithmic traders increasingly resemble those of quantitative researchers. Both groups often hold university degrees in subjects like mathematics, physics, computer science, or engineering (Borch and Lange 2017), and many of my informants held advanced degrees in these fields from prestigious institutions in the US and Europe. An extreme example of this shift was recounted by William, a quantitative researcher. At his firm, the boundary between traders and analysts had almost disappeared with the rise of automated trading. "We don't really have traders anymore. . . . We call ourselves quantitative researchers." For such roles, he added, "We'd probably hire [hard science graduates] from Cambridge, Oxford, Imperial. And then Ivy Leagues in the US. And very much French Grandes Écoles."

This distinction suggests that the recruitment pathways for these roles tend to be more specialized compared to other parts of the finance industry. For example, in her study of Wall Street hedge funds, Megan Tobias Neely (2022, ch. 2) identified four primary tracks into that sector: (1) the social circle track, where elite social network ties, often familial, lead to job opportunities; (2) the investment banking track, where internships or similar roles at investment banks serve as a stepping-stone to hedge fund positions; (3) the trading track, where a background in floor trading provides sufficient expertise to enter a hedge fund trading room—though, as Neely notes, the shift away from interhuman trading has made this track increasingly rare; and (4) the academic track, where a (PhD) degree in a nonfinancial subject from a prestigious university opens the doors to a hedge fund.

My interviews indicate that in automated trading, the academic track is the most dominant, although social networks also play a role.[15] A prime example of this is John, head of quantitative research at a bank, whose entry into automated trading was a mix of happenstance and networking, along with his mathematical expertise. John initially pursued a PhD in experimental physics, which led him to work for a nanotechnology firm after his postdoc. A former postdoc colleague had transitioned into finance and reached out to John with a job offer, saying, "'If you're interested, we're hiring.' . . . I didn't even know these types of jobs existed.

. . . I wasn't enjoying what I was doing, . . . so I thought, 'Well, let's give it a try.'"
John's experience aligns with Neely's observation that quantitative and analytical
skills are more crucial for entering automated trading than any prior knowledge
of finance or economics. Similarly, William noted that although he had pursued a
PhD in economics, the content of his dissertation turned out to be "all useless" for
his role as a quantitative analyst, because academic economics relies on "very thin
assumptions" that are largely "irrelevant to the industry." On the other hand, the
mathematical and statistical expertise he had gained through a dual degree in statistics proved invaluable for identifying complex patterns in financial data.

While recruitment patterns in automated trading differ from those in hedge
funds, the overlap in the academic track reveals broader implications. Neely (2022,
73) makes the important observation that "the trading track is one of the few avenues through which working- and middle-class opportunists, mostly men, without
elite pedigrees can enter the inner workings of Wall Street." With that pathway effectively closed because of the disappearance of interhuman trading, and given that
"the academic track benefits class-privileged white men in particular" (2022, 78),
the recruitment process for first-generation automated trading is likely to render
trading firms more elitist and homogeneous than in the past. Reflecting this, although I interviewed a few nonmale, nonwhite individuals, they represented a mi-
nority (however, the increasing prominence of ML may lead to greater diversity
within the industry, particularly as it attracts talent from a broader range of racial
and ethnic backgrounds).

This homogenization of staff unsurprisingly manifests in the daily culture of
trading firms. As previously mentioned, the quiet atmosphere of these offices mirrors the demeanor of those working there. For example, one of my informants, Jim,
had previously worked at a firm populated by former pit traders who had imported
their "rowdy macho" culture, complete with frequent eating contests. In contrast, at
Jim's current firm, where pit traders have been replaced by quants, "It's like a library.
People are coding. Jokes are about coding."[16]

A Culture of Secrecy

Another significant cultural aspect of automated trading is its pervasive secrecy. As
I have mentioned repeatedly, this is a field cloaked in confidentiality. This secrecy
shapes both the organizational culture and the structure of many firms specializing in first-generation automated trading, as explored in depth by Lange (2016). In

her seminal article, she describes how the algorithmic traders she observed ethnographically went to great lengths to protect their strategies from being copied, even by other traders within the same firm. For instance, traders employed "filters on their screens so that their codes could only be viewed when facing the screen directly" (2016, 237). Additionally, traders frequently responded to Lange's inquiries with "That I don't know." Initially, Lange assumed this was a professional tactic to police the flow of information, creating strict boundaries on what they would share with her. However, she gradually realized that these responses were likely sincere. In the firm where she conducted her research, individual traders lacked access to the underlying code base of the trading system. While they could bolt their strategies onto the system—with assistance from software developers who worked for multiple traders—these traders had limited knowledge of how the core software architecture was designed and coded.

As Lange (2016, 240) observes, by ensuring that "the operation of the [underlying] trading system as a whole remained opaque" to the traders, the organizational structure was deliberately designed to "create an atomized team culture." While collaboration between traders and developers did occur, the traders were pitted against one another, with none knowing how their individual strategies interacted. What is the rationale behind this form of organization? The answer Lange's fieldwork provides is straightforward: by compartmentalizing the traders and ensuring they had no access to the full framework, the firm safeguarded itself against the loss of intellectual property. At most, traders could take their personal strategies to another firm, but doing so would not destabilize the core foundation of the firm.[17]

My own fieldwork partially corroborates Lange's findings. Although I did not observe traders using screen filters, several informants emphasized that, in some firms, a competitive culture is ingrained in the organizational structure. One CEO vividly described many first-generation automated trading firms as "Balkanized portfolios of individual self-interest," where traders essentially plug their algorithmic strategies into the firm's underlying hardware and software infrastructure with little concern for what other traders in the firm are doing. Alex echoed this sentiment: "There are firms that bring traders in, give them capital and [follow a] 'You eat what you kill' kind of thing. . . . If you're at a [prop] shop where each trader is his own aggregation unit, then they keep the source code on their desktop encrypted. They keep as much intellectual property to themselves as possible."

The compartmentalized approach to developing the underlying code infrastructure for automated trading, as described by Raymond, was closely tied to concerns about security and intellectual property protection. Each person would be tasked with coding only one pillar of the software architecture to mitigate risks:

> You have to think about the safety, people stealing things. So how do you split the work? What access do you give to some people? Who's allowed on the production machine? . . . That's why . . . we split the system [with] one person basically doing one task . . . so that the information was retained within one person. . . . People worked on separate components. We had encrypted machines. . . . We were working separately so things were never exposed. . . . From my strategy side, I would build an encrypted library which I would then pass on, which would then be unencrypted at one time on a secure production box. . . . We really have to be careful about this. This is everything. If somebody gets that, your competitive edge is much reduced.[18]

While my fieldwork indicates that concerns around secrecy are prevalent in the industry, two important qualifications should be noted. First, I encountered the perspective that the emphasis on the secrecy of first-generation trading systems is often overstated when considering the importance of the infrastructure needed to operate them. Lange makes a similar point, noting that in the context of HFT, "The information that is considered highly proprietary is not the strategies but the technology that is involved in reducing latency" (2016, 242). Alex expanded on this idea:

> [At] the firm I worked at, they said we could publish what we do on the front page of the *New York Times* and we still wouldn't worry about competition because the algorithms and the equations are a part of the puzzle, but the infrastructure required to run it—all the colocated servers, telecommunications lines, and the cost schedules with the brokers—would take so long to implement that it would take [others] a year or two years to get there, and then everything has changed.

Second, several informants reported working in collaborative environments where internal secrecy was seen as less important and in some cases was viewed as a barrier to success. For instance, Alex mentioned that at his firm, "Everybody could see all the source code because you really want everybody to win." Frank shared a similar sentiment, noting that collaboration among traders and quantitative analysts, particularly in developing and optimizing strategies, allowed for deeper, more long-term thinking. "I don't have to think just 'Will this trade make me money today?' but [rather,] 'What's the long-term utility of what we're doing?'" Likewise, Brett, a seasoned quant, explained that at his firm traders even open-sourced their ideas to gather input from others. Additionally, some informants noted that the physical layout of the office was intentionally designed to foster collaboration and reduce secrecy. For example, John lamented that the bank where he worked was generally "fairly siloed," but he made an effort to have "people from trading and technology ... sit very close together" so that everyone has "some kind of understanding of what's going on."

The Embedding and Disembedding of First-Generation Automated Trading

While my primary aim in this chapter has been to shed light on how and why trading firms engage in first-generation automated trading, as well as some of the challenges they face, I want to conclude by addressing broader questions about the implications of this market arrangement. One central question concerns the impact that automated trading has on markets—and on how to sociologically understand them: Do markets benefit from the rise and spread of first-generation automated trading systems?[19]

Assessing the implications of automated trading for financial markets has long been a major focus for financial economists, yet their findings remain inconclusive. When examining HFT, some economists argue that this form of automated trading helps reduce volatility (Boehmer, Li, and Saar 2018; Hagströmer and Nordén 2013), while others suggest it may exacerbate it (Jarrow and Protter 2012). Some maintain that both arguments have merit and that much depends on the specific market context (Biais and Foucault 2014). Similarly, some scholars contend that automated trading has narrowed the bid-ask spread—a key measure of trading costs—thus making markets more efficient (O'Hara 2015). However, other researchers have pointed out that low-latency automated trading systems, and the arms race they fuel, make trading more expensive for slower market participants. One estimate suggests that these systems effectively impose a "tax" on markets, amounting to around "$5 billion per year in global equity markets alone" (Aquilina, Budish, and O'Neill 2021, 494).

A particularly thorny issue involves liquidity. MacKenzie (2018a) has shown that for many professionals in automated trading, the distinction between providing and taking liquidity—that is, between placing passive orders for others to execute, as market makers do, and actively hitting those orders to remove them from the order book—carries a moral weight. Providing liquidity is viewed as a positive contribution to the market, while specializing in taking liquidity is seen as purely speculative and therefore morally questionable. This moral distinction touches on a larger debate about automated trading and liquidity. Some studies argue that automated trading has increased market liquidity (Hendershott, Jones, and Menkveld 2011), making it easier for participants to trade when they need to, even under stressful conditions (Brogaard et al. 2018). While this is considered a positive outcome, others argue that much of the liquidity provided is illusory, as automated systems quickly cancel their orders when market conditions turn unfavorable (Degryse et al. 2020). Mattli succinctly captures this concern:

> A distinctive feature of high-speed traders is their high rates of order submission and cancellation during a very short time period—seconds, milliseconds, even microseconds. Excessive cancellation rates (or high order-to-execution ratios) may reflect the need to quickly adjust their orders to rapidly changing prices to avoid adverse execution, or they may simply be an expression of predatory "spam and cancel" strategies that seek to manipulate prices or otherwise disadvantage institutional investors. Such strategies create a misleading sense of liquidity known as "phantom" liquidity—the orders quickly disappear when a "slow" market participant seeks to interact with them. (2019, 164)

Some of my informants voiced similar concerns. Jack was particularly critical, arguing that low-latency market makers do not deserve that title. "A market maker is supposed to make a market by posting orders that are meant to be executed," he said, but the practice of quickly "posting things that come and go" does not "represent an actual willingness and ability to trade."[20]

Discussions about fake, or phantom, liquidity connect to broader questions about the relationship between automated trading and the real economy. Low-latency automated trading systems primarily focus on order-book data and related trade data, whereas macroeconomic indicators—such as unemployment, inflation, and growth rates—play no tangible role in their subsecond strategies. While this may differ for algorithmic systems with longer time horizons, it is evident that low-latency systems are effectively disconnected from the real economy. To borrow from Karl Polanyi (2001), these systems might be described as disembedded—detached from the fundamental workings of the economy, operating in a speculative orbit of their own.

This interpretation holds some weight, suggesting that first-generation automated trading can be viewed as part of a long-standing tradition in which finance has been closely linked to speculative ventures (de Goede 2005; Fourcade and Healy 2024; Stäheli 2013). In fact, many first-generation automated trading systems seem to reflect the significant shift identified by Aris Komporozos-Athanasiou (2022) in contemporary capitalism—from *homo economicus* to *homo speculans*. However, in this context, *homo speculans* is clad in algorithmic garb, representing an *algo speculans*.

That said, caution is warranted before declaring first-generation automated trading, even in its low-latency forms, entirely disembedded from the real economy. There are both theoretical and empirical reasons for this. On the theoretical side, Martijn Konings (2018, 2021) has argued that critiques of financial speculation and its detachment from the real economy are often rooted in a problematic, yet "persistent foundationalism," which insists on a strict separation between a fictitious speculative domain and an ontologically real economic sphere. Drawing on postfoundational theories, Konings challenges this distinction. In particular, he invokes German sociologist Niklas Luhmann's (2013) concept of self-reference, which suggests that all social systems create, reproduce, and connect to their own operations without needing to be grounded in an external foundation. From this perspective, speculation is no more fictitious than the "real" economy: both are self-referential domains, governed by their own logics and driven by their own contingencies. Following Konings, one might therefore argue that speculation remains speculative but that its self-referential detachment from the economy is not fundamentally different from the way other social realms are detached or disembedded from their environments.

While this offers an important corrective to simplistic critiques of speculation, there are also empirical observations that challenge the idea that first-generation automated trading is completely detached from the real economy. One is that even though many first-generation systems primarily focus on order-book data, the dynamics of the order book are still influenced by key economic indicators released on a regular schedule. For example, when unemployment figures come in worse than expected, stock prices often react negatively.[21]

More fundamentally, in many of my interviews with people working in automated trading, the informants emphasized that financial markets had changed significantly since the 2008 financial crisis. Most notably, the quantitative easing (QE) programs implemented in several countries in response to the crisis—where central banks engaged in substantial asset purchases to stimulate the economy—not only injected considerable liquidity into the markets but also, because of this buying spree, caused volatility to drop. As Jim put it more dramatically: volatility had "absolutely collapsed." Since the profitability of many automated trading strategies, particularly for market makers, relies less on whether the market trends upward or downward and more on the degree of movement, this plunge in volatility had direct consequences. One informant explained that a strategy of his, which had delivered "double-digit returns until 2012," had to be abandoned because QE had reduced volatility—expressing a "hope for volatility to come back." Combined with high fixed costs for connectivity and data transmission, the drop in volatility forced many firms out of business, while others struggled to adapt. Consequently, the frequent job transitions I observed among industry professionals were often attributed to these effects.

The key point here is that, despite the seemingly myopic (speculative) focus on order-book and trade data, even low-latency automated trading strategies can be significantly affected by developments in the "real" economy. In fact, this empirical evidence suggests more of an attachment (or embedding) rather than a detachment (or disembedding) between the two.

THREE

Creating Trading Automatons

The Rise of Second-Generation Systems

LOCATED IN THE CITY OF LONDON, on the fourth floor of a high-rise filled with financial services and tech firms, Cormac Trading Group might, at first glance, appear
no different from other automated trading companies. Access to its main office is
tightly controlled; an admission card is required to enter. The front door opens onto
a compact reception area. From here, the space expands into the main room, a large
open-plan area divided into rows of desks, each brimming with computer screens.
To the right, hallways lead to a sizable kitchen stocked with games for staff, meeting
rooms of various sizes (their whiteboards covered in formulas), a library, and another section of the firm housing departments less reliant on technology—such as
HR and overall financial operations. The main room is home to most of Cormac's
roughly sixty employees, who work in an environment marked by a low hum of
activity, punctuated occasionally by bursts of laughter, often initiated by the CEO's
lighthearted engagement. This room is an open space, devoid of strict dividers, yet
staff are subtly grouped according to their roles, and spontaneous intermingling is
common.

This overall quiet, screen-dense open office layout resembles those of many
firms focused on first-generation automated trading systems. However, Cormac's
approach diverges sharply. Its chief mission is to develop an ML system capable of
autonomously devising its own trading strategies, guided by a deep-seated belief

that such systems can outperform human traders in identifying profitable opportunities and adapting to shifting market conditions.

In this chapter, I use Cormac as my primary "model case" (Krause 2021) to explore trading automatons: the aspirations driving their development; the dominant ML architectures underpinning them; the skills and procedures required to design, test, deploy, and oversee them; the organizational structures that facilitate these processes; and the key limitations these automatons encounter. Toward the end of the chapter, I broaden the analysis to consider the forms of embedding and disembedding that new types of financial data make possible within ML-powered automated trading.

I acknowledge that Cormac may not represent the entire industry. For instance, the firm's second-generation system, focused on market making, relies on a specific ML technique—deep neural networks. While this is a widely adopted approach, other firms specialize in alternative models. To illustrate this diversity, I discuss another approach I encountered during my fieldwork—genetic programming—supplementing the examination of Cormac with insights from two firms that focus on this technique, Sentient Technologies and Ragin Capital. Nonetheless, regardless of the particular ML technique employed, my informants consistently cited similar reasons for using ML in trading, entrusting machines with the capacity to make trading decisions that they believed were superior to those made by humans.

It is also important to note that, while I briefly introduce the overall logic of various ML architectures, my analysis will intentionally avoid technical details. My interest lies in understanding how trading firms attempt to create trading automatons, as well as the challenges this pursuit entails, without delving deeply into the complex technicalities of ML applications (a topic thoroughly covered in other works, e.g., Dixon, Halperin, and Bilokon 2020; López de Prado 2018, 2020).

Why Create Trading Automatons?

The use of ML for trading financial assets has been made possible by three critical resources: relatively affordable computing technologies (such as NVIDIA chips), access to extensive datasets, and the growing pool of ML expertise among university graduates and other professionals. However, these enabling factors alone do not explain why trading firms have developed a demand for ML. My interviews indicate that the motivations for adopting second-generation systems build on the reasons that initially supported first-generation systems: scalability, cost efficiency, and cognitive capabilities are key drivers behind the pursuit of trading automatons. As discussed in chapter 2, firms specializing in first-generation systems often justified automated trading by citing its ability to address the cognitive limitations of human traders. These systems can observe and respond to market developments across multiple asset classes and time zones, and they do so at near-lightning speed, vastly extending the cognitive reach of trading firms. Furthermore, barring bugs or unforeseen internal feedback loops, once human trading strategies are encoded into software, they operate with a strict if-then logic, executing trades in a deterministic manner without the influence of human moods—unless manual intervention is specifically triggered.

The motivations for deploying ML techniques differ somewhat but remain linked to those that initially inspired first-generation systems. Howard, Cormac's CEO, expressed a view shared by many of my informants: the trading industry is growing "more complex, more competitive, and more costly." The competitive edge gained by moving from manual, screen-based trading to automated trading has intensified the race for reduced latency, driving up basic operating costs associated with essential technological infrastructure.[1] This costlier, more complex, and fiercely competitive market environment has led many participants to consider alternative strategies: If further gains in speed come only at prohibitive costs, could smarter, more sophisticated algorithmic systems offer a more cost-effective route to profitability? The adoption of ML techniques represents an affirmative response to this question.

Indeed, a key motivation for using second-generation systems is that ML uniquely excels at identifying patterns in data—patterns that humans might not detect without extensive effort, labor resources, and significant costs. With massive amounts of market data generated each day, ML systems hold the potential to uncover patterns that human traders have overlooked, transforming these insights into profitable trading opportunities. Kristian Bondo Hansen (2020, 4) emphasizes this point, stating that ML systems serve as "technical aids firms use as a way of compensating for the limited information processing, calculative, and information storage (memory) capacity of humans." Reflecting this perspective, at Cormac and similar firms focused on second-generation systems, there is a strong conviction that ML systems outperform humans in identifying profitable trading strategies. Ian, Cormac's CTO, explicitly and repeatedly declared their ambition to build an automated trading system that would become "the best trader in the world," surpassing any fully human-designed system.

This reliance on ML is seen as a path to competitive advantage in automated trading. Another related factor is the perceived limitation of first-generation systems—their nonadaptive nature. These systems are entirely deterministic; ideally, they behave exactly as programmed. While this rigidity helps eliminate emotional biases from trading, it also means that first-generation systems do not learn from their interactions in the market. Their approach remains static, and any changes to their behavior require modifications to the underlying code—a process necessary to address the model decay discussed in chapter 2. In contrast, a central motivation for deploying second-generation systems is their capacity for adaptation to evolving market conditions, albeit with certain constraints (which will be discussed later in this chapter). This adaptability is crucial for Cormac and forms the basis of what they call their "goal-directed, adaptive trading products (GDAP)" (internal document, June 2017, Cormac Trading Group). These products (the rationale for using the term *product* will be explained later) "use a disciplined objective (*goal*) that balances risk and return, but they constantly *adapt* their behaviour to their observed environment by re-evaluating which inputs gain or lose predictive power. The adaptive nature of machine learning is particularly suited to problems that deal with vast amounts of noisy, dynamic input data such as the high-frequency order book data seen by market makers" (internal document, June 2017, Cormac Trading Group; original emphases). Simon from chapter 1 echoed this sentiment, stating that "the artificial intelligence style of trading where you let the computer figure out the rules is much stronger" than the style of first-generation systems because the rules it generates are "more dynamic." The adaptability of trading automatons means they do not require constant, granular human tweaks and recoding.

The idea that automated adaptability could potentially reduce the need for manual programming points to a final cost-related rationale for specializing in ML. Traders and quants who develop first-generation systems command high salaries, making them expensive hires for trading firms. By automating their work—their trading strategy generation—firms could potentially achieve significant cost savings. One CEO was candid on this point, viewing the high salaries earned by traders and quants behind first-generation systems as often unwarranted. Referring to them generally as quants, he said:

We wanna automate as much as we can, because, let me tell you a dirty little secret, quants are expensive, and in my honest opinion they're worth shit. I've seen more quants burn up more cash and deliver so little that I find it, from the financial perspective, one of the worst returns on capital . . . I've ever seen in my life. But you're seduced by the few that really make it. We have seen young grads coming up, freshly armed with a PhD from schools like yours, and they're twenty-six, twenty-seven years old, and they're like, "Why not pay me five hundred [thousand pounds] a year?" Do you know what I need to make [to make this sustainable]? So we want to automate as much as we can. . . . A [first-generation quant] trader will know exactly how much they made [on the profit side]. Ask them how much it cost [the firm] to make that? Oblivious. . . . So, when we talk about a [trading] system, we're also very conscious about what we call the cost/income ratio. . . . One way to look at machine learning is continuing the industrial propagation of automation to more highfalutin jobs. So instead of paying quants to come up with hypotheses . . . we say, "Actually, let's automate that role and make the rules by using AI."

My interviews suggest that the pursuit of machines capable of realizing the various hopes invested in trading automatons began gaining momentum in the 2010s. Since the mid-2010s, in particular, the exploration of ML approaches has become widespread within the industry. Consequently, while many firms still focus on first-generation systems, others have fully transitioned to second-generation systems, and still others are experimenting with incorporating ML elements into their first-generation setups. To clarify what is specific to second-generation systems, I will focus on firms that specialize exclusively in these systems, examining how they are designed in practice. I propose that their design can be analyzed along two main dimensions: the algorithmic architecture of the trading system itself and its organizational embedding, including the diverse types of human expertise required to develop, test, deploy, monitor, and, when necessary, correct the ML system and its market behavior. I begin by discussing the former, followed by an analysis of the latter. When addressing the organizational dimension, I will explore how the forms of expertise and divisions of labor outlined in chapter 2 take on slightly new configurations in firms specializing in second-generation systems. Since the types of organizational secrecy analyzed in connection with first-generation systems also apply to firms developing second-generation systems, I will not revisit this aspect here.

The Architecture(s) of Trading Automatons

Regardless of the specific ML architecture in use, the core concept behind ML-based approaches, from a high-level perspective, is to provide the algorithmic system with an objective function—a mathematically defined goal, which in a trading context often translates to "maximize profits within given risk parameters." The system is then trained on vast amounts of data, from which it extracts patterns that enable it to make actionable predictions (also referred to as "rules" or strategies) by placing orders to buy or sell financial assets. After training, the model's performance is tested on new, previously unseen data to assess whether the patterns identified during training generalize to other scenarios. If the results are suboptimal, the model may be adjusted, retrained, and tested again on fresh data. But if the results prove strong, the strategy may then be deployed in live markets.

Just as first-generation systems can execute a range of strategies, so can second-generation systems align with diverse approaches and operate across various time horizons. For instance, many firms feed their systems only order-book and trade data, pursuing low-latency strategies based on this limited input. Cormac exemplifies this approach. Similarly, the head of another proprietary trading firm using ML-based methods stated, "I don't use analyst recommendations, completely out, [and] I don't use news." Other firms, however, train their systems to operate with longer-term outlooks. For example, the CEO of an ML-driven hedge fund explained that their system was designed to make stock market predictions up to ninety days in advance. Longer-term horizons are often built upon a wider array of data sources beyond the order book. Since the early 2010s, a surge in new data sources has led to rapid growth in ML applications that extend beyond low-latency trading, aiming to predict prices for minutes, hours, weeks, or even months into the future. These additional data sources, often discussed under the term *alternative data,* will be further explored at the end of this chapter.

Among the firms where I interviewed that specialize exclusively in second-generation trading, two primary ML approaches emerged: artificial (or deep) neural networks and genetic programming. Originally inspired—though less so today—by the idea that the brain functions as a neurological network (McCulloch and Pitts 1943; Rosenblatt 1958), the fundamental concept of artificial neural networks is to construct a network of information-processing units (neurons) that can learn through iterative adjustments within the network. The neurons are connected by synapses, which transfer information across the network. Synapses also link neurons to inputs and outputs, with each synapse assigned a variable weight. Figure 3.1 presents an example of a simple, single-layer artificial neural network.

In contrast to such "shallow," single-layer artificial neural networks, "deep" neural networks contain two or more hidden layers. An example of a deep neural network is presented in figure 3.2. This deep neural network has five sources of input data, and it makes one output prediction, with two "hidden layers" placed between the input and output layers. Note that for simplicity, figures 3.1 and 3.2 have only one neuron in the output layer (they make just one prediction), but depending on the task at hand, there could be multiple outputs.

Regardless of the type of neural network design, neurons in each layer receive

Figure 3.1: Simple neural network.

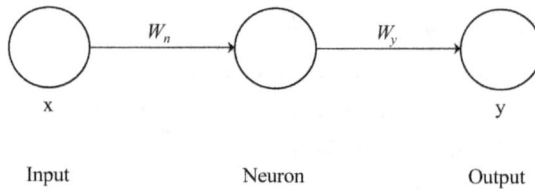

Source: Author.

Figure 3.2: Deep neural network.

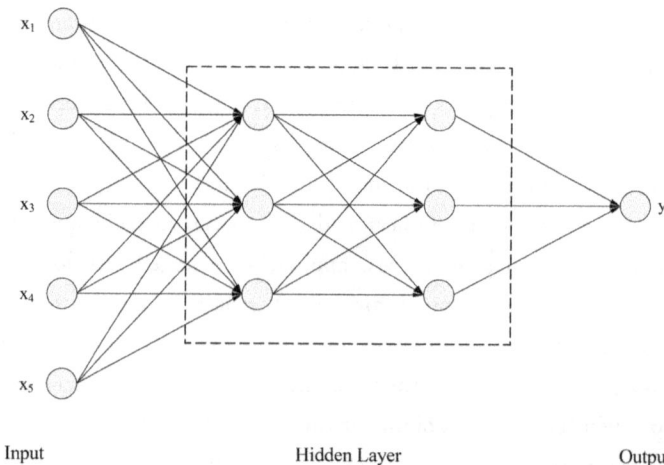

Source: Author.

input from the preceding layer. Each synapse transfers input multiplied by its assigned weight (see figure 3.1), so a neuron's input is the sum of these weighted inputs from neurons in the previous layer. A neuron activates if its weighted input reaches a certain threshold value. Once activated, it forwards its output to neurons in the next layer, once again adjusting by the weights of the relevant synapses. If a neuron does not activate, no information passes from it to the next layer.

Various types of activation functions are available, with more complex learning tasks generally requiring nonlinear ones. More challenging tasks also typically demand greater neural capacity. This can be achieved by adding neurons to a single-layer artificial neural network or introducing additional hidden layers to a deep neural network. Each new hidden layer processes the input at a more complex representational level. For example, in natural language processing, one layer might recognize individual words, while subsequent layers could identify word pairings or common phrases. The final prediction from such an ML algorithm might suggest the next search term on Google or provide a full-sentence translation.

Of course, this description is simplified, and designing and optimizing neural networks involves numerous challenges. One common issue, which Ian also mentioned, is the risk of *overfitting*—where the ML system identifies patterns in the training data that are actually tied to noise, rendering these patterns nontransferable to new, unseen data (for a general discussion of overfitting, see Shin 2025). In other words, a model that performs well on training data may struggle on test data, leading to subpar outcomes in practice.

One example of a neural network application in finance is a specific type of deep neural network known as *recurrent neural networks,* which are particularly well suited for processing sequential data, such as time-stamped order-book data. A recurrent neural network is structured so that a neuron in a hidden layer receives input not only from neurons in the preceding layer but also from itself. As a result, the value of this neuron at time t depends both on the input from other neurons and on its own value at time $t - 1$. This architecture enables the recurrent neural network to retain memory of the data it has previously processed (Alpaydin 2016; LeCun, Bengio, and Hinton 2015). Recurrent neural networks can be used to determine whether, for instance, the returns of certain stocks at time $t + 1$ can be predicted based on stock returns up to time t. If the model can make such predictions, it could form the foundation of "an automated trading policy" that helps to "decide at time t which stocks to buy, hold or sell" (Alonso, Batres-Estrada, and Moulin 2019, 266). Cormac's automated trading system is built around a recurrent neural network architecture. The network is fed vast amounts of historical market data so that the system may develop a set of automated trading rules—that is, formulate and execute independent trading strategies.

The other key ML technique I encountered during my fieldwork is genetic programming, a subset of evolutionary computation. Drawing inspiration from the principles of natural selection, genetic programming seeks to generate a set of candidate solutions to a problem through evolutionary iteration. The process involves the following steps: (1) define a population of individual candidate "agents" that aim to achieve a specific purpose in a given environment (for example, agents might represent trading rules with certain parameters aimed at generating profit); (2) assign a fitness function to each, which measures how well the purpose is fulfilled; (3) run simulations to evaluate the performance of the agents and then select the best candidates (such as those generating the highest returns within specific risk conditions); (4) create a new population by (a) directly carrying over some selected candidates into the new population ("reproduction"); (b) generating new candidates by randomly recombining elements from selected individuals ("crossover"); and (c) introducing new candidates through random changes to elements of selected candidates ("mutation"); and (5) repeat steps (3) and (4) until a set of optimized candidates has evolved (Koza and Poli 2014). Thus, in this approach, learning is an evolutionary process, honed through successive generations of refinement.

Babak Hodjat is now the CTO of AI at Cognizant, but when I first interviewed him he was the cofounder and chief scientist of Sentient Technologies, a firm specializing in genetic programming. Babak explained how Sentient Technologies used this ML technique "to evolve rule sets that do the trading." In other words, they leveraged genetic programming to automatically generate rules that specified the conditions under which specific actions should be taken in the markets. To initiate the process, human experts defined an objective function and a set of "indicators," or a "feature set"—essentially variables like price and volume that characterize the market. With these inputs, the ML system generated "rule sets [that] key off the indicators." Specifically, "[The rule sets] take a subset of those features and combine them into various different ranges for those features or lack thereof. For example, 'Is this feature in a certain range or is this feature not within a certain range, and, and, and?' so that you have what we call a condition string of features strung together by evolutionary computation." Put differently, the system automatically defined the conditions that needed to be satisfied to trigger different types of actions. Next, "Each rule triggers an action, and again that action is evolved. The actions that we have, for example, are not just 'Go long' or 'Go short but cover your short' and so forth, but it's also the order models: 'Go short, but go short with a limit order at this particular price normalized by volatility with respect to the prior close.'"

The result was a complex rule set. Babak noted that there "could be up to 128 rules, and each rule could be up to sixty-four conditions," meaning that multiple conditions had to be satisfied before a single action was triggered. A critical part of this process involved applying these rules to time-series data:

> The rule set is running looking at this minute, and then the next minute and then the next minute, and part of what it is considering as indicators is what we call introspective indicators: you have a rule set that is stateful. For example, it knows whether or not it entered a position, how long ago did it enter a position, how is it doing with that position—is it losing money or making money—and it can keep a tab on that every minute so it can decide what to do next. . . . This stateful rule set . . . essentially defines the behavior of the traders.

In line with the process described above, the firm continuously evolved the trader agents generated through automation: "These traders are evolved over hundreds of thousands of compute nodes over months, and continuously we harvest from these runs. The best of the best is kept on the server side on the server farm within our data centers and very regularly—I think right now it's every three hours or so—we have this process that goes through that list of the best and it harvests the more promising and less correlated strategies." Once these rules and actions had been produced through training, the resulting strategies were then "run on unseen sets— these are calendar-exclusive and sometimes stock-exclusive stratified data that is un- seen—to validate that the system is actually generalizing." Finally, the firm grouped the different trading agents to create "different profiles of behavior that can be used when trading."

Babak emphasized that this process was designed as "automatic programming," meaning that instead of humans manually defining the rules and actions, these ele- ments evolved dynamically through a complex, genetically inspired system. The key point that emerges here applies to all trading automatons: *while humans design their overarching ML architecture, the strategies that trading automatons ultimately pro- duce are not conceived by humans.* This is why I describe them as *semi-independent.*

Semi-Independent Machines

To grasp the semi-independent nature of trading automatons, it is essential to accurately understand the relationship between their human design and curation, on the one hand, and the rules or strategies they generate, on the other. Human influence manifests across multiple levels. The adage that ML systems are only as good as the data on which they are trained—commonly phrased as "Garbage in, garbage out" (e.g., Davidson 2025)—underscores that the selection of training data profoundly shapes the strategies a system can produce. In ML, this includes the process of "feature selection," which involves determining what input data are included during training. These decisions are far from trivial, as I will elaborate shortly, but they are accompanied by an even more foundational question: To what extent do human decisions about the overarching ML design shape the trading strategies the system ultimately generates?

When asked where and how humans influence the actions of a trading automaton, informants such as Simon pointed to the objective function. As noted, the objective function serves as a mathematical articulation of the system's overarching goal—typically, to generate profit. However, it is also the mechanism by which desired and undesired behaviors are encoded. Simon explained that the specifications for what he and his colleagues want the automaton to do—or avoid doing—are embedded within the objective function: "If you don't want to hold onto positions for too long, whatever it is, stuff you don't like, you put that in there." Depending on the ML architecture in use, human designers may adjust the objective function by adding rewards to promote specific behaviors or penalties to deter others. Ian offered an example, referring to their ML-based system called DEPS (the abbreviation will be explained below): "The objective function that we give [DEPS] is reasonably complicated. It says things along the lines of 'Make money, but I want you to do it smoothly and don't hold risky positions ever. . . . Maybe . . . you get lucky by holding a risky position, but it was still risky, so I don't want you to do that.'"

The objective function therefore serves as a critical relay for human input, not only setting the overall direction of the ML system but also defining priorities related to central trade-offs, such as those between risk and returns. A system designed with a high-risk objective function is likely to develop rules that exhibit greater risk tolerance compared to a system whose objective function imposes stricter constraints on risk. Furthermore, the decisions human designers make about how the objective function is *optimized* during training play a crucial role in shaping the rules the system ultimately produces. ML offers various optimization techniques, particularly for neural networks, where these techniques adjust weights during training to better align with the objective function. As Ian described, when they are training their deep neural network, "The optimizers job is to update the weights," specifically determining how to adjust them so that "given the market, the optimal action to take to maximize my objective is X." However, because different optimization algorithms come with distinct advantages and drawbacks (Aggarwal 2018), decisions about which algorithm to use and how to configure it can significantly influence both the speed at which the system learns and the extent to which its rules generalize beyond the training data. As Jeff, the quant, explained, "You might want to use different objective functions on different parts of the model because you want to train certain part of the model faster and other parts of the model in a more precise and accurate way." Additionally, as one informant noted, because markets evolve, it can be important to retrain an ML model, sometimes assigning greater weight to recent data than to older data. Although this process can be automated, decisions about where and when to adjust data weighting are inevitably shaped by human judgment and will influence the model's eventual predictions.

Importantly, however, while human design decisions undoubtedly shape the rules an ML system generates, these rules do not flow directly from those decisions. Unlike first-generation systems, the rules governing trading automatons are not written by humans. As Howard put it, "We don't write rules for [DEPS]." Despite the human specification of the objective function, along with any incentives or penalties incorporated into the system, the automaton exercises a degree of discretion in how it navigates these inputs. Ian emphasized this point:

> DEPS has the entire responsibility to take information in aggregate over years and come up with an action policy. So basically, all the humans can ever do is give DEPS information, incentives, and penalties, and it's up to DEPS entirely to come up with the trading policy. We can't do it. We can inform, we can enforce risk controls, like "You can't put on more than 100k of margin," right?[2] Of course, we have controls that are of that form, but we don't have rules where a human comes up with a rule. We try to capture their intuition as information representation. A wiggly line that DEPS gets to see, and then DEPS decides if that wiggly line is meaningful or not. So DEPS, on some level, gets to choose from the options that the people give it. That's part of it. Also, we can give it sometimes quite broad options so that it can choose on its own, and it can just ignore what it doesn't want.

This sentiment was echoed by informants specializing in genetic programming. Babak, from Sentient Technologies, explained that when their team of quants selected technical indicators—such as price, volume, and volatility over time—they could attempt to steer the ML system in specific directions, for instance by embedding certain volatility preferences into some of the system's agents. Still, Babak underscored that such human influence remained inherently partial, indirect, and nondeterministic. "The system being evolutionary, if the indicator has value, it will be picked up. If it doesn't, it won't."

Bruce, the CTO of Ragin Capital, whose work also involves genetic programming, expressed a similar perspective. He explained that their quants generate ideas for trading opportunities but that ultimately the ML system itself is responsible for "constantly generating new strategies and new signals [i.e., trading opportunities] that feed into the overall strategy." When asked to confirm whether the ML system, rather than human staff, detects these signals, Bruce replied, "That's right." The key takeaway is that human input matters only insofar as the evolutionary iterations and their unpredictable outcomes validate its relevance. Beyond this type of indirect influence, the process by which the trading automaton generates strategies is entirely automated and independent.

Ian offered an analogy, likening human influence on the trading automaton to designing a curriculum for a student to maximize their learning potential (for a discussion of a similar analogy, see Airoldi 2022, 61–66). "You could think of us as coming up with a learning curriculum," he explained. "We have a trajectory of learning that happens; we have to give [DEPS] the right things at the right time, the right objectives. Sometimes early learning is different than late learning." Similarly, Howard described the efforts of staff to "coach" DEPS, leveraging their domain expertise to guide the system's development.[3]

From a conceptual perspective, the interplay between human influence and machine semi-independence can be understood through Luhmann's (2012) theorization of the distinction between systems and their environments (Borch 2022a). According to Luhmann, social, psychic, and other systems are "operationally closed" entities, maintaining strict boundaries that prevent external operations from directly influencing them. Because systems are operationally closed, System A cannot directly interfere with the operations of System B. At most, System A may produce an external "irritation" for System B, but any effect this irritation has on System B depends entirely on how System B chooses to respond (Luhmann 2012, 56). This dynamic mirrors the relationship between humans and trading automatons. While humans design the automaton's architecture, the rules it ultimately generates are not directly or deterministically derived from human decisions or the input provided. Instead, human influence is reduced to an irritation between operationally closed systems: humans offer their complexity (knowledge and understanding of markets) to the automaton, but it is up to the automaton to determine which irritations are relevant and whether—and to what extent—they should inform its trading rules. This distinguishes trading automatons from first-generation systems, which directly enact human-conceived rules and lack operational closure relative to their inventors.

That said, humans may impose boundaries that trading automatons cannot cross. The risk controls mentioned by Ian exemplify this. Similarly, at Cormac, DEPS is designed to learn continuously from its actions in the market, automatically updating its weights daily. However, if these weight updates deviate significantly from one day to the next, the system raises alerts. Ian explained that, "for lack of a more scientific term," this process reflects "the brain of the system" adapting to market changes. Using a tool that provides a snapshot of the system's brain, the firm compares daily scans and immediately blocks updates if substantial changes are detected:

> The norm is that as long as we measure it and it's within normal brain change for day over day, it's fine. If it is outside of band, then it's management by exception. It gets escalated to a human who can go in there and say, "All right, I have the tools to go in there and analyze and see what's really happened. It's trading more volume. Is that good? Is that bad?" And they can kind of drill in as arbitrarily as is needed. Once the appropriate roles have been involved, they can say, "Okay, I'm happy for this to be released, or not."

If an updated version of DEPS is blocked, the prior version continues to operate. This monitoring of daily brain updates does not compromise the fully automated nature of the trading process; it merely introduces a layer of control to the system's adaptability. Informants across firms were clear that automated trading—whether first- or second-generation—would lose its purpose if humans began questioning the automation itself and intervening in its actions. As one remarked, "You run into [a] pretty big issue if you start to second-guess your algorithm. . . . You have to let the algorithm run 100 percent autonomous because otherwise, you cannot trust your result."[4]

Manufacturing Trading Automatons: Reshuffling Expertise

While firms like Cormac, Ragin Capital, and Sentient Technologies each focus exclusively on a single type of ML architecture, other organizations often pursue hybrid approaches. As mentioned, this hybridity sometimes involved combining first- and second-generation systems. For instance, several firms—particularly banks—with extensive experience in electronic screen trading and first-generation systems are now experimenting with incorporating ML components into their trading and asset management strategies.

A similar form of hybridity becomes apparent from an examination of Cormac's historical trajectory. Before establishing the firm, Kenny, its founder, had worked on the trading desk of a bank, where he specialized in market making for various interest rate derivatives. To gain a competitive edge, Kenny developed a sophisticated spreadsheet that allowed him to quote prices faster than his rivals. "I wanted to be the quickest; I wanted to be the fastest at quoting," he recalled. Eventually, Kenny left the bank and secured a seat in a trading arcade, a popular organizational model in the 1990s and early 2000s, reflecting the broader shift from interhuman to electronic screen trading. These arcades provided traders with shared office spaces and access to essential electronic trading infrastructure (Cameron et al. 2010). Initially working independently, Kenny later partnered with a former colleague who had a vision of transforming Kenny's trading style into a fully automated system. "He wanted to take the way I traded and systematize it, turn it into a static algorithm. That was our first iteration of algorithmic trading," Kenny explained. This collaboration laid the foundation for Cormac Trading Group, which was established in the early 2000s. The firm initially focused on electronic screen trading and the automation of Kenny's strategy, embodied in a first-generation system called "Alpha." The firm thrived for several years, expanding steadily. However, increasing competition eventually pushed Kenny to reassess the company's direction. In the mid-2010s, recognizing the need for adaptation, he brought in a new management team to help chart the firm's future.

Howard and Ian, the new CEO and CTO respectively, identified several issues with the firm's existing approach. On the technology side, Alpha "was still just patched together," Ian explained, lacking a cohesive, strategic plan for leveraging technology to advance their automated trading ambitions. According to Ian, the firm's early years were characterized by what he described as an "accidental business model, or a series of independent trades": "We used to have a [firm] which is like, you find the trade, you exploit it, you find another trade, you exploit it." In Howard and Ian's view, this made the firm indistinguishable from many other first-generation automated trading companies. Howard elaborated on the typical model of such firms:

> They tend to be platforms, that is to say, once I have my risk management in place, once I have my plant in place, my technical infrastructure, once I have my capital infrastructure in place, I just need to bolt on more guys, bolt on teams, bolt on traders. "Hey, you've got an algo? You're a good guy, come on in, we'll bolt you in, we'll bolt you on." We've taken a distinctly different view. . . . Rather than bolt on, we want to build out.

Determined to reinvent the firm's approach, Howard and Ian developed a new business model named Delta, a title that also gave rise to the ML system's name: the Delta Product Suite (DEPS). This new model positioned DEPS at its center, signaling a strategic shift that highlighted the stark contrast between Alpha and DEPS, as Ian explained when discussing their relationship:

> They are totally different beasts. You can think of Alpha as being a specific thing and DEPS being less of a specific thing. I mean [Alpha] was, just from a first-principle or design perspective, it was intended to do one thing that there's no way to generalize away from. And because of that it was a successful one-trick pony, but there's literally no way to make it go lateral or move in any other direction. There's a distinction: a trade or a business. So it was a successful trade; however, I wouldn't call it a business.

Implementing Delta required phasing out the firm's first-generation automated trading systems—a process completed in 2019—and reorienting the entire organization around its ML system. This shift focused on how to best design, nurture, deploy, monitor, and improve the system. Specifically, the Delta model aimed to leverage the firm's domain expertise in markets where it had traditionally excelled and to develop an ML system that could perform well in these markets, with the potential to expand into others.

Ian described the transition as comprising a "cleanup" phase, which involved dismantling the first-generation system, and a "setup" phase, which introduced a business model centered entirely on ML as the firm's technological priority. This transformation required significant organizational changes, particularly in what Ian called the "people's space." Staff whose skills and expertise were misaligned with the new direction were replaced with individuals who could develop and support the ML system's various functions. While the firm still needed software developers and experts in the technological infrastructure that connected its algorithms to the markets, other functions, areas of expertise, and their hierarchical relationships were fundamentally reshaped.

On the quant side, the shift to ML marked a move away from valuing broad quantitative skills toward prioritizing specialists with deep data science expertise in the nuances of ML. This distinction was emphasized by several informants. One individual from an investment management firm described the difference between the skill sets required for first- and second-generation automated trading systems as "completely different" (see also K. Hansen 2020). For first-generation systems, stochastic calculus was paramount: "That is just a model that you come up with to describe the evolution of financial assets . . . and come up with a price and risk characteristics." In contrast, second-generation systems demand an entirely different focus. The emphasis shifts to "having a clean set of data, organizing data, and because the amount of data available these days is much bigger than it was before, you have this need for people to be skilled around how to manipulate these big sets of data, and to present it in a way that is usable." However, recruiting data science experts with general data-manipulation skills alone might not suffice. Ian highlighted the challenges of finding ML specialists who could navigate the specific complexities of finance:

> We've interviewed several people from machine learning backgrounds outside of finance that are trying to apply things to finance and they're often extremely naive in these areas. They will apply extremely naive views on the data and extremely naive views on the simulation. And they—my phrase is unicorn chasing—they invent a fantasy land that they become wealthy within, and they chase the unicorn over the rainbow. But it's actually a fantasy land and that will just be bad for them, essentially.

This sentiment echoed a broader consensus among many informants: pure ML expertise must be combined with domain knowledge—in this case, a deep understanding of market microstructure—to be truly effective.[5] This point is also reflected in the broader sociological literature (see Preda 2025; Rella et al. 2024). To be sure, larger firms may prioritize pure data science expertise over domain knowledge when recruiting, operating on the belief that market expertise can be acquired on the job (K. Hansen and Souleles 2023, 435). At Cormac and similar firms, however, the preference is for data science experts who already have experience applying ML to practical financial problems.

As outlined in chapter 2, firms developing first-generation systems often rely on a clear division of labor: traders serve as idea generators, funneling their concepts to quants, who refine and test them. At Cormac, this traditional model was turned on its head. Staff with ML expertise were elevated to the center of the organization, while the roles of the few remaining human traders were reimagined. These traders, all with significant nonalgorithmic trading experience, formed what became known as the Delta Trading Team. Led by Phil, a veteran with over twenty years of experience in pit and electronic screen trading, the team no longer traded directly. Instead, their role evolved into collaborating with the firm's ML experts to interpret, mentor, and shape DEPS's behavior, while addressing its "blind spots," as Phil described. This organizational restructuring reflected Cormac's pivot from first- to second-generation automated trading. The Delta Trading Team consisted of just three members, while the Research Engineering Team, comprising the ML specialists, expanded to seven. The remaining fifty staff were primarily divided between developers, responsible for code implementation, and IT personnel, who maintained the firm's technological infrastructure as part of the Infrastructure Team.

The firm's material infrastructure—or stack (K. Hansen 2024)—also reflected what was both retained and renewed in its trading activities. During its first-generation phase, the firm developed a comprehensive software and hardware infrastructure, similar to what is described in chapter 2. This included a low-latency platform for accessing and communicating with exchanges, as well as in-house simulation-based testing for prospective strategies. This structure, known as the "Delta trading platform," was preserved as the foundational "chassis" upon which the new ML strategies would be deployed.

Howard and Ian consistently emphasized the "product" aspect of their ML operations, both in internal documents and during conversations with us. They deliberately chose the term *product* over the more conventional *strategy*. As Ian explained, describing DEPS as a product "connotes more the idea that many people are necessary to come together to build this thing," whereas *strategy* suggests something proprietary to an individual. This terminology underscored the firm's belief that successful ML-based trading is inherently a collective achievement. It also aligned with another principle central to Cormac's approach to second-generation trading: the conception of trading operations as a form of *industrial manufacturing*.

"The Delta manufacturing approach encompasses the entire production workflow from the selection and prioritisation of development tasks to design, development, review, testing and deployment of software" (internal document, June 2017, Cormac Trading Group). This manufacturing mindset was reflected in the way the firm referred to its infrastructure: the Delta trading platform as the "chassis" and DEPS as the "engine" driving it.

According to Ian, the idea of applying the language and principles of industrial production to the manufacturing of trading automatons emerged through internal discussions about how organizational designs and practices from other industries might inform their own work:

> We studied the airline industry and the automotive industry and paid a lot of attention to development from these industries and tried to understand how they might be applicable to ours. . . . The airline industry is great at learning from errors. How can we do that? . . . We obviously learned a lot from the vehicle manufacturing system. We looked at Tesla's Gigafactory and how they do automation of their world. [And we are] deeply inspired by Toyota, in particular. . . . Our manufacturing [approach], really the language of chassis and engine, comes very much from considering what is appropriate from that domain, to project it onto ours. Also, the transparency that comes along with that.

The focus on learning from errors ties into broader themes of organizational control wrappers, which I will examine further in chapter 4. Transparency is closely linked to ML explainability, a subject I explore in chapter 5.

For now, my focus is on how Cormac conceives of its manufacturing process. This process is structured around several key phases, which I discuss in detail below. The first is the *data preparation* phase, where data are collated and cleaned for ML training. Once this step is completed, the training phase begins. Here the firm's ML engineers conduct experiments on historical data, priming DEPS to generate new trading rules or "candidate models." This is followed by the *experimentation* phase, where promising rules or models are identified for further testing. Candidate models that show potential then move into the *delivery* phase, which involves rigorous checks. Their performance is tested against both historical data and near-live market developments, and the implications of deploying the new models are assessed in relation to existing models. If a model passes all these tests and receives the necessary internal approvals, it advances to the *deployment* phase. At this stage, the model is released into the market, where its behavior requires continuous and careful monitoring.

Preparing Data

The data preparation phase offers a vivid illustration of both the overlap and the divergence between first- and second-generation automated trading systems. As noted in chapter 2, issues with data quality present one of the primary challenges for first-generation systems. Erroneous data used in back-testing can undermine the validity of a strategy: the patterns identified by traders and quants might not reflect real opportunities but instead be artifacts of flawed data. The stakes are equally high for second-generation systems. Much like an image recognition system that struggles to identify cats when its training images are insufficient or poorly rendered, a trading automaton cannot produce reliable market predictions if its training data are contaminated or of poor quality. Similarly, just as an image recognition system trained only on soda can images will not learn to identify cats, a trading automaton trained solely on equities data will not produce profitable predictions for FX markets. The importance of clean and reliable data for training trading automatons— regardless of their underlying ML architecture—was underscored by Babak, who remarked, "The biggest headaches that we have had have to do with data: how well curated the data is and all that sort of stuff. Lots and lots of headaches. . . . In actual fact, a good 65–70 percent of our time goes to the mundane."

Reflecting the heightened need for rigorous data hygiene in second-generation automated trading, Cormac employs staff whose primary responsibility is to ensure data quality. During one of our visits, we spoke with Matthieu, a data engineer at the firm, who detailed their processes for managing data. Cormac collects order-book data directly from exchanges and also sources them from market data vendors, who buy and resell data from trading venues. Once acquired, the data are validated and reformatted for DEPS:

> Matthieu: In the process of doing that we find problems, because the data is not perfect, either because the exchange made a mistake or because the vendor didn't record it properly. There's a whole lot of problems that could occur.
>
> Christian: So it's cleaning up [the data] basically?
>
> Matthieu: Yeah, exactly. We deal with two main exchanges, [Exchange A] and [Exchange B]. And we have a good story for our [Exchange A] data, and we're just in the process of getting a better story for our [Exchange B] data. We spent a lot of time, during the last year, trying to clean up the [Exchange A] data and make it easier to answer questions about it. Our [Research Engineering] Team might be looking at something and they might say, "This looks a bit weird, what happened? Was there a problem?" And it was very difficult to find out what that was.

To address these challenges, Matthieu developed several tools to improve data accuracy and reliability. The primary function of one such tool, the "Consolidator tool," is to automatically detect "any issues with the data from the vendor." Matthieu recounted an incident where a vendor had "stopped reporting stuff [i.e., certain market data] for two months. . . . They told me about it when I started poking around, but that was a very intensive manual process." While large-scale lapses like this are uncommon, even minor omissions—such as missing specific data points—can prove critical by distorting the ML system's understanding of market dynamics. "That's where the Consolidator comes in and tries to fill [any gaps] from other sources that we might have, or other sources [the vendor] might be able to give us," Matthieu explained.

The Consolidator also addresses another technical issue the firm encountered: one vendor's system reversed the sequence of certain orders, creating a false picture of which orders were responses to others. This type of error has significant implications for training ML systems that depend on precise sequences to model market behavior. Another tool Matthieu described, the "data console," provides a real-time heat map of incoming exchange data. Using a color-coded system (red, yellow, green), the console displays the quality of various data streams feeding each DEPS product. This allows the firm's ML experts to assess the reliability of the data underlying their experiments and to consider its impact on DEPS's actions in the market.

A related concern, which also arises in the context of first-generation automated trading, is the accuracy of time stamps. All order-book data are time-stamped by trading venues and data vendors, but for low-latency automated trading, where events occur on the scale of micro- and nanoseconds, extreme precision is essential. The quality of the data hinges on vendors' ability to provide highly accurate time stamps. Matthieu highlighted particular challenges with historical market data: "In the past, [trading venues] didn't do a good job" of ensuring the accuracy required for such granular data. He elaborated: "Clocks from computers are [often] very inaccurate. . . . Unless you have a good system for keeping that on track, you can make quite a mess. We've seen that in the data in the past. It's very clear that the vendor's clock was all over the place." In keeping with their broader approach to data quality, the firm addressed time-stamp issues by cross-referencing and triangulating data across multiple sources. "Each [order] message has an ID or a sequence number, so we can grab a message from one [data] source and a message from another source and look at the offset between the two and then adjust that recording," Matthieu explained.

To repeat, the overlap in data challenges and solutions between first- and second-generation systems is significant. Regardless of whether a human or a machine ultimately identifies patterns in the data, the data must be carefully prepared and cleaned. Moreover, because data are sourced externally, firms working with either generation of systems face the persistent risk that third-party errors can seep into their pattern-recognition processes if robust internal controls—like data triangulation mechanisms—are not in place. I explore this type of risk in greater detail in chapter 4.

That said, the data challenges encountered by second-generation systems can manifest in more extreme ways. A key reason for this is the adaptability of ML systems. As Babak described in relation to their genetic programming approach:

> The whole name of the game is the fact that these [trading] rules start adapting very quickly to their environment. Their environment is the stock data information that they're seeing. Good examples are when our data has been corrupted. Early on we got data from cheap sources, and for one source of data we suddenly realized that our genes [trading agents] are making tons of money, so what's going on? Well, it turns out that the data was corrupted in that the daylight-saving hours had shifted and that was not accounted for. Every year you had a month or two where the open of the market was one hour into what we thought was the market open. Of course, you have very little volatility, and suddenly you have a volatility spike and the price changes one way or the other. But the fact is that these genes had adapted to that. They knew that if they saw a certain profile of volatility, they would start to pile on as soon as they hit the one hour. They would capture the direction and pile on, and then make a ton of money either on the long side or the short side.

Bruce offered another example, illustrating the challenges ML systems face when making longer-term predictions using data on companies' dividends:

> In the finance and investment world, there's plenty of data. It can be expensive to get, but there's quite a bit of it. The real challenge is that it's very, very easy to accidentally time-travel one way or another. You need to have an infrastructure that completely prevents that. And it can be very subtle. For example, many [data] vendors, when they're reporting on dividends, they will—if a company has never issued a dividend—put "NaN" and not a number for the value of that dividend. As soon as that company offers a dividend in the future . . . , they will backfill all those "NaNs" with zeroes. Your clever little machine learning algorithm could pick out if a dividend is zero that that company's going to do well because at some point in the future they're going to offer a dividend.

Of course, a corrupted dataset can also mislead a human trader designing a first-generation system into spotting patterns that do not actually exist in the markets. However, the distinction lies in control: an ML system identifies patterns autonomously, leaving its human designers with far less influence over what it uncovers and how it adapts to the data. Unlike a human, an ML system might proceed undeterred by issues that would appear nonsensical or erroneous to a trader, diligently trying to detect patterns even when none exist. This is a variant of the overfitting problem: the strategy produced by a trading automaton may be based on artifacts from contaminated data that bear no resemblance to genuine historical market events. Naturally, the odds of such a strategy succeeding in live markets are minimal. So, while noise is a well-recognized issue in contemporary finance, as detailed by Preda (2017, 2020), it presents a distinct challenge in the context of ML. Beyond ensuring that machines do not confuse noise with meaningful information, particular attention must be paid to minimizing the noisiness of the training data itself.

Training Experiments

As Ian explained, "Training is, in essence, we take data, we apply some machine learning configuration, and we say, 'Go off into a computer for as many days or weeks as it takes for you to finish your learning.'" While the specifics of their ML configurations—the settings governing the training process—were considered proprietary and thus not shared by my informants, certain insights can still be drawn. First, in their daily work designing and training models, many informants utilized general ML libraries like TensorFlow and PyTorch (see also K. Hansen and Thylstrup 2024). One ML expert likened the flexibility of these tools to playing with building blocks: "TensorFlow is like Lego. You have the pieces and then you build the models you want." Second, as with first-generation systems, developing trading automatons relies on a twofold infrastructure. This includes not only large volumes of clean, well-prepared data but also a sophisticated simulation environment that closely replicates the operation of trading venues. Ian underscored the importance of this aspect of the training phase: "The natural counterpart of the data is the simulation of trading that goes hand in hand with the data. So the data is an input, but the other input is the simulation of how the exchange works, given that data. And exchanges work in many different ways."

The simulation environment holds particular significance in second-generation automated trading because of the adaptability of ML systems. Just as ML systems can quickly adjust to the data they are fed, they can also adapt to the nuances—or shortcomings—of the simulation environment in which they are trained. Ian cautioned, "Machine learning is very powerful. If your simulation is naive, it will find false things. So that's another very important aspect to machine learning, making your simulation be truly robust and representative." He likened the issue to training automated vehicles in a simulation that fails to accurately reflect real-world traffic conditions, then releasing them onto public roads: "It's very analogous [in finance] and that is the natural counterpart of the data. . . . [With ML] you have to be paranoid that you're fooling yourself. . . . If you give the machine anything false . . . you have to really guard for that."

Since the tradeable patterns an ML system detects are shaped not only by the training data but also by the market environment modeled in the simulation, many informants emphasized the importance of domain expertise in configuring robust second-generation systems. Markets are inherently dynamic, and their microstructure often evolves in response to new regulations or other external factors. As with first-generation systems, maintaining up-to-date simulation environments is therefore important when developing trading automatons, requiring staff with a deep understanding of the technical intricacies of market microstructure. Babak highlighted the need for this ongoing alignment between market microstructure and ML training and testing environments: "The microstructure does change. It's gradual. It is not pervasive. It's overlapping. That's my sense of how it operates, but there is fundamental change, and if your system isn't able to keep up with that, then it goes stale very quickly. Your processes and your system have to be able to keep up with that."

Once the proper data and simulation environment are established, the training phase can begin. During training, the automaton ideally learns to identify exploitable patterns in the data. At Cormac, this stage was described as generating a "candidate" or "candidate model," a potential new rule that, if successful, could be put into production and integrated into the overall strategy or "product." Staff categorized candidates into four types—"skill," "scale," "scope," or "signal"—and tailored experiments to develop each. A *skill* update focuses on refining DEPS's existing trading capabilities. Edwin, a senior software engineer at Cormac, explained: "A skill change we might talk about is the character of its liquidity interaction. So, how effective is DEPS in interacting with liquidity? How effective is it in managing its positions?" *Scale* refers to the volume DEPS trades in specific market conditions, with training experiments aimed at producing candidate models to either increase or decrease its market presence. *Scope* involves expanding the markets in which DEPS operates—for instance, training it on equities data when it originally focused on futures markets. Finally, *signal* relates to "What's it seeing in the data? What's driving it, its trading experience?" Edwin noted that new training experiments might enable DEPS to detect previously unnoticed patterns in the data, offering fresh opportunities for exploitation. Regardless of the type of experiment, the training phase can be both time-intensive and uncertain. As Ian described: "You might say, go off for a month and there are nice web tools and so on and people will look and see the progress of training. And they will abort various [candidates], 'These are clearly not going to succeed, let's kill them.' Others, we'll typically let them run for a while and you see their evolution during training." Informants from other firms shared similar experiences. Jeff, for instance, explained that growing a new strategy through training often required "a few weeks to six months of work," with most experiments ultimately proving unsuccessful. However, if a training experiment produces a promising candidate, that candidate moves to the next stage in the manufacturing process: delivery.

Performance Tests

Cormac's delivery process is overseen by a team of "delivery managers," individuals with IT expertise and extensive experience in software coding and testing. Alongside their team of "testers," the delivery managers act as intermediaries, much like quants in firms specializing in first-generation systems. Their responsibilities include testing candidate models, conducting additional evaluations requested by the ML experts, and coordinating with developers and IT staff to address any compatibility issues between the Delta platform's "chassis" and "engine."

The delivery phase involves multiple steps, all aimed at rigorously testing candidate models under conditions not included in the training phase. The goal is to determine which candidates are suitable for deployment in production. At Cormac, this process revolves around a "performance environment," where candidate models undergo a series of evaluations akin to the back-testing and paper trading used in first-generation systems. Back-testing examines a candidate model's performance using historical test data distinct from its training data. Similarly, the performance environment enables testing in a simulated market that closely mirrors real market conditions but lags by one minute. This shift from historical data to near-real-time simulation reflects the need to account for the context-dependent nature of training data. Historical data may represent market conditions or patterns that no longer exist, potentially rendering the learned strategies ineffective in current contexts. For instance, an ML system trained on data from highly volatile markets might excel at identifying patterns that become irrelevant in a low-volatility environment. Simon highlighted the impact of such shifts: "[Volatility surges are] usually good because then you get more trading signals, there're more opportunities, whereas if you go from a high-volatility to a low-volatility regime you're used to lots of opportunities and then there're none. That usually kills the strategy, whereas the other way around in my experience is just beneficial." The performance environment is designed to catch such mismatches—not only dramatic regime changes like shifts in volatility but also subtler discrepancies between the market conditions reflected in historical data and those of present-day markets.

Testing candidate models in the performance environment serves a crucial additional purpose: ensuring that individual product improvements contribute positively to the overall system. It is entirely possible, for instance, that a candidate model emerging from a training experiment shows skill improvement for DEPS when evaluated in isolation but causes poorer overall performance when integrated into the larger trading framework. One such scenario could involve self-trades, where the system inadvertently trades with itself—buying the very assets it intends to sell. Most exchanges prohibit intentional self-trades, as they create a misleading impression of market activity. To prevent such issues, Cormac staff conduct "integration tests," which, according to an internal document, examine "the interaction between multiple components [that is, model candidates]" to "evaluate the correct interactions between the newly developed component and all other components of [the] platform or product" (internal document, June 2017, Cormac Trading Group).

The various tests evaluate candidate models using an array of performance metrics. While some metrics may yield clear-cut results, others can prompt deeper discussions about the underlying behavior of a candidate model. For instance, the head of trading might be consulted to assess the model's performance from the perspective of an experienced human trader. As Ian explained, "We'll say, 'How do you like this new skill? Is the behavior in line with what you're expecting?'" If the head of trading raises concerns based on his domain expertise, these would be discussed with the ML experts, potentially triggering new rounds of training.

Just as training experiments can lead to aborted models, so too can the delivery phase uncover shortcomings that prevent a model from meeting all test requirements. Such models may be discarded outright or sent back for further training.

Even models that perform well in the performance environment might still exhibit behaviors that warrant closer scrutiny in simulation. For example, a candidate model might appear profitable but behave unpredictably compared to expectations derived from historical data performance. In such cases, ML experts may choose to run additional tests, causing the candidate model to step back in the manufacturing process for further refinement.

Models that pass the performance tests are subjected to stress tests, as mandated by regulation (see chapter 4). At Cormac, "Stress testing encompasses exposing the newly developed [candidate models] to unusually high load (e.g. high data frequency, burst of input data) and evaluating their robustness. . . . They need to be able to cope with simulated stress loads that exceed maximum historically observed peaks by at least a factor of two" (internal document, June 2017, Cormac Trading Group).

If a model clears the stress tests, it moves to the final approval stage. Here delivery managers prepare a "release pack" summarizing the test results. This release pack is then submitted to the Product Control Group (PCG), which reviews any material changes to DEPS. These changes might involve adjustments to its skills, scale, scope, or signals—essentially, "changes that have the potential to impact the performance, risk, and/or market conduct profile" of DEPS. Examples include "the trading of additional contracts, modifications to the objective function . . . , and changes to the quoting frequency" (internal document, June 2017, Cormac Trading Group).

The PCG comprises the CTO, the head of trading, and the chief risk officer. Its discussions focus on evaluating the individual candidate models. Some models may receive immediate approval, while others are sent back for additional testing or refinement. Edwin explained: "We might have prepared everything, but if somebody [from the PCG] has any concern then you might . . . pause it, review something, and then come back. And we have had examples where we have actually gone through all the delivery process and then someone was like, 'No, it's not going yet.' And you'll have to work it out and then come back to usually the market integrity, or something like that."[6] Another type of PCG discussion focuses on comparing competing model candidates that have successfully passed all necessary tests but are not all slated for release. As Ian explained:

> The comparison is very difficult. On some level, you can say, does [the candidate model] make more money? That's an easy question, on some level, but it's never that straightforward. The consistency of the return? What kind of losses does it have? How did it do on certain special events? So the process of comparison between models, to decide the criteria for going forward, is typically manifold again. . . . It's

like when you're hiring people. . . . I can say on one dimension [A is] more advanced and on another dimension [B is] more advanced. But I can't say that A is greater than B, unless I subset dimensions to choose on. It's a similar problem for promoting a machine learning agent. Sometimes there's a clear dominance and that's great and it makes it easy.[7]

While I have focused primarily on the manufacturing process for developing new ML products, Cormac applies the same manufacturing logic to the Delta infrastructure that enables DEPS to trade in markets. Any proposed improvements to the infrastructure undergo a comprehensive evaluation process, akin to the testing and approvals required for candidate models in the performance environment. As Edwin explained, "Any change to the Delta platform is considered to be a material change, and it goes through a rigorous set of testings and approvals and peer reviews in order to get into the market."

Release: Monitoring Market Action

Release marks the moment when a candidate model enters production, becoming part of the active portfolio of trading rules deployed in the markets. However, this step does not conclude the manufacturing process. At Cormac, an essential component of ML manufacturing involves automated postrelease monitoring and conduct surveillance. I will only touch on this briefly here because I discuss conduct surveillance in more detail in chapter 4 and because, in many respects, postrelease monitoring is similar across first- and second-generation systems.

At Cormac, postrelease monitoring includes ongoing checks of DEPS's behavior. The rationale mirrors that of first-generation systems: because DEPS is tested in a performance environment where it does not actively interact with live markets (i.e., it does not send actual orders), its potential market impact cannot be fully accounted for during simulation. Even with rigorous performance tests and in highly liquid markets, there remains a risk that DEPS's real-world behavior will deviate from expectations or elicit reactions from other market participants that simulations cannot replicate or anticipate. Postrelease monitoring is therefore critical for quickly identifying and addressing any such discrepancies. Like firms operating first-generation systems, Cormac also employs kill switches, which can be manually activated by the Delta Trading Team to withdraw orders from the markets in case of exceptional events.

Monitoring at Cormac is handled jointly by the Delta Trading and Infrastructure Teams. While automated software alerts infrastructure staff to unexpected activity, human oversight remains indispensable whenever DEPS is active in the markets.[8] As with first-generation systems, for the Delta Trading Team, observing DEPS's actions can yield insights into its underlying trading logic, potentially inspiring new training experiments aimed at refining its skill, scale, scope, or signal. However, unlike first-generation systems, DEPS's semi-independence and the inherent complexity of its neural net–based decision-making processes make its behavior less immediately interpretable. As a result, one of the primary post-trade tasks of the Delta Trading Team and the Research Engineering Team is to better understand why DEPS engages in specific behaviors. This understanding can then inform efforts to nudge the system in desired directions. I delve further into this interpretability challenge in chapter 5.

Comparing First- and Second-Generation Systems:
Decomposition, Adaptability, Intuition

This chapter has explored the motivations for adopting second-generation automated trading systems, their perceived advantages over first-generation counterparts, and the steps involved in Cormac's manufacturing process—from data preparation and ML training to experimentation, performance testing, and post-deployment monitoring. As discussed, the manufacturing of trading automatons shares key similarities with the setup of first-generation systems. These overlaps are especially evident in the underlying infrastructure needed to communicate with trading venues. The basic chassis required to support automated trading remains consistent across both generations and demands ongoing updates to account for market microstructure developments. Similarly, some challenges—such as issues related to data quality—are common to both generations. Systems of either type will struggle if their strategies are based on limited or poor-quality data.

That said, there are also fundamental differences between first- and second-generation systems. First-generation systems are explicitly designed to enact human-conceived strategies, which means, in principle, that their human inventors maintain complete control over them. However, as noted in chapter 2, various practical factors can limit this control. Code bugs may lead to unexpected behaviors; adding new components to an already-sprawling, million-plus-line codebase can introduce unforeseen interaction effects among its parts; and unanticipated, difficult-to-simulate interaction dynamics can emerge in markets. While these issues contribute to the model risk inherent in first-generation systems, their underlying strategies remain *decomposable*. Humans can take apart the system's engine— the strategy or set of strategies it follows—to analyze its action and, when necessary, correct its course.

Second-generation systems present a fundamentally different set of challenges. The model risk associated with these systems stems from factors such as data quality, overfitting, adaptability, opacity, and lack of explainability—all of which heighten the likelihood of loss-producing or otherwise undesirable behaviors (Cohen, Snow, and Szpruch 2021). Despite the extensive human curation required to set them up, the strategies these systems generate are far more difficult to decompose. The complexity of this decomposition depends significantly on the ML technique involved. As I discuss in chapter 5, explaining a system's decisions is particularly challenging for deep neural network–based systems.

As previously noted, the lack of direct human involvement in the steps from input to output, whether through a deep neural net or a genetically evolved system, presents a significant *adaptability* challenge. Trading automatons quickly adapt to the data and simulation environments on which they are trained. This adaptability can take nonintuitive forms, including detecting seemingly exploitable patterns where causal relationships are either reversed or nonexistent. The semi-independent nature of their pattern detection therefore demands vigilant oversight. The challenge here is twofold. First, ML systems are prone to fitting to noise—random fluctuations—rather than identifying genuine patterns in the training data, resulting in patterns that do not translate to test data or real-world conditions. Second, this overfitting or curve fitting (referred to by various names) occurs autonomously, detached from human intuition or expertise. This independence is critical: while a human trader might also identify a spurious pattern and design a first-generation system around it (as Alex's anecdote in chapter 2 illustrates), the trader would have attributed certainty to the pattern, likely comparing it to their experiential understanding of how markets operate. Achieving this kind of intuition-based evaluation is vastly more difficult with second-generation systems. One informant, the CEO and cofounder of a small HFT firm, aptly described this problem. He explained their attempt to transition from first- to second-generation automated trading in response to growing competition:

When we did [first-generation] high-frequency trading, we knew exactly why we were making money. We could pinpoint the exact market inefficiency that we were exploiting. And we also knew when it would disappear because it disappeared gradually and then, at some point, [the strategy] just became unprofitable. Whereas when you try to apply more sophisticated data-driven models, it starts to get hard to understand why [they detect which patterns]. Why should this set of data contain any predictive value? There are so many ways that you can fall into this trap and do, essentially, curve fitting—like the data you selected, the model that you've selected, the way the system that you have selects the models. And the more advanced it gets, the more risk there is that somewhere in the system, you simply just have some bias which is then exploited by the algorithm, and not a real market inefficiency. . . . The nice thing about [first-generation] high-frequency trading—if it actually works—is that you can almost predict how much you're going to make, basically down to a daily level. And you also know very, very quickly if your model works or not. With the models that we tried to create using more advanced machine learning, there was a little more uncertainty in whether we were actually curve fitting or whether we were exploring some underlying anomaly that would make us money over time. We had to take on a lot more risk, and that was . . . problematic for a small company.

As the uncertainty and associated risks persisted and profitability remained low, the founders of this firm ultimately decided to shut down their operations. While this was an extreme outcome, many other informants voiced similar concerns about the overfitting risks inherent in second-generation systems. In particular, informants specializing in first-generation systems were often critical of ML because of challenges surrounding overfitting, nonintuitive decision-making processes, and the difficulty of decomposition. Jonathan, the first-generation automated trader mentioned in chapter 1, succinctly summarized his skepticism: "Fancy machine learning optimization techniques will tell you that you've found a signal very easily when you're just optimizing on noise. You can actually give most machine learning strategies pure noise and it will give you an answer. It'll say that it found a signal even if it's a random number generator." Charles, introduced in the previous chapters, expressed similar reservations:

I'm not a big fan of machine learning, and I know I'm gonna live to regret this, but . . . if you don't understand fundamentally what the [system's] decisions are, then how do you improve it? . . . I feel like it's a buzzword. Sure, if you want to get into a credit card fraud classification problem, . . . that's a great spot for machine learning, but markets are fairly random in terms of their short-term movements. [So,] if you don't construct the problem right, you're gonna come out with crap anyway, and then how much faith are you gonna put in that? So I struggle to see [ML] as being a core part of what we do.

Nick, another informant, recounted his team's attempt to deploy deep learning models to develop optimal execution algorithms. Despite their initial enthusiasm, the models were ultimately abandoned due to their nonintuitive complexity: "If you use more intuitive models and something doesn't work right, you have a simple way to do attribution analysis. You can actually figure out what went wrong, what didn't work. If you're using complicated nonlinear models, they're hard to say what went wrong. There's no simple way to decompose deep learning structure into simple blocks."

My interviews revealed various iterations of this theme and underscored why many market participants specializing in automated trading continue to favor first-generation systems. Unlike second-generation models, first-generation systems are built on a foundation of human intuition—a human-conceived idea that, while requiring numerous algorithmic components to implement in markets, allows each individual part to be isolated and analyzed if the system behaves unpredictably. Achieving such intuition and decomposability with a deep learning system is far more challenging. Therefore, as Kristian Bondo Hansen (2020, 2021b) has demonstrated, even as complex ML models gain traction, many in the industry remain committed to simpler, more intuitive approaches. These models help avoid the specific risks associated with second-generation systems: the opacity and operational challenges of managing highly complex, difficult-to-explain algorithms.

As discussed earlier in this chapter, a central motivation for designing trading automatons is their dynamism. Unlike first-generation systems, which are limited by the ingenuity of their human creators and require direct code modifications to change behavior, second-generation systems are designed to improve their market behavior automatically, without human intervention. Ironically, however, one of the advantages of simpler first-generation models lies precisely in their static nature: their human designers tend to have a clearer understanding of their limitations when markets undergo radical changes. Second-generation systems may be more flexible, but that flexibility comes at a cost. Their ability to adapt to historical data and simulated environments can produce overfitting. And that same adaptability does not automatically extend to live-market conditions. What appears as dynamism in theory often runs aground in practice, bounded by the epistemic limits embedded in the systems themselves.

One key limitation is a version of the "out-of-distribution generalization" problem widely recognized in ML. This refers to an ML system's inability to make accurate predictions in a domain that diverges substantially from its training data—a phenomenon akin to the "cats and soda cans" issue discussed earlier. In finance, this problem might manifest during the deployment of a strategy trained in a simulation environment that uses one order-matching principle (FIFO) in a market operating under a different one (pro rata). Because the order-book dynamics in these two settings are fundamentally different, strategies learned in one are unlikely to succeed in the other. Even when an automaton is deployed in a market that aligns with the order-matching principle from its training phase, it can encounter other generalization challenges. For instance, a system trained on high-volatility market data might perform well under similar conditions but falter if the market shifts to a low-volatility regime.

In ML, this challenge is a variant of the "nonstationarity" problem, which refers to how the statistical properties of a dataset—such as price volatility or market liquidity—change over time, rendering previously detected patterns obsolete. An example discussed in chapter 2 is how post-2008 financial crisis QE programs affected market liquidity and price volatility. The CEO of one hedge fund argued that the nonstationarity created by QE posed a greater challenge to ML-driven approaches than the data quality issues mentioned earlier. He described datasets compiled during the QE era as essentially "manipulated," reflecting a period of heavy central bank intervention. According to this informant, a trading automaton trained primarily on such data would develop a skewed and highly unrealistic understanding of how markets operate.[9]

Another variation of the generalization problem arises in one-off situations or rare events not reflected in training data, leaving the automaton without patterns to guide its market behavior. Examples include Brexit and the market turmoil of March 2020 caused by the COVID-19 pandemic, which saw prices plummet and volatility surge to unprecedented levels. Brexit was a singular event, offering no historical precedent to help an automaton predict its market implications. Similarly, while pandemics have occurred before, their rarity and the vastly different contexts in which they have unfolded provide no reliable data for market prediction. One might argue that because trading automatons are designed to adapt, nonstationarity should not pose a problem. In theory, if markets change, the automatons should follow, continuously learning to refine their market actions. While this is the ideal, informants acknowledged clear limits to the types of changes an automaton can absorb. Marc from Cormac's Delta Trading Team put it succinctly: "Humans can adapt extremely quickly. You could literally diverge from your past within an instant. . . . Machine learning, the way that it relies on consistency through data over long periods of time, it's very difficult for it to [adapt] just on the flip of a coin."[10] Phil, the head of the Delta Trading Team, offered a similar critique of DEPS's limitations. Comparing the system's market actions to his own extensive trading experience, he found himself underwhelmed:

> There was this big assumption that the machine will learn to do everything, and it would learn quickly. I wasn't seeing that. . . . Markets [are] very quick these days. Liquidity's very itinerant. So [DEPS] needs to learn quick or it's not going to learn at all in the long run. There might not be a long run if there's no short run. . . . I mean it's good with price patterns. It's good with capitalizing on patterns. But if you're gonna see an outsize risk move, or what we refer to as a VAR [value at risk] shock or a volatility shock, it's not gonna be so good with that. It can't preempt, it can only react to the now. It's the machine learning algorithm walks into a bar, the barman says, "What will you have?" "I'll have what everyone else is having." So it just sits there doing what everyone else does. It will not actively go out and construct a position to deal with the potential onslaught of volatility coming towards it.

Phil also highlighted the machine's shortcomings in politically charged market conditions. "When politics and markets collide, politics usually wins," he observed. DEPS, designed to interpret a world of electronic order books, struggled to grasp the complexities of politically influenced situations:

> One of the things DEPS, or machine learning, can't do is see into the future, but you know as a human. You can tell when there's potentially bad news in the newspaper. DEPS doesn't read newspapers, and machines don't read newspapers very well. They will in the future, no doubt, or they probably do but not on a trading level just yet, and they can't always work out the paths of where the market may go. Humans tend to have a better idea of the fight and flight.[11]

It is hardly surprising that experienced human traders view themselves as better equipped than machines to handle the nonstationarity of market data. What stands out at Cormac, however, is how the traders' critiques of DEPS's shortcomings gradually influenced a broader recognition—even among the ML experts—that the machine's short-term adaptability left room for improvement. To harness human domain expertise and intuition in this area, Cormac's Research Engineering Team initiated ongoing conversations with the Delta Trading Team. These discussions focused on the traders' insights into how markets respond to news, political shifts, and economic developments, using this input to refine and enhance DEPS's adaptability.

Embedding or Disembedding through Data

In chapter 2, I argued that first-generation systems resist easy classification, as they can appear either disembedded from or embedded in the real economy, depending on the aspect being considered. A similar duality applies to second-generation systems. If trained exclusively on order-book and trade data, trading automatons are likely to produce strategies that are as speculatively disembedded as those seen in low-latency first-generation systems. Conversely, systems incorporating financial metrics such as dividends are more likely to generate strategies that reflect a closer connection to corporate performance within the broader economy. Moreover, the caveat I raised about first-generation systems applies equally to trading automatons: order-book and trade data are not limited to speculative activity. They also encode real-economic dynamics, such as the volatility effects driven by QE programs. Thus, even automatons trained solely on order-book data might mirror—and even exhibit bias toward—a specific real-economic scenario. This suggests that, even in low-latency speculative strategies, significant linkages emerge between trading automatons and the real economy.

SYNTHETIC DATA

That said, the potential data universe for second-generation systems is markedly broader, as these systems can be trained on a wider range of data types. For instance, trading automatons may draw not only on *actual* historical data but also on *synthetic data*—artificially generated data produced by one ML system for use by another, often through generative AI (Ferrari and McKelvey 2023; Jacobsen 2023, 2024). Synthetic data can mimic the properties of real data, much as a chatbot generates sentences that closely resemble human speech. Additionally, synthetic data can expose ML systems to scenarios absent from—or insufficiently represented in—their training data, enhancing the generalizability and adaptability of trading automatons.

Consider the case of training an automated vehicle to navigate traffic. Conventional training data consist of images of typical road conditions (Kim and Canny

2018). While such datasets capture most common scenarios, they may lack examples of rare road users—such as a penny-farthing—leaving the vehicle unprepared to respond appropriately. Synthetic data can generate such rare instances, supplementing the conventional training data to better equip the automated vehicle for unusual situations (Jacobsen 2023). In finance, a similar approach involves generating synthetic data that model entirely different market configurations or scenarios, such as varying volatility regimes, sudden liquidity collapses, or extreme market stress, and training the trading automaton on these simulated environments (Assefa et al. 2020).

The potential gains from synthetic data are significant, and a range of firms—including Gretel, Hazy, and Syntho—have emerged to produce and sell synthetic datasets to the finance industry and beyond. By training trading automatons on both real and synthetic data, firms can better address the nonstationary nature of financial markets and enhance their systems' ability to handle black swan events, such as sudden, rare market disruptions. Despite this promise, my interviews suggested that synthetic data are not yet widely deployed in the development of trading automatons, although one ML expert mentioned that a division of his firm—a major investment management company—was investing heavily in generating its own synthetic data for training purposes. In fact, informants offered differing perspectives on the usefulness of synthetic data. Jeff, for example, argued that for firms specializing in low-latency automated trading, the challenge is rarely a lack of data but rather navigating an overwhelming surplus of it. As he explained: "If you train a model on order-book data, you have everything you need. However, small stocks, they don't have so much data, . . . so that's where you might need to use synthetic data, but in high-frequency trading, I never heard anybody being successful by doing that." By contrast, another informant, an ML expert specializing in portfolio management, saw enormous potential in synthetic data. He was sharply critical of the conventional market theories taught in "finance school or economic core theories," dismissing much of these as overly reliant on multilinear regression, which he deemed "pretty much wrong." Instead, he advocated for a paradigm shift toward "experimental finance, just like people are doing in the research lab in physics or in biology." He noted a key limitation in finance: "The only problem is that in finance you cannot recreate the same conditions of the experiment because the lab is the market." Synthetic data, he argued, could bridge this gap by enabling ML researchers to design experiments in controlled synthetic environments where models can be rigorously trained and tested.

Despite the justifications offered for training automatons on synthetic data, this practice introduces a profound disembedding from the real economy. What a trading automaton learns from synthetic data may bear little resemblance to reality; indeed, it could be trained on wildly implausible counterfactual scenarios. The risk of such disembedding is mirrored in concerns surrounding the rise of large language models like ChatGPT. Scholars have warned that training ML models on synthetic data creates a looming threat of "model collapse," described as "a degenerative process affecting generations of learned generative models, in which the data they generate end up polluting the training set of the next generation. Being trained on polluted data, they then mis-perceive reality" (Shumailov et al. 2024, 755). The central example underpinning this critique involves a large language model generating synthetic data (output), which then serve as training data (input) for a subsequent model. This iterative process leads to conceptual inbreeding, producing outputs that deviate from the world depicted in the original real data (Shumailov et al. 2024). Such critiques underscore the necessity of maintaining a baseline of original, nonsynthetic training data alongside synthetic inputs (Shumailov et al. 2024, 759).

The extent to which the risk of model collapse affects finance depends on how synthetic data are deployed. If these data constitute part of the training set—intended, for instance, to address issues like market nonstationarity—there is a tangible risk of collapse. Mitigating this requires balancing the degeneration risk (and excessive disembedding) by integrating robust real-market data, whether from order books or fundamental economic metrics. Conversely, if synthetic data are used solely to *test* automatons in extreme or anomalous market scenarios rather than to train them, the risk of collapse diminishes. But even when they are used solely for testing, there remains a risk of overreliance on scenarios that carry inherent biases from synthetically generated data (see also Cohen, Snow, and Szpruch 2021, 9).

ALTERNATIVE DATA

While synthetic data—particularly in their degenerate forms—risk severing ties to the real economy, so-called alternative data hold the promise of embedding trading automatons more deeply into the fundamental layers of economic activity. *Alternative data* refers to finance-relevant information sourced from unconventional origins (Denev and Amen 2020; K. Hansen and Borch 2022, on which the following draws). Unlike traditional datasets—such as order-book, price, or trade data, typically obtained from financial exchanges or data vendors—alternative data might include satellite imagery of wheat fields or retail parking lots, offering predictive insights into crop yields or retail earnings months in advance. Other examples include corporate disclosures, such as quarterly earnings reports, which ML algorithms can process at scale, or social media activity, where real-time chatter about specific stocks might anticipate price movements mere minutes ahead.[12]

The definition of alternative data, as outlined above, is admittedly imprecise (K. Hansen and Borch 2022). In an effort to refine the concept, Alexander Denev and Saeed Amen (2020, 6) identify several distinguishing features. According to them, alternative data are often "less commonly used by market participants," may "be more costly to collect, and hence more expensive to purchase," and frequently pertain to subjects "outside of financial markets," such as satellite images of parking lots. Furthermore, these datasets typically have a "shorter history" than conventional ones; unlike order-book data, for instance, they may lack records spanning multiple years. Their use also often entails significant technical challenges.

The growing interest in alternative data reflects a dynamic, self-reinforcing cycle: data vendors are increasingly offering alternative datasets for sale, while new ML techniques are being deployed to uncover tradeable patterns within these datasets. Some vendors focus on aggregating and reselling alternative data, which may be provided either in raw, unstructured form—requiring buyers to handle the processing themselves—or in a structured, more readily usable format. Notable examples of such vendors include RavenPack, Refinitiv (acquired by the London Stock Exchange Group in 2021), and Quandl (acquired by Nasdaq in 2018).[13]

As noted, the expansion of alternative data offerings parallels and is further driven by advancements in ML that enable the extraction of patterns from large datasets. For instance, automating the identification of patterns in satellite imagery relies on progress in ML-based image recognition.[14] Similarly, when detecting and leveraging patterns in text, techniques from the field of natural language processing (NLP) are critical. Several firms where I conducted interviews (though none mentioned so far in this chapter) specialized in market predictions using NLP, with social media sentiment analysis as a central method. In such cases, the process typically involves (a) collecting a substantial volume of social media data, (b) determining the overall sentiment related to specific assets, and (c) developing an automated trading strategy based on this sentiment. The core assumption underpinning this approach is that the extracted sentiment can serve as a predictor of asset prices (early academic work in this area dates back to the early 2010s; see K. Hansen and Borch 2022).

One of my informants, David, is the principal researcher at a firm that formerly aggregated tweets about approximately four thousand US stocks, totaling nearly five hundred million tweets daily. As David explained, their focus was on "looking for comments that are expressed on Twitter about how people view the stock, how people are trading the stock, and just their general commentary about the company." Crucially, therefore, "We're not measuring transaction activity [as registered in order-book or market data], we're measuring comment activity," though the ultimate aim was to determine how social media sentiments corresponded to subsequent stock price movements.

The specific method used to achieve this goal unfolded as follows. Of the five hundred million tweets available daily, the firm's NLP algorithms filtered out roughly 90 percent to eliminate noise from duplicates and spam retweets. The system then calculated an average sentiment for the remaining tweets, capturing positive, neutral, and negative statements—along with nuanced variations of each—and aggregated these to create a sentiment score for each stock. When analyzing tweet content, the firm relied on a sentiment dictionary containing approximately twenty thousand unigrams (single words) and four hundred bigrams (two-word phrases). As David described:

> You can make various measures of positive statements—not just like good or bad. The example that we use a lot is like we'll see tweets that say, "Apple gapped up $5 on the open. They're having a good day." It's a positive statement. We'll see other tweets that would say things like "Apple broke through a resistance level right after the open. It's going to run to this level. I bought five hundred shares." That, in a trading context, is a more positive measure of market statement than the first example, and we capture that type of granularity. Where the first one is moderately positive, the second one is very positive from a financial trading standpoint.

Building on this foundation, the firm's NLP algorithms calculated changes in sentiment for each stock (for more details, see K. Hansen and Borch 2022).[15] Notably, this firm did not trade on the basis of the sentiment scores it generated. Instead, it sold these scores to other market participants—such as hedge funds or institutional investors—who could then use them as tradeable signals.

I interviewed other informants working at firms with similar business models. Although extracting tweets has become more challenging over time, NLP-based sentiment analyses can now be applied to other types of social media data. However, I did not encounter firms that relied exclusively on social media analytics for automated trading or investment decisions. Instead, these analytics were typically one component of a larger portfolio of potential signals. Reflecting this, David remarked, "I don't believe any hedge fund would trade solely on social media data. I would hope not! But it is a component of a broader strategy."[16] Another informant from a firm specializing in alternative data, Rado Lipuš, the CEO of Neudata, echoed this point, describing social media analytics as a tool for refining financial models: "It's very rarely used as a stand-alone factor, but it goes into a model where maybe it has 5, 10, 20 percent impact on the final trade," he said.

One significant risk of basing an automated trading strategy solely on social media sentiment is the potential for manipulation. Social media posts can be fabricated to influence sentiment intentionally, leading to schemes such as "pump and dump." Here individuals tweet positively about a stock to encourage others to buy it, driving up its price, at which point the manipulator sells for a profit. These tactics have been documented in the realm of penny stocks (valued under five dollars) that are traded privately outside traditional exchanges (Murphy and Stafford 2021). However, my informants noted that similar manipulative practices also occur with exchange-traded stocks. David explained that this risk is one reason his firm filters tweets: "It's possible you could jam a stock, so you have to have a way to detect that, and we think that some of our metrics help do that." Elaborating on these manipulative practices, the CEO of an asset management firm specializing in social media analytics observed:

> Most of what we see are pump and dump schemes, but we see very, very sophisticated ones. . . . We found that there are some groups of people or groups of robots who post all of the same information at different times on different message boards. They use different usernames and what they do is they cultivate relationships with actual humans. They'll post noncommittal, benign messages like "Great call" or "Good job," or "That's very interesting," and what they do over time is that they send these random but very generic messages to develop relationships with real humans and start following them. And so, after twelve months of developing a relationship, simultaneously, every one of them will promote the same stock, even though they never promoted a stock before. So you see this very organized racket of very sophisticated pump and dump schemes in social media.

Not surprisingly, prospective buyers of alternative data are acutely aware of these risks, raising questions about the data's reliability and value. The chief scientist of a large investment management firm captured this concern, remarking, "There's a lot of buzz about [alternative data], certainly from the people selling it. I'm sure that probably the only guaranteed people making money out of alternative data are people that are selling it." He highlighted a major challenge in turning alternative data into viable investment strategies: "Most of this new data has very short history," making it exceedingly difficult to conduct robust back-tests "if you only have two years of data." While he was particularly critical of social media–derived data—"all these tens of millions of fake accounts that people can buy and fund and spoof with"—he saw greater potential in large-scale weather data for commodities trading, as such data are less prone to manipulation.

So when alternative data capture specific underlying phenomena—such as crop yields, parking lot activity analyzed through image-recognition systems, or extensive collections of financial statements processed via NLP algorithms—they enable a deeper embedding of second-generation systems within real-economic fundamentals. In contrast, manipulation drives disembedding rather than embedding, severing any strategies unable to detect manipulative content from their connection to real-life fundamentals. Concerns about manipulated alternative data have been voiced by US regulators (Gensler 2021; K. Hansen 2022), highlighting broader debates about how automated trading might increase the likelihood of certain forms of market misconduct compared to earlier market arrangements. This example points to a broader landscape of risk, which I explore in more detail in the next chapter.

FOUR

Risk, Reliability, Regulation

THE HISTORY OF FINANCIAL MARKETS charts a narrative of steadily advancing technological sophistication, driving the evolution from one dominant market arrangement to the next. This trajectory, however, is equally marked by crashes and crises, encompassing both minor disruptions and global financial collapses. Predictably, these twin histories are interwoven. Specific technologies not only enable market participants to exploit opportunities—such as improved latency and enhanced financial information processing—but also introduce significant risks. These risks often necessitate corresponding forms of mitigation, which, more often than not, arrive belatedly through regulation.

The risks posed by technological innovations extend both to the individual firms deploying these systems and to the broader markets they inhabit. As markets become increasingly interconnected—geographically and through complex financial products—the potential for one firm's technological failures to ripple outward grows considerably. A salient example is the dramatic collapse of Knight Capital, a US broker-dealer, in August 2012. Knight Capital relied on automated systems to direct clients' orders to the market for execution. In the lead-up to its downfall, the firm conducted an update to its order-routing system, SMARS, which turned out to be fatally flawed. Not only did the system retain dormant code tied to an order-routing functionality discontinued seven years earlier, but on August 1, 2012, that outdated code was unexpectedly triggered on one of SMARS's eight computer servers—a server that had not been updated. The result was catastrophic: the firm mistakenly sent millions of erroneous orders to the stock market, triggering a chain of events that culminated in extraordinary financial losses. Specifically, the system generated "4 million executions in 154 stocks for more than 397 million shares in approximately 45 minutes. Knight inadvertently assumed an approximately $3.5 billion net long position in 80 stocks and an approximately $3.15 billion net short position in 74 stocks. Ultimately, Knight realized a $460 million loss on these positions" (SEC 2013, 6). Because of the massive losses, Knight Capital was swiftly acquired by a competitor (Kirilenko and Lo 2013, 65). However, the repercussions of the malfunctioning system extended far beyond the firm itself. According to the SEC (2013, 6), as Knight was already a major player in the market,[1] its deluge of orders on August 1, 2012, caused significant immediate disruptions. For some of the stocks it traded, prices were moved by more than 10 percent, creating substantial ripple effects in a market shared by numerous other participants.

Another stark example of the risks generated by financial interconnectedness is the so-called Quant Meltdown of August 2007. Faced with mounting losses, quantitative hedge funds began liquidating large portfolios to raise cash or reduce leverage. As Andrei Kirilenko and Andrew Lo (2013, 61) explain, "The subsequent price impact of this massive and sudden unwinding caused other similarly constructed portfolios to experience losses," triggering a downward spiral of cascading liquidations.[2] Then there is the Flash Crash of May 6, 2010. As I have examined this event and its competing explanations extensively elsewhere (Borch 2016, 2020), I will limit myself to a brief summary here, relying on the official joint CFTC and SEC (2010) report issued a few months after the crash.[3]

The Flash Crash unfolded in an already-jittery market environment shaped by the European sovereign debt crisis. On May 6, 2010, an asset management firm using an execution algorithm initiated a substantial sell order of seventy-five thousand "E-Mini S&P 500" contracts—CME-traded futures linked to the S&P 500 stock index—valued at over $4 billion. Initially, HFT algorithms absorbed part of the sell order. However, after ten minutes, with the sell execution still ongoing, many HFTs began unwinding their positions. This sell pressure compounded the execution algorithm's increasing pace, pushing prices sharply downward. A frenetic "hot potato" effect ensued, with HFTs rapidly buying and selling among themselves (CFTC and SEC 2010, 3). The resulting pressure caused the prices of the E-Mini and related assets, including stocks, to plummet. Approximately fifteen minutes after the sell order began, the CME's systems automatically triggered a five-second trading pause. While the E-Mini's price rebounded when trading resumed, stock markets continued to decline for another fifteen minutes—partly because of the withdrawal of many market participants—before recovering. The entire event spanned about thirty minutes and constituted one of the largest intraday price collapses in the history of US financial markets, temporarily wiping out roughly $1 trillion in value, with the steepest decline occurring in under five minutes.

The Quant Meltdown, the Flash Crash, and the collapse of Knight Capital all took place before the widespread adoption of second-generation systems within the finance industry. These events, in other words, can largely be understood as reflecting risks associated with first-generation systems. This raises a critical question: If specific technologies are tied to particular forms of risk, what kinds of risks does the increasing use of ML in trading introduce? Specifically, does the shift to second-generation systems create novel risks for firms and markets, and if so, what are they? And what strategies can be employed to mitigate risks unique to ML?

To delve into these issues, I analyze the risks posed by both generations of systems, highlighting their distinct characteristics and assessing strategies for mitigating these risks. My analysis begins with sociological theories on the risks posed by complex technological systems and the potential to address those risks through the creation of reliable, risk-mitigating organizational designs. This theoretical lens provides a valuable entry point for understanding how both first- and second-generation systems could implode in ways reminiscent of the Knight Capital debacle and identifying measures to prevent such outcomes. Yet, while this framework is instructive, I contend that the risks of automated asset trading require a broader analysis. This expanded perspective must account for how individual firms' systems depend on external infrastructures—such as connectivity or data—and how their market actions directly affect other participants, creating a fertile ground for risk to spiral both inwardly and outwardly. I demonstrate that existing regulations governing automated trading in Europe and the US acknowledge these risks and aim to address them by requiring market participants to implement risk-mitigating protocols. However, these regulations remain vague about what such measures entail in practice. To shed light on what effective risk management might entail on the ground, I examine how Cormac seeks to manage the risks arising from its reliance on external infrastructures. While I contend that infrastructural risks and their mitigation are similar across both first- and second-generation systems, the latter face unique challenges in avoiding inadvertent engagement in illegal manipulative practices.

The chapter concludes by exploring two dimensions that partly extend and partly transcend these considerations. The first concerns a paradox: efforts by individual firms to mitigate risk may unwittingly exacerbate systemic risk, defined as "the risk that events or failures involving one actor, either a firm or individual, or one market sector propagate out to negatively affect the broader financial system and the economy at large" (Gensler and Bailey 2020, 15–16). This paradox is relevant to both generations of automated trading systems. The second dimension, however, is unique to trading automatons. It involves the risk that these systems, developing strategies semi-independently yet often drawing on similar (order-book) data and employing analogous ML architectures, might inadvertently converge on identical strategies, heightening the likelihood of herding in markets.

Normal Accidents, High-Reliability Organizations, and Financial Markets

Since technological risk is not limited to financial markets, my discussion begins outside the realm of finance. Specifically, I start with Charles Perrow's now-classic sociological account of technological risk, *Normal Accidents* (1999), originally published in 1984. In this work, Perrow challenged the idea that technological failures are merely isolated mishaps caused by random or occasional events. To illustrate the broader dynamics often at play, Perrow examined the 1979 accident at the Three Mile Island nuclear power plant in Pennsylvania. During this incident, a failure in a cooling system escalated into a partial reactor core meltdown, resulting in the release of significant amounts of radioactive gases. For Perrow, this disaster was not merely a matter of human error or poor decision-making—although those factors were present. Rather, he argued, it stemmed from the way system components were tightly coupled and complexly interconnected. Examining numerous similar examples across industries such as chemical plants, aircraft and air traffic control, and nuclear weapons, Perrow concluded that certain technological systems are inherently prone to large-scale accidents. This insight formed the foundation of his "normal accidents theory" (NAT): in systems marked by both "complex interactions" and "tight coupling," accidents are not just possible but inevitable.

Complex interactions occur when system components interact in "unfamiliar . . . or unplanned and unexpected sequences" that are "either not visible or not immediately comprehensible" (Perrow 1999, 78). By contrast, linear interactions are those that follow predictable paths among system components. Even if unplanned, they are at least visible and can be addressed directly. An assembly line serves as a quintessential example of a system with linear interactions: one component or step naturally feeds into the next, and any disruption is easily identified and resolved. In comparison, a nuclear reactor exemplifies a system where components might engage in complex, unforeseen feedback loops.

Technological systems are considered *tightly coupled* when their components exert direct, immediate effects on one another. Such tight coupling can lead to rapid domino effects, leaving humans with insufficient time to intervene vis-à-vis an incident. Conversely, loosely coupled systems allow components to operate with greater independence; a failure in one part need not trigger adverse effects throughout the system.

Technological systems can be assessed along these two axes: the degree of complex versus linear interactions and the extent of tight versus loose coupling. Perrow argued that systems with linear interactions and loose coupling may experience incidents, possibly even frequently, but that these events rarely escalate into large-scale accidents. In stark contrast, systems designed with both complex interactions and tight coupling are far more vulnerable. In such systems, isolated incidents can swiftly escalate into full-scale accidents. More provocatively, Perrow's theory contends that catastrophic accidents in these systems are not merely possible—they are bound to happen. They are a "normal" consequence of the way these systems are built. As Perrow (2010, 310) observed, "My formulation of system [or normal] accidents expressly argues that these accidents occur even where everyone tries as hard as they can to avoid system failures. They are built into the system, and though generally rare, are inevitable." As a result, Perrow's analysis casts a somber light on the inherent risks of complex technological systems, underscoring their immanent hazards.

The pessimistic, semideterministic perspective of NAT faced significant challenges from organizational scholars during the 1980s and '90s. Like Perrow, these researchers examined technologically advanced organizations—including nuclear aircraft carriers, submarines, power plants, and air-traffic control systems—where failures could have devastating and potentially fatal consequences (e.g., Bierly and Spender 1995; La Porte and Consolini 1991; Roberts 1990). However, rather than concluding that systems characterized by complex interactions and tight coupling are inevitably destined for catastrophic failure, this body of work argued that the risk of large-scale accidents could be mitigated through carefully designed organizational structures, cultures, and procedures. In essence, they contended that "high-reliability organizations" (HROs) could be engineered to manage and reduce the dangers associated with complex technological systems.[4]

What, then, defines an HRO? Two HRO scholars, Karl Weick and Kathleen Sutcliffe (2001), identified five key characteristics:

1. Preoccupation with failure identification and reporting: The organization prioritizes identifying, acting upon, reporting, and learning from even minor incidents to prevent larger accidents.

2. Reluctance to simplify interpretations of incidents: To achieve a nuanced understanding, the organization mobilizes diverse forms of expertise when analyzing incidents.

3. Sensitivity to operational aspects: Emphasis is placed on frontline operations, fostering a culture where staff are encouraged to report issues and incidents without hesitation.

4. Commitment to resilience: Clear procedures are established to ensure the organization can continue functioning effectively despite errors or disruptions.

5. Deference to expertise over hierarchy: Incident response is guided by those with the most relevant expertise rather than being automatically escalated through formal hierarchical channels.

So this research suggests that organizations can mitigate their susceptibility to the technological catastrophes predicted by Perrow by fostering a culture centered on the core features of HROs. By incentivizing practices that prioritize detecting, reporting, acting on, and learning from minor incidents before they escalate, organizations can reduce the risks associated with complex systems (Fraher, Branicki, and Grint 2017; Weick and Roberts 1993).

At first glance, these insights might seem distant from discussions about financial markets. Indeed, and somewhat surprisingly, financial markets and the organizations operating within them have not been extensively studied through the lenses of NAT or HRO. To the extent that HRO scholarship has focused on finance, it has primarily critiqued financial organizations for failing to implement HRO procedures (Bush, Martelli, and Roberts 2012; Weick and Sutcliffe 2015; Young 2011/12).[5] NAT research, by contrast, has shown somewhat greater interest in financial markets, although they were absent from Perrow's original *Normal Accidents*. In the expanded 1999 edition, however, he devoted a few pages to "financial systems," noting that "an obvious place to apply NAT would seem to be the financial world, which everyone agrees has increased in complexity and, in something close to the notion of tight coupling, volume" (1999, 385). Perrow identified several factors contributing to complex interactions and tight coupling in financial markets: the proliferation of sophisticated financial instruments (especially derivatives), global market interconnectedness, arbitrage strategies that link disparate markets and instruments, currency pegging, and the rise of computerized trading, including high-speed trading.[6]

Speaking to the latter, the collapse of Knight Capital offers a compelling illustration of key insights from both NAT and HRO research. The SEC's report on the incident underscores how it fits Perrow's definition of a system accident, or normal accident—an event marked by "the *unanticipated* interaction of two or more failures that would be acceptable individually" (Perrow 2010, 312, original emphasis). In the Knight case, multiple failures unexpectedly interacted (far too many to detail fully here). Among these were the outdated piece of code that was unintentionally activated on one of the firm's servers and a series of controls that were either absent, partially implemented, or ineffective. Compounding the issue, staff lacked a sufficient understanding of the system's complexity, leading to confusion as they attempted to diagnose the problem when SMARS began erroneously routing millions of orders. In their efforts to resolve the issue, staff made matters worse by uninstalling updated code from the seven servers where it had been deployed correctly, thereby exacerbating the crisis (SEC 2013, 8).

While the Knight Capital case highlights the risks inherent in systems characterized by complex interactions and tight coupling, it also underscores the relevance of HRO principles. A central critique from the SEC was that Knight had failed to adhere to existing regulations regarding risk management controls, technology governance, and supervisory procedures—elements that align with foundational HRO practices. Compliance with these measures might have mitigated or even prevented the accident. For instance, Knight lacked formalized procedures for reviewing and testing new code:

> Knight did not have written code development and deployment procedures for SMARS (although other groups at Knight had written procedures), and Knight did not require a second technician to review code deployment in SMARS. Knight also did not have a written protocol concerning the accessing of unused code on its production servers, such as a protocol requiring the testing of any such code after it had been accessed to ensure that the code still functioned properly. (SEC 2013, 8)

As a result, flawed pieces of code could inadvertently be added to the system, while outdated ones could persist, creating complex interactions. This reflects a broader issue in the evolution of first-generation systems, where new rules are continually layered onto existing ones. This accumulation process is exacerbated by the observation I made in chapter 2: because of fierce competition among trading firms, the window during which first-generation automated strategies remain profitable is constantly shrinking. Exploitable opportunities are quickly seized by competitors or otherwise disappear, leading traders to focus heavily on developing new strategies or tweaking old ones to extend their viability (Borch and Lange 2017). Although each piece of code added in this iterative process may be individually comprehensible, the interactions between these accumulating system components become increasingly complex and harder to understand. Ian, Cormac's CTO, highlighted this issue, noting that because first-generation systems often comprise "millions of lines of code," they eventually "become quite brittle because basically what happens is you keep inventing new rules that get added on new rules that get added on new rules, and eventually you go down some path that is intentional but not intentional really." This brittleness is a recipe for normal accidents.

For second-generation systems, the challenge is different but equally serious. In particular, deep learning–based systems are notoriously difficult to explain. Even the architects of a deep neural network, those who design its architecture, objective functions, and other parameters, often struggle to understand how the system transforms inputs into actionable outputs. The combination of their adaptability and the opaque nature of their inner workings makes it especially challenging to prevent second-generation systems from exhibiting complex interactions and tight coupling or otherwise becoming exposed to significant risks. Although I argue below that the types of risk management and governance protocols Knight failed to implement are critical for both first- and second-generation systems, the latter require far more extensive HRO measures.

This underscores the relevance of NAT and HRO scholarship for understanding the risks associated with automated trading. However, firms specializing in first- and second-generation systems must also grapple with a dimension that falls outside the primary focus of NAT and HRO research: the risks stemming from the interconnectedness of automated trading systems with systems and resources *in their environment*.

Beyond Insulated Analytics: Infrastructural and Mutual Enactment Risk

On the surface, it is a straightforward observation: market participants constantly factor in each other's behaviors, and trading venues serve as pivotal infrastructures that facilitate these interactions. Beneath this apparent simplicity, however, lies a more intricate reality. When numerous automated trading systems simultaneously observe and respond to developments in the order book—doing so at ultra-low latency—each system's actions are shaped by the behavior of others. The result can be unforeseen, extraordinarily complex interaction dynamics that are neither easy to predict nor readily understood. Furthermore, as explored in previous chapters, both first- and second-generation systems depend critically on various external inputs, with data being among the most significant. Operational reliability hinges on consistent access to these inputs and the seamless functioning of infrastructural connections to trading venues. When external data streams falter or infrastructural ties are severed, firms cannot sustain the functionality of their automated trading systems. Consequently, automated trading does not unfold within insulated entities that might generate discrete accidents, as described in NAT. Nor does it occur within isolated organizations that may manage their high-risk technologies through the rigorous, fail-safe protocols championed by HRO theory. Instead, this activity takes place within a market arrangement where individual firms and their automated trading systems are profoundly interconnected with their environment. In such a setup, the risk of accidents arises significantly from these interconnections themselves.

It is notable that, while Perrow acknowledged that technological systems "will have at least one source of complex interactions, the environment, since it impinges upon many parts or units in the system" (1999, 75), this recognition did not evolve into a systematic analysis of the environment's role. In *Normal Accidents*, Perrow (1999, 176, 251) often treated the environment as little more than a backdrop, citing examples like bad weather for marine officers or falling rocks for miners, which are challenging but narrowly framed conditions. There are two exceptions to this pattern in *Normal Accidents*. One is Perrow's discussion of military early-warning and response systems—systems designed to detect and respond to missile attacks. Here he examines "a system where the environment is intentional and self-activating" (1999, 292). These systems are tightly integrated with their environment, where enemy systems operate under identical conditions, continuously observing and responding to the same environmental cues. The second exception involves Perrow's treatment of coast guard and air traffic control systems. Both aim to prevent collisions among vessels and aircraft, and in both cases, significant risks stem from interactions between individual systems and their broader environments. While Perrow recognized the importance of such system-environment interrelations, he did not develop a comprehensive theoretical framework to analyze them.

A similar pattern exists within HRO scholarship. While these studies offer rich, detailed accounts of the internal functioning of HROs, they show far less engagement with the environmental contexts in which these organizations operate. Karlene Roberts (1990, 161, 71), for instance, notes in passing that HROs "face very uncertain environments," as in the case of aircraft carriers encountering unexpected weather conditions (see also Bigley and Roberts 2001; Sutcliffe 2011). Likewise, Weick and Sutcliffe's (2007, 85) exploration of organizational environments is limited to the observation that a mindful HRO approach is particularly relevant "in contexts that are dynamic, ill structured, ambiguous, or unpredictable."

That said, some HRO studies have taken steps to recognize the significance of the environment (La Porte 1996; Roberts, Stout, and Halpern 1994). The most developed exploration comes from Paul Schulman and Emery Roe (2018), who argued that organizations interconnected through larger networks can develop mutual interdependencies, making HRO principles critical across these organizations. Relatedly, Roe and Schulman (2018) analyzed the interplay of reliability and risk within infrastructures—such as telecommunication networks or power grids—that link organizations and enable their operations. When these infrastructures are interconnected, the failure of one can cascade, adversely affecting others and raising more complex HRO challenges than those considered in earlier literature.

Although Schulman and Roe did not address financial infrastructures, these have been the focus of systematic inquiry among sociologists of finance (Handel 2022; Kennedy 2017; MacKenzie 2021; Pardo-Guerra 2019; Petry 2021; Pinzur 2021a, 2021b). Particularly notable is Pardo-Guerra's (2019) historical study of financial infrastructures, which maps how different market arrangements have depended on distinct infrastructures. Pardo-Guerra's work highlights that the complex sociomaterial infrastructures underpinning contemporary automated trading are the products of both deliberate and incidental processes. But more than that, these infrastructures are central to the functioning of automated trading, down to the granular mechanics of order-book queuing. This centrality also renders markets acutely vulnerable to infrastructure failures. The implication aligns with Roe and Schulman's insights: when organizations depend on external infrastructures, their localized HRO practices must account for the risks of those infrastructures breaking down.

In the market arrangement of automated trading, managing technological risk therefore involves more than addressing intrafirm concerns. It requires attention to how firms' automated systems connect with others in their environment and with external infrastructures, including data. To frame this within NAT-HRO terminology, complex interactions and tight coupling occur not only *within* individual technological systems but also *across* them. Building on this, I propose to analyze HRO measures in automated trading as fundamentally addressing these interconnections. To function as an HRO in this domain means grappling with technological risks that can spiral inward—entering an organization as externally generated threats if defenses are inadequate—or spiral outward, affecting others if the organization fails to contain them effectively.

While the terminology of NAT can be broadened to account for complex interactions and tight coupling that transcend the boundaries of single technological systems, it is also productive to move beyond the deterministic framework NAT often implies. To that end, I propose distinguishing between two types of environment-related risks. *Infrastructural risk* refers to the vulnerability arising when external infrastructures falter, making it hazardous for automated trading systems of either generation to function effectively in markets. This risk necessitates the implementation of HRO procedures capable of swiftly managing any infrastructural failures within the environment. The second category, *mutual enactment risk,* emerges from the design of automated trading systems, which are often programmed to observe and respond to one another's actions in markets. Both risks reflect the combination of complex interactions and tight coupling: the dependency on underlying infrastructures and the interconnectivity of trading systems responding to the same order-book data further intensify the presence of complex interactions and tight coupling in automated trading, increasing the risks for individual market participants and markets as a whole, as disruptions in either dimension can escalate rapidly. Before delving into these two forms of risk, it is important to distinguish them from the model risks discussed in previous chapters. *Model risk* pertains to deficiencies in the design, input data, testing, or deployment of trading models, which can result in inaccurate outputs or unintended consequences. In contrast, infrastructural and mutual enactment risks transcend the individual trading system and its internal design, focusing instead on the broader interdependencies in which these systems are embedded.

In the trading context, infrastructures encompass any external elements essential for the efficient operation of a trading system. These include trading venues, the technological infrastructures connecting firms to these venues, and data transmission systems—such as microwave networks—used to relay information between colocated servers at different venues with minimal latency. The failure of any of these infrastructures can severely disrupt the automated trading systems they support, making continued operation highly risky. For example, trading venues frequently experience technological glitches that may halt trading or prevent them from correctly processing order flows (e.g., Bloomberg News 2024; Robertson and John 2024). Such failures directly affect automated trading systems operating on the disrupted venues and may also ripple outward, impairing operations on other venues where related assets are traded. Similarly, automated trading systems of either generation depend on real-time access to market and order-book data. Any disruption—whether from exchanges or third-party data providers—can significantly hinder these systems' ability to place and execute orders effectively.

Naturally, the failure of certain infrastructures poses greater risks than others, and this depends in part on how easily those infrastructures can be substituted. For instance, there is only one objective representation of market data: the orders placed and the trades executed. However, because market data can be obtained from multiple sources, it is often possible to substitute one failing source with another, at least temporarily. By contrast, connectivity infrastructures are far more challenging to replace quickly. They involve a higher degree of infrastructural lock-in, which increases the associated risk. In the terminology of NAT, this is fundamentally a question of coupling: the less substitutability available, the tighter the coupling, and thus the greater the infrastructural risk.

The concept of mutual enactment risk is admittedly less intuitive but no less significant. I borrow the term *enactment* from Weick (1977, 268), who described it as the process by which organizations "create the environment that they make sense of." He used the finance industry to illustrate this dynamic, pointing out that investors not only respond to an external market but also shape that market every time they invest in financial assets. In essence, they "impose the environment that imposes on [them]" (1977, 269). As participants cocreate the environment—the market—to which they then react, "the distinction between organization and environment becomes hopelessly blurred," argued Weick (1977, 269). While this blurring is apparent in financial markets, it is not absolute. A more accurate interpretation is that trading firms and their automated systems are tightly coupled through mutual enactments, and this coupling produces complex interactions. When one automated system submits orders to a venue, those orders not only *respond* to the market but also actively *reshape* it, prompting other automated systems to respond. These systems, operating at high speed, then decide whether to keep, cancel, or modify their orders, which in turn alters the market once more, eliciting additional responses, and so forth.

This intricate entanglement in automated trading is a primary source of risk exposure, captured by the term *mutual enactment risk*—or more precisely, the risks arising from the complex interactions and tight coupling generated by mutual enactments. The 2010 Flash Crash provides a vivid example of this phenomenon, where a single large sell order set off a chain reaction of frenzied activity among automated systems, triggering cascading effects across the market. However, mutual enactment risk also manifests in less dramatic ways. For instance, trading systems are vulnerable to the misconduct of other systems. If one firm's automated trading system engages in manipulative practices, such as market abuse, the ripple effects of its behavior may adversely affect numerous other firms through these mutual enactments.

Manipulative practices in financial markets include activities such as "spoofing," which is prohibited under the US Commodity Exchange Act and is defined as "bidding or offering with the intent to cancel the bid or offer before execution" (CFTC 2013, 1). *Spoofing* involves placing a large volume of orders in the order book to mislead other market participants into perceiving substantial buy or sell interest, then exploiting this false impression before canceling the orders. For instance, a spoofer holding a significant number of shares and seeking to sell them at a higher price might submit numerous buy orders, aiming to drive the price up. Once the price rises, the spoofer quickly sells the shares and cancels the buy orders (Lange 2020; Lange, Lenglet, and Seyfert 2024; MacKenzie 2022). Since these buy orders were never intended to be executed and were placed solely to mislead other market participants, this behavior is considered manipulative and is therefore illegal.[7] Importantly, spoofing exploits the tight coupling of market participants through mutual enactments, wherein one participant's orders alter the market environment, prompting others to respond.

The US Commodity Exchange Act also prohibits a wider range of manipulative strategies beyond spoofing, including "(i) submitting or cancelling bids or offers to overload the quotation system of a registered entity, (ii) submitting or cancelling bids or offers to delay another person's execution of trades, (iii) submitting or cancelling multiple bids or offers to create an appearance of false market depth, and (iv) submitting or cancelling bids or offers with intent to create artificial price movements upwards or downwards" (CFTC 2013, 2). While the latter two examples align with spoofing, the first two are typically discussed under the label of "quote stuffing." As the term suggests, the aim of *quote stuffing* is to flood a trading venue with a large volume of bids or offers within a brief time frame, creating congestion in the matching engine. This congestion delays order-book updates and slows the processing of others' orders. Additionally, it marginally increases the time other market participants require to process these updates. In both cases, the increased latency can be exploited for cross-venue arbitrage purposes before the quote-stuffed orders are canceled. As Mattli (2019, 139) notes, "Quote stuffing can involve the placing and canceling of over 25,000 orders of a stock per second—spread either over the entire second or in particularly disruptive bursts within a second." A 2010 analysis of US equities markets, which examined all trades and quotes for NYSE- and Nasdaq-listed stocks across multiple venues, found that quote stuffing occurred daily, affecting more than 74 percent of the stocks studied (Egginton, Van Ness, and Van Ness 2016).

Two points are critical when considering quote stuffing. First, as Mattli (2019, 140) emphasizes, "Quote stuffing is unequivocally harmful. It creates a false sense of demand and supply—or 'phantom' liquidity—widens spreads, and raises volatility, thereby degrading market quality." Quote stuffing exemplifies how the actions of one automated trading system can negatively affect others. Specifically, this practice exploits the low-latency infrastructure of modern financial markets, as well as the mutual enactments of automated trading systems. By inundating the order book with quotes, the practice alters the market to which other participants must respond, disrupting their ability to react promptly to changes in the order book. These effects are immediate because of the tight coupling among automated trading systems, while the complex interactions among them may create unpredictable outcomes. Importantly, as with infrastructural risk, quote stuffing is not a direct, NAT-like result of tight coupling and complex interactions. However, it introduces unique risks for market participants precisely because of their interrelations through these mechanisms.

Second, the primary reason quote stuffing does not qualify as a NAT-like system failure is that it stems from human malfeasance. As defined, quote stuffing is characterized by the deliberate *intent* "to overload the quotation system of a registered entity" or to delay other participants. However, something *resembling* quote stuffing can also arise unintentionally through the interactions of automated trading systems, resulting in a NAT-like event. This occurs when tight coupling and mutual enactments between systems unintentionally trigger cascading quoting activity:

Large episodic spikes in quoting activity may be generated for technological reasons where two algorithms interact with each other and fail to converge. For example, one algorithm submits a quote that causes another algorithm to reply, causing
the first algorithm to respond. If this process of multiple algorithms "chasing" each
other continues, a large burst of quotes will be generated. Although the large burst
of message flow may not be part of a nefarious plan to manipulate the market, these
quoting episodes may still be associated with degraded market conditions. (Egginton, Van Ness, and Van Ness 2016, 584)

Let me finally note that infrastructural and mutual enactment risks are not exclusive to automated trading; they are relevant to other market arrangements as well—
whether in the form of a late nineteenth-century stock ticker linking markets in
Chicago and New York City or a late twentieth-century monitor connecting an
electronic screen trader to a global financial network. However, the fully automated
nature of both first- and second-generation trading systems makes their actions
and interactions in markets far more dependent on technological infrastructures.
This dependency is particularly acute for low-latency strategies, where any environmental failures may unfold too quickly to be effectively mitigated through human
intervention. Additionally, the simultaneous observation and response of numerous automated trading systems to changes in the order book at low latency render
these systems more vulnerable than nonautomated participants to manipulative
enactment risks. This heightened exposure underscores the need for carefully tailored HRO measures to protect trading firms and their automated systems from
these cross-technological risks. While existing regulations provide some guidance,
as I will discuss below, they ultimately fall short of addressing these challenges
comprehensively.

Regulatory Attempts to Curb Risk

Three regulatory bodies oversee US financial markets: the CFTC, the SEC, and
FINRA. Despite their distinct responsibilities, all three aim to protect investors,
uphold market integrity, ensure fair and efficient markets, and prevent market
abuse, including in the realm of automated trading. In 2015, the CFTC introduced
Regulation Automated Trading (Reg AT), emphasizing risk control and compliance for automated trading firms, clearing firms, and Designated Contract Markets
(DCMs)—regulated exchanges for futures contracts and related derivatives.

Under Reg AT, firms employing automated trading systems were mandated to implement robust *risk controls,* such as "pre-trade risk controls (maximum order message and execution frequency per unit time, order price and maximum order size parameters), and order cancellation systems." They were also required to follow stringent *development, testing, and monitoring standards,* which included "keeping the development environment separate from the production environment; testing prior to implementation; a source code repository; real-time monitoring of such systems; and standards to ensure that systems comply with the Commodity Exchange Act and Commission regulations." Additionally, firms had to submit annual *compliance reports* to DCMs, detailing "their risk controls as well as copies of written policies and procedures developed to comply with testing and other requirements" (CFTC 2015, 2). DCMs were similarly tasked with implementing risk controls for incoming orders and providing test environments for trading firms to validate their systems, effectively creating a dual layer of testing and risk mitigation.

In 2020, the CFTC withdrew Reg AT and introduced "Electronic Trading Risk Principles" (2021) as its successor. This new framework outlined three specific risk principles, all of which DCMs were required to enforce: "the implementation of exchange rules applicable to market participants to prevent, detect, and mitigate market disruptions and system anomalies associated with electronic trading; the implementation of exchange-based pre-trade risk controls for all electronic orders; and the prompt notification of Commission staff by DCMs of any significant market disruptions on their electronic trading platforms" (2021, 2048). Although the Electronic Trading Risk Principles were directed exclusively at DCMs, their intended impact extended indirectly to trading firms. Firms operating on these platforms would need to align with the principles, ensuring compliance with the DCMs' regulatory frameworks.[8]

The introduction of the Electronic Trading Risk Principles reflected a broader acknowledgment among US regulators of the systemic vulnerabilities within the financial markets—what I described as infrastructural risk. For instance, in 2014, the SEC implemented "Regulation Systems Compliance and Integrity" (Reg SCI), a response to the increasing fragility introduced by automation. As the SEC noted: "Given the speed and interconnected nature of the U.S. securities markets, a seemingly minor systems problem at a single entity can quickly create losses and liability for market participants, and spread rapidly across the national market system, potentially creating widespread damage and harm to market participants, including investors" (SEC 2014, 72253). Reg SCI offered concrete examples of minor technological failures—such as network connectivity outages or an inability to process sudden surges in order-message rates—that had forced exchanges to suspend trading. To mitigate such risks, Reg SCI mandated that critical market infrastructure entities, including national securities exchanges, major alternative trading venues, clearing agencies, and "plan processors" (entities responsible for consolidating trade and quote data), establish robust policies and procedures. These measures were aimed at ensuring that their systems possessed adequate capacity, integrity, resilience, availability, and security to maintain operations and support fair and orderly markets. Additionally, the regulation required these entities to conduct rigorous "testing of the operation of their business continuity and disaster recovery plans, including backup systems" (SEC 2014, 72252).

While Reg SCI was designed to prevent market disruptions, such as trading halts caused by technological failures within parts of the financial system, other regulatory measures have been introduced to intentionally impose such halts under specific circumstances—most notably during sudden and dramatic price movements. Although rapid price swings may stem from substantive financial causes, they can also arise from automated trading systems interacting in unpredictable ways, as seen during the 2010 Flash Crash. In that event, prices plummeted without clear cause, draining liquidity and destabilizing the market. To mitigate the risk of such situations—where undesired spillover effects could escalate into systemic risk—exchanges are now required to implement automated "circuit breakers." Strengthened in the aftermath of the 2010 Flash Crash, these mechanisms temporarily suspend trading for durations ranging from fifteen minutes to the rest of the trading day, depending on the severity of the price movement. The rationale is to grant market participants time to reassess conditions and restore stability (e.g., NYSE 2020).

European financial market regulation, particularly in the context of automated trading, is less fragmented than its US counterpart but incorporates many similar principles. The cornerstone of the EU regulatory framework is the Markets in Financial Instruments Directive II (MiFID II), agreed upon in 2014 and enacted in January 2018. MiFID II emerged as a response to the 2008 financial crisis, reflecting the EU Commission's determination to strengthen oversight of financial markets. It built upon the earlier MiFID framework, which had been adopted in 2004 and implemented in November 2007. The MiFID II recitals explicitly addressed the dual-edged nature of automated trading, outlining both its advantages and its risks:

> [Automated] trading technology has provided benefits to the market and market participants generally such as wider participation in markets, increased liquidity, narrower spreads, reduced short term volatility and the means to obtain better execution of orders for clients. Yet that trading technology also gives rise to a number of potential risks such as an increased risk of the overloading of the systems of trading venues due to large volumes of orders, risks of algorithmic trading generating duplicative or erroneous orders or otherwise malfunctioning in a way that may create a disorderly market. In addition, there is the risk of algorithmic trading systems overreacting to other market events which can exacerbate volatility if there is a pre-existing market problem. (European Parliament and EUC 2014b, Recital (62))

Against this backdrop, MiFID II introduced a range of measures designed to mitigate risks arising from this market arrangement. Some measures targeted exchanges, requiring them to "be able to identify, by means of flagging from members or participants, orders generated by algorithmic trading, the different algorithms used for the creation of orders and the relevant persons initiating those orders" (European Parliament and EUC 2014b, Recital (67), Article 48(10)). However, the majority of risk-mitigating measures were directed at firms deploying automated trading systems. MiFID II specified the following:

> An investment firm that engages in algorithmic trading shall have in place effective systems and risk controls suitable to the business it operates to ensure that its trading systems are resilient and have sufficient capacity, are subject to appropriate trading thresholds and limits and prevent the sending of erroneous orders or the systems otherwise functioning in a way that may create or contribute to a disorderly market. Such a firm shall also have in place effective systems and risk controls to ensure the trading systems cannot be used for any purpose that is contrary to Regulation (EU) No 596/2014 or to the rules of a trading venue to which it is connected. The investment firm shall have in place effective business continuity arrangements to deal with any failure of its trading systems and shall ensure its systems are fully tested and properly monitored to ensure that they meet the requirements laid down in this paragraph. (European Parliament and EUC 2014b, Article 17(1))

Like US regulations, MiFID II addressed both infrastructural risks and mutual enactment risks. It emphasized that trading firms must be prepared to handle external incidents and ensure that any internal failures—whether technical or behavioral—do not spiral outward to disrupt broader market stability. Mutual enactment risks, particularly those associated with disorderly market conduct and market abuse, were the specific focus of the Market Abuse Regulation (MAR), adopted alongside MiFID II and effective as of July 2016. MAR provides a general definition of market manipulation, which includes:

(a) entering into a transaction, placing an order to trade or any other behaviour which:

(i) gives, or is likely to give, false or misleading signals as to the supply of, demand for, or price of, a financial instrument, a related spot commodity contract or an auctioned product based on emission allowances;

(ii) secures, or is likely to secure, the price of one or several financial instruments . . . at an abnormal or artificial level; . . .

(b) entering into a transaction, placing an order to trade or any other activity or behaviour which affects or is likely to affect the price of one or several financial instruments . . . , which employs a fictitious device or any other form of deception or contrivance. (European Parliament and EUC 2014a, Article 12(1))

Although US and European regulation of automated trading and its associated risks might appear comprehensive—and it is, indeed, more extensive than this brief overview suggests[9]—both frameworks face a critical shortcoming: a lack of specificity. Key terms such as *suitable risk control systems, effective business continuity arrangements,* and *proper monitoring* of trading systems remain largely undefined.[10] The European Commission's 2017 Regulatory Technical Standards (RTS), issued to complement MiFID II, provide the most detailed guidelines for regulating automated trading.

According to the RTS, the testing of automated trading systems under MiFID II's Article 17(1) includes both "conformance testing" and the use of "testing environments." Conformance testing ensures that a trading firm's automated system "interacts with the trading venue's matching logic as intended," with such tests required whenever significant changes occur in the venue's systems (European Commission 2017, Article 6(2)). For testing environments, the RTS mandates that trading firms maintain a strict separation between these and their production environments. Additionally, the RTS requires annual self-assessments, including stress tests that involve

(a) running high messaging volume tests using the highest number of messages received and sent by the investment firm during the previous six months, multiplied by two;

(b)   running high trade volume tests, using the highest volume of trading reached
      by the investment firm during the previous six months, multiplied by two. (Eu-
      ropean Commission 2017, Article 10)

The RTS also elaborates on "means to ensure resilience," requiring firms to implement mechanisms such as kill switch functionalities, automated MAR surveillance
systems, real-time monitoring of trading activities, pre- and post-trade controls, and
robust business continuity arrangements. The latter must include

(a)   a governance framework for the development and of the deployment of the
      business continuity arrangement;
(b)   a range of possible adverse scenarios relating to the operation of the algo-
      rithmic trading systems, including the unavailability of systems, staff, work
      space, external suppliers or data centres or loss or alteration of critical data and
      documents;
(c)   procedures for relocating the trading system to a back-up site and operating
      the trading system from that site, where having such a site is appropriate to the
      nature, scale and complexity of the algorithmic trading activities of the invest-
      ment firm. (European Commission 2017, Article 14(2))

Despite such specifications, both US and European approaches to automated trading grapple with a persistent issue: even if firms establish procedures addressing the
risk-mitigation requirements set by regulators, the implementation of these procedures can vary widely. As a result, formal compliance does not necessarily translate
into effective risk mitigation. As explored in earlier chapters, firms specializing in
automated trading typically conduct rigorous back-testing, implement strategies
incrementally, and maintain kill switches to halt trading when necessary. However,
the determination of whether these measures are suitable, effective, and appropriate is ultimately left to the firms themselves. Although many of my informants
acknowledged the necessity of financial market regulation, some expressed frustration over its lack of clarity. For instance, the CEO of a London-based proprietary
trading firm noted that "because of the lack of clarity" in MiFID II, the regulatory
framework introduced considerable uncertainty for the industry. A head of compliance similarly highlighted the challenges posed by this ambiguity, observing that
it encouraged a highly diverse and individualized range of approaches: "In trying
to understand best practice, it'll come down to the skills of the individual compliance officer, how maybe broad-minded that compliance officer is, as to how they
approach the problem."

Against this backdrop, I now shift focus from regulation to provide an inside view of what HRO-like risk-mitigation strategies might entail in addressing infrastructural and mutual enactment risks. Additionally, I explore whether second-generation trading systems present distinct challenges in this regard. I argue that, because the underlying infrastructure connecting second-generation systems to venues and data providers remains similar to that of first-generation systems (as detailed in chapter 3), the strategies for mitigating infrastructural risks through HRO measures are largely analogous across both generations. By contrast, mutual enactment risk takes on a fundamentally different character in second-generation systems.

Dealing with Connectivity Outages

Firms specializing in automated trading confront a spectrum of infrastructural risks, necessitating considerations informed by HRO principles to mitigate such vulnerabilities. As outlined in the MiFID II RTS, these considerations include assessing a trading firm's capacity to manage sudden disruptions at trading venue "data centres or loss or alteration of critical data," as well as verifying that its automated trading system "adequately processes the data flows downloaded from the trading venue" (European Commission 2017, Articles 6(2), 14(2)). Yet the scope of infrastructural data connectivity risks extends beyond these examples, encompassing the transmission networks that link firms to exchanges. To illustrate these risks and potential HRO-inspired responses, I return to Cormac and an incident the firm faced in 2017 (drawing and expanding upon Min and Borch 2022).

Based in London but trading, among other venues, at what I refer to as "Exchange A" in Chicago, Illinois, Cormac colocates its computer servers at Exchange A's data center. This arrangement reduces latency: while DEPS is trained in London, its specific trading strategies are executed via the Chicago servers—so, instead of sending order-book updates back and forth between London and Chicago to make trading decisions, all real-time processing and order responses occur at the colocated servers. However, to enable oversight and system management, Cormac contracts with a third-party network provider for a transatlantic data transmission network connecting its London office to Chicago. This network spans Illinois to New York and then crosses undersea transatlantic fiber-optic cables to London. Although this connection is unsuitable for low-latency trading because of the physical distance, it is essential for monitoring and manual intervention. For instance, staff in London rely on this network to observe DEPS's market activities and, if needed, intervene manually—up to and including activating the kill switch to remove DEPS from the market. While not instantaneous, data transmitted along this connection typically reach their destination in under one hundred milliseconds, a speed sufficient for monitoring and management functions.

To bolster redundancy and resilience, the network provider operates two widely separated fiber-optic cables—a primary and a secondary route—enabling simultaneous transmission of identical data along both lines. If the primary cable experienced a failure, the secondary cable would ensure continuity. However, on a Monday afternoon in late February 2017, a ship's anchor inadvertently severed both undersea cables. At 14:05 GMT, Cormac's Infrastructure Team received notification from the provider that the primary cable had been damaged. Howard, the CEO, recounted that the Infrastructure Team promptly informed the Leadership Team, stating, "We were running on a nonresilient connection." By 14:41, the secondary backup cable had also failed. This left Cormac without full visibility or control over its automated trading operations at Exchange A, although trading itself continued unaffected. Limited monitoring was still possible through a standard software tool for tracking orders and fills provided by Exchange A. However, the staff deemed this solution suboptimal because of its slower processing speed. An internal postmortem analysis of the event stated that, following consultation with leadership—including the head of trading, who had been notified after the primary cable failure—the firm took the following action: "At 15:10 the decision was taken to pull all our orders from [Exchange A] in all products as we could not guarantee safe participation in the market, with reduced visibility and control over the products" (internal document, February 2017, Cormac Trading Group). The transatlantic network connections were restored at 2:22 a.m., 12 hours after the initial cable outage. Despite this, Cormac's staff decided to delay resuming active participation in the market until they had conducted additional checks. These checks began at 7:00 a.m., and trading in Chicago recommenced at 8:15 a.m.

Three central lessons can be drawn from this incident. First, it underscores the infrastructural risks associated with connectivity technology. Because Cormac does not own its undersea fiber cables, it is critically reliant on the capabilities of a third-party network provider to maintain functional data transmission between its London office and the exchanges on which it trades. Although it is theoretically possible for Cormac to manage its own fiber-optic network, the costs would be prohibitive, and even such a system would not be immune to rare but high-impact outages or the challenges of rapid repair. Second, connectivity infrastructures are not easily replaced, amplifying the consequences of failures. The cable incident demonstrates this clearly: while Cormac has the option to switch network providers, doing so cannot be achieved instantaneously. For its daily operations, therefore, the firm is effectively bound to the complex connectivity infrastructure it relies on.

Third, Cormac's response to the incident reflects adherence to classic HRO principles, extending these beyond the firm's internal systems. This ranges from incident reporting to conducting thorough postmortem analyses designed to extract lessons from critical events. Howard, the CEO, noted that Cormac's approach to the cable failure was informed by lessons from prior disaster management cases. He specifically cited the 1982 Tylenol case, in which bottles of Johnson & Johnson's widely used Tylenol pills were tainted with cyanide, resulting in seven deaths. Johnson & Johnson responded by swiftly initiating a complete recall of Tylenol products, setting a benchmark for decisive crisis management (Wright 2017, 122–24). Drawing a direct parallel, Howard explained:

> What was the first thing [Johnson & Johnson] did? They pulled everything. They didn't go, "Oh, we found out that it's an episode in California, maybe."[11] They pulled everything, everywhere, globally, gone. When we had the [transatlantic cable] hit, we didn't go, "Hmm, you know, maybe it will last an hour or two, let's leave [DEPS] in." We were told and within two minutes we pulled, we hit the kill switch. That was our Tylenol moment, literally inspired by that.

It did in fact take the firm twenty-nine minutes from the moment it confirmed the total loss of connection to hitting the kill switch and withdrawing DEPS from trading at Exchange A. While this might seem reasonably fast, the Knight Capital case serves as a cautionary tale of how even a half-hour delay can prove catastrophic when a low-latency automated trading system veers off course. What distinguishes the cable incident from Knight Capital's collapse, however, is that DEPS continued trading without issue; it did not deviate or malfunction. In this sense, the incident was noncritical to Cormac's core trading activities. Even so, because the disruption affected the firm's customized, high-speed monitoring and system management tools—less advanced alternatives were accessible via Exchange A's monitoring portal—the staff deemed it safest to pull the system.

This type of infrastructural risk is common to both first- and second-generation automated trading systems, as both rely on connectivity for real-time monitoring. Firms operating either type of system could benefit from adopting and potentially enhancing the kind of risk-mitigation practices exemplified by Cormac. While these infrastructural risks and their management are consistent across system generations, other risks are unique to second-generation systems. One prominent example involves market abuse.

Watching for Market Abuse

In discussing mutual enactment risk, I highlighted market abuse practices such as spoofing and quote stuffing. Since a firm's buy or sell orders inherently alter the market and influence other participants, any manipulative or distortive behavior can have far-reaching negative consequences. How, then, is market abuse prevented? Setting aside cases where interactions among automated trading systems unintentionally mimic spoofing or quote stuffing without malicious intent, first-generation systems engage in market abuse only if deliberately programmed to do so. Thus, the primary strategy for preventing such behavior in first-generation systems is to increase the likelihood of detection and enforce severe penalties. Both measures are challenging. As noted in chapter 1, the sheer volume of daily orders complicates the task of identifying abusive patterns (Mattli 2019). Moreover, proving intent—a requirement for effective sanctioning—is notoriously difficult (MacKenzie 2022).

The landscape is different—but equally intricate—for second-generation systems. These systems generate semi-independent strategies, making the issue of market abuse less about the human designers' intent and more about whether the trading automaton might autonomously develop abusive strategies. If the training process focuses narrowly on short-term profit and loss (P&L) objectives, it is conceivable that the system could learn to maximize profits by engaging in occasional market abuse. The challenge is compounded when the automaton's strategies are difficult to explain—when human designers struggle to understand the rationale behind specific order decisions. To mitigate the potential for market abuse in second-generation systems, I argue that measures must move beyond focusing solely on human malintent and instead incorporate and deepen certain HRO recommendations.

At Cormac, staff have already made efforts in this direction. For instance, in designing and training DEPS, they have aimed to instill a long-term perspective in its behavior. Ian, the CTO, explained, "We specifically ... structured [DEPS] so it has that sort of longer-duration objective set, as opposed to make the most money you can today." Additionally, the firm collaborated with a third-party market surveillance software provider—I refer to it as "Detect"—to develop a solution for identifying potential market abuse at every stage of the manufacturing process. Instead of merely checking whether DEPS's postrelease trading complies with regulations like MAR, Cormac evaluates potential market abuse during the early stages of strategy development and testing. Practically, this involves incorporating Detect-based MAR assessments into the "release pack" that the Product Control Group reviews before approving new models. Delivery managers collect these assessments to ensure that candidate models are back-tested and evaluated not only for profitability but also for compliance with MAR.

More specifically, "The Detect back-tests provide information primarily on the character of the product," meaning its ability to operate with integrity (internal document, November 2017, Cormac Trading Group). Interviews with Cormac staff and internal documents consistently emphasized the importance of market integrity: "A product that has integrity of character does not distort its markets, mislead other market participants, or add disproportionate noise. A product with integrity is a healthy and welcome market participant" (internal document, November 2017, Cormac Trading Group). In alignment with this principle, the Detect software not only assesses whether DEPS engages in spoofing or quote stuffing but also flags behaviors considered undesirable by Cormac staff, even if they are not illegal. For instance, Detect identifies "pinging," a practice where small orders are sent to the market to detect whether a large hidden parent order is being executed by another participant. If, for example, a series of small sell orders is quickly filled, it could indicate the presence of an active large buy order. A low-latency strategy might exploit this by purchasing the asset in anticipation of a price increase. Similarly, the Detect software monitors compliance with venue-specific rules, such as message rate limits. If a trading system sends numerous order messages to an exchange but rarely executes trades, it may indicate the presence of phantom liquidity. Many trading venues impose order-to-trade ratio limits to curb such practices.

Given the limitations of back-testing discussed in earlier chapters—and the inherent adaptability of trading automatons—a system that demonstrates high integrity in a simulated market environment may still engage in market abuse when operating in live markets. This highlights the importance of continuously monitoring its MAR conduct and of having robust procedures in place to respond swiftly to suspected market abuse, preventing it from having broader market impact. At Cormac, real-time monitoring of DEPS's conduct via Detect is integrated with protocols for responding to MAR alerts. For instance, DEPS products are monitored for patterns that could lead to "a trading loop with a market participant on the exchange." If such a pattern is detected, "the product will stop placing orders for that side/contract until the next price is available or 5 sec have passed or a fill is received. If this control fails, the Detect Market Surveillance tool will detect [it] and raise an alert" (internal document, November 2017, Cormac Trading Group). An alert can prompt different responses depending on the severity of the suspected behavior. If DEPS violates exchange rules, this triggers "an audible alarm on the floor" and automatically halts its trading (internal document, November 2017, Cormac Trading Group). Restarting DEPS after such an incident requires approval from the head of trading and must be manually executed by the Infrastructure Team.

When a trading automaton's decision-making is opaque—meaning its human designers cannot clearly explain its actions—it becomes critical not only to monitor its behavior for MAR compliance but also to subject any MAR alerts to thorough postmortem analysis. As previously noted, a trading automaton that appears to act with integrity during testing may later adopt unwanted behaviors. Following the HRO principle of learning from incidents, MAR alerts serve as a valuable opportunity to examine this risk. However, because individual alerts might point to deeper, systematic issues, collecting broader statistical data is equally important. To this end, in addition to daily reviews of MAR alerts, Cormac compiles monthly alert statistics "to determine whether an algorithmic trading product repeatedly generates similar alert patterns" (internal document, June 2017, Cormac Trading Group).

Min and I gained access to Cormac's "monthly conduct" reports covering the period from April 2018 to January 2019. These reports provide detailed insights into various conduct metrics, including order resting times, the number of MAR alerts, the "top MAR alert trigger for [the] month," the number of confirmed MAR incidents, and the frequency of "kill switch activations" across the firm's primary trading markets. Over this ten-month period, a total of 196 MAR alerts were recorded, predominantly in two markets, while no alerts were generated in one of the other markets. Two primary types of alerts—quote stuffing and pinging—were most frequently triggered. In both cases, postmortem analyses revealed that the alerts occurred in rapidly moving markets where DEPS adjusted its passive orders in ways that resembled quote stuffing or pinging but did not involve actual market manipulation. For instance, one postmortem report noted: "The Pinging and Quote Stuffing cases detected in [name of] contracts show another market participant improving their bid/(offer) and then quickly removing their quote, DEPS then followed passively. Examples were shared with [the firm's ML experts] for further analysis. No further action to be taken" (internal document, July 2019, Cormac Trading Group).

This analysis indicated that the MAR alerts were likely triggered by the behavior of other market participants, which influenced DEPS to adjust its own quotes. As a market maker, DEPS must continuously respond to order-book changes, and in rapidly shifting markets this necessitates frequent submission of new quotes and cancellation of existing ones. This activity, while essential to market making, can superficially resemble quote stuffing or pinging. Similar conclusions were drawn for other alerts during this period. Since these behaviors did not indicate any intent to distort markets, no actual MAR incidents were logged in the ten monthly reports, and no kill switch activations occurred. Reflecting on spoofing specifically, Ian, the CTO, remarked: "We have never encountered spoofing behavior. We have encountered a detection of a pattern that could be construed as spoofing perhaps and there's a difference. We believe that the system is structured in a way so that it actually can't [spoof], but that doesn't mean that sometimes the pattern of messages can look something like it." This echoes the earlier observation about quote stuffing: the interaction of automated trading systems can inadvertently produce patterns resembling quote stuffing, even when none of the systems involved is pursuing a deliberate quote stuffing strategy. As I have argued, the risk of such occurrences increases with the proliferation of automated trading, which amplifies the prevalence of mutual enactments. This observation underscores that market abuse remains a critical issue for both first- and second-generation systems, albeit in distinct ways. For first-generation systems, market abuse typically stems from human malintent being encoded directly into the system. In contrast, second-generation systems face the more nuanced challenge that market abuse might emerge organically, almost as an "acquired taste" developed through their interactions with the market—an outcome unintended by their human designers. While this risk may partially stem from human designers defining overly short-term objective functions, it is equally conceivable that such abusive strategies are learned and adopted through the system's adaptive engagement with its market environment.

This brings me back to the discussion of NAT and HRO, and their failure to adequately address how organizations and their technological systems interact with external systems. For trading automatons, the issue of market abuse—and its broader implications for market stability—is not confined to the internal components of the system. Instead, it stems from the automaton's ability to adapt to its environment while simultaneously influencing it. Given this, any HRO-inspired measures aimed at mitigating market abuse must address both internal and external factors. Internally, this includes considerations such as how the objective function is defined and the extent to which market integrity is prioritized alongside profitability during training. Externally, it involves scrutinizing how the automaton interacts with the market and adapts its behavior on the basis of these interactions.

Risk Mitigation Spiraling into Systemic Risk

I have argued that infrastructural and mutual enactment risk reflect and intensify complex interactions and tight coupling within the market arrangement of automated trading. Moreover, I have suggested that such risks can be mitigated through practices akin to those associated with HROs. However, the logic underpinning the HRO tradition, even when adapted to system-environment relations, may encounter significant limitations in financial markets, where complex interactions and tight coupling extend beyond individual systems to link multiple automated systems across the broader market landscape. Indeed, under certain conditions, the very strategies that individual firms adopt to adhere to HRO principles might inadvertently destabilize markets rather than stabilize them (Min and Borch 2022). In this sense, actions intended as precautionary at the organizational level could paradoxically produce adverse effects on the market as a whole. The Flash Crash of May 2010 provides an illustration of this possibility.

While the exact causes of the event remain disputed, it is well established that NYSE experienced significant delays in its data feed on May 6, 2010. An unanticipated combination of high message rates during the crash and concurrent technical issues arising from an upgrade to the systems feeding data into the Consolidated Quotation System—the public feed aggregating quotations across US markets—resulted in substantial delays in the data sent to the consolidated feed. According to the official joint CFTC and SEC report on the Flash Crash, some stocks experienced delays averaging more than twenty seconds, while the proprietary NYSE feed—delivered directly to subscribing market participants—reported an average delay of just over eight milliseconds (CFTC and SEC 2010, 77). Many automated trading firms rely on the public feed as a "data-integrity test" (MacKenzie 2021, 229), using it to verify the accuracy of direct feeds. When the two feeds fell out of sync, many firms activated "feed-driven integrity pauses" (CFTC and SEC 2010, 36), withdrawing their automated systems from the market as a precautionary measure. Paradoxically, this prudent action further exacerbated the crash by causing additional liquidity to vanish (Min 2020).

The CFTC and SEC report concluded that feed-driven integrity pauses did not play a "dominant role" in the Flash Crash (CFTC and SEC 2010, 5n10). However, subsequent analyses of the event have challenged this assertion. Scholars have argued that the data feed issue was, in fact, a critical factor in the market turmoil (Aldrich, Grundfest, and Laughlin 2017). Building on this, MacKenzie contends: "Failed data-integrity checks plausibly exacerbated the effects of the big, fast, algorithmic selling that seems to have been the trigger [of the Flash Crash]. . . . If that is correct, it is a fascinating example of individually prudent, rule-bound behavior (checking data integrity *is* prudent) generating potentially damaging, unruly, collective turmoil" (2021, 229, original emphasis).

The example of the data-integrity check exposes a broader dilemma concerning the relationship between risk mitigation and its potential unintended consequences. In environments marked by complex interactions and tight coupling, efforts to mitigate risk can paradoxically amplify the very dangers they aim to address. Even a seemingly straightforward mechanism, such as stop-loss orders—automated orders designed to sell assets once a predetermined price threshold is reached—illustrates this point (see again Min and Borch 2022). Stop-loss orders are a prudent market tool, intended to limit losses by allowing a trading system to exit its position when the market moves against it. In this sense, they can be categorized among HRO-inspired measures, functioning as automated responses to sharp downward market movements.

However, because automated trading systems enact the market through the order book, the activation of one stop-loss order inevitably drives prices lower by increasing sell pressure. This decline, in turn, may trigger the stop-loss orders of other market participants, further depressing prices and potentially activating additional stop-loss orders, creating a self-reinforcing cascade. The risks of such feedback loops are magnified by the tight coupling of financial assets across trading venues, where abrupt price shifts in one market can quickly propagate to others. Given that each automated trading system has its own, undisclosed trigger thresholds, these cascades are inherently unpredictable, embodying the complex interactions described by NAT (Borch, Skar-Gislinge, and David 2025; Min and Borch 2022). Moreover, the speed at which these automated responses unfold often outpaces human intervention, necessitating mechanisms like exchange circuit breakers to temporarily calm the market.

These examples are not confined to either first- or second-generation automated systems. Both can be enveloped in risk-mitigating procedures that paradoxically generate systemic risk. That said, second-generation systems introduce additional challenges. Beyond the risk of inadvertently engaging in misconduct, as previously discussed, they pose a deeper problem: when *more* trading algorithms converge on similar actions—whether illicit or legitimate—the potential for systemic instability increases dramatically.

Automatons Marching in Step

In February 2024, the then SEC chair Gary Gensler delivered a talk at Yale Law School titled "AI, Finance, Movies, and the Law."[12] Drawing on films like *Her* and *Harry Potter* to illustrate his points, Gensler explored the growing integration of AI in the finance industry, the risks this evolution poses, and the regulatory challenges it introduces for financial markets. The central themes of his talk—also aired in other public appearances (Palma and Jenkins 2023)—echoed concerns outlined in a 2020 paper, "Deep Learning and Financial Stability," coauthored with Lily Bailey during his tenure as a professor at MIT (Gensler and Bailey 2020). Unlike the cinematic flair of his Yale speech, the paper, though structured into "acts," avoided references to popular culture. Instead, it offered a somber narrative in which the protagonist, deep learning, was portrayed as an agent of financial instability.

At the heart of the Gensler and Bailey thesis lies the contention that deep learning techniques, when adopted by the finance industry, create financial models that diverge radically from those of earlier eras. These models are distinguished by their nonlinearity, their complexity, and their dynamic, adaptable nature. Yet they also introduce significant challenges around data dependency, explainability, fairness, and bias. This aligns closely with the central argument of this book: second-generation automated trading systems represent a fundamental departure not only from their first-generation predecessors but even more so from the models employed in preautomated market arrangements.

That said, Gensler and Bailey's scope differs from mine in both narrower and broader dimensions. Their focus is narrower because they examine only deep learning–based systems, while I have also discussed trading automatons built using other ML techniques. This distinction carries significant implications, particularly regarding risks such as explainability, which is a pressing concern for deep learning but not for genetic programming (see chapter 5). At the same time, their focus is broader in that they address the deployment of deep learning across multiple areas within the finance industry—ranging from credit underwriting to fraud detection, risk management, and trading—whereas I concentrate exclusively on its application in financial asset trading. This divergence has its own important consequences, especially in relation to issues of bias and fairness.

A substantial body of literature across diverse disciplines explores how ML systems can perpetuate social biases—for example, related to gender or race. These systems, if trained on biased data, are likely to generate biased predictions, negatively affecting those subjected to decisions influenced by these predictions (e.g., Alegria 2025; Brayne 2017; Buolamwini and Gebru 2018; Burrell and Fourcade 2021; Noble 2018). In finance, these challenges are well documented, as in the case of credit scoring, where ML systems guide decisions on extending credit. For instance, research has shown that ML techniques "can be used to infer creditworthiness based on multiple data sources, including social media behavior, consumption patterns, and browser footprint information (e.g., location geolocated from IP addresses), which can end up inadvertently working as proxies for race" (Spears and Hansen 2025, 342).

Whether similar issues extend to trading automatons is less straightforward. On the one hand, successful trading automatons may generate substantial financial gains for their creators and users, thereby reinforcing financial inequality that spills over into broader societal inequities (as discussed by Godechot 2012). On the other hand, the issue of biased training datasets perpetuating social inequalities does not apply as directly to the trading context. Order-book data, often used to train trading automatons, may reflect past and present market power structures, but it is qualitatively different from datasets containing facial images, income records, or residential data—and thus less likely to yield directly biased outcomes for individuals. Moreover, while models trained on alternative datasets may grapple with bias—or raise ethical concerns, as when computer vision models rely on data labeled under precarious conditions in the Global South (Borch 2025; Spears and Hansen 2025)—such models are not deployed to make decisions about individuals. As I elaborate in chapter 6, this does not entirely preclude certain embedded biases in second-generation systems, but the nature of these biases differs from those rightly critiqued in broader discussions about ML reproducing racial, gender, or other forms of social inequality.

With this caveat in mind, let me return to Gensler and Bailey's central argument: the widespread adoption of deep learning systems is likely to introduce systemic risk into the financial system. Similar to aspects of my analysis based on NAT, Gensler and Bailey argue that specific behavioral, infrastructural, and regulatory factors enable issues at the level of individual firms to cascade through the broader financial ecosystem. For instance, if a firm deploys models that, intentionally or not, are also widely adopted by other market participants, its trading behaviors may mirror those of others or react similarly to identical signals. This alignment increases the likelihood of triggering unanticipated market-wide disruptions, as seen in the Quant Meltdown or the Flash Crash. Similarly, when many market participants rely on a single technology provider, disruptions at that provider can reverberate across the entire ecosystem. For example, several of my informants noted their reliance on cloud computing for back-testing and training simulations (see also Asgari 2024), leaving them vulnerable to outages at their cloud service providers (K. Hansen and Thylstrup 2024). As well, if regulatory gaps exist in specific areas, such as those concerning technologically driven forms of market manipulation, the likelihood of such actions destabilizing the broader market increases.

The most intriguing and contentious element of Gensler and Bailey's argument is their claim that deep learning systems might converge on similar behavioral patterns, thereby fostering herding or crowding that could precipitate rapid and widespread market instability. One of the key observations supporting this assertion is that deep learning models require vast amounts of data, which are both difficult and costly to amass. As a result, market participants employing deep learning techniques may increasingly depend on a small number of dominant data providers capable of aggregating and reselling massive datasets for training purposes (K. Hansen and Thylstrup 2024). Such concentration among data providers would introduce clear infrastructural risks. Overreliance on a few dominant players for data services makes the financial system more vulnerable to disruptions caused by issues affecting those providers. But the implications extend further. A concentration of data sources also raises the risk of uniformity, as deep learning systems trained on the same datasets may generate highly correlated behaviors. Gensler and Bailey emphasize this point:

> Models built on the same datasets are likely to generate highly correlated predictions that proceed in lockstep, causing crowding and herding. The risk of uniformity—and thus systemic risk—increases as the data provider moves further up the value chain, from simply providing raw data; to standardized, normalized, and regularized data; to summarized data; to analytics and insights generated from the data. Highly concentrated data providers, similar to cloud storage companies, are a source of network interconnectedness risk—new single points of failure to the network. (Gensler and Bailey 2020, 21)

This argument carries weight. In automated image recognition, for instance, the ImageNet dataset, created in 2009–10, became the dominant training set for deep learning systems in the field. Its widespread adoption resulted in models that (a) inherited biases embedded in the dataset and (b) produced similarly biased predictions (Denton et al. 2021).

But how does this apply to trading automatons trained on financial data? Could diverse deep neural networks, trained on the same order-book and market data but equipped with varied objective functions, end up developing identical strategies? In one of my interviews with Simon, the ML expert introduced in chapter 1, he expressed strong conviction that this is indeed a significant risk. When asked how likely it is that different ML-based trading systems might produce the same strategies, Simon responded, "I would think extremely likely," adding, "I would be surprised if that's not the case." He identified two key reasons for this convergence.

One reason for ML models converging on similar predictions, Simon explained, lies in the nature of financial markets themselves. Market data are notoriously noisy, and the number of tradeable signals embedded in them is inherently limited. As Simon put it, "There's only so many ways you can trade. So if you start throwing these machine learning models [on market data], [they are] going to end up doing the same thing." While this could lead to the kind of herding that Gensler and Bailey warn about, Simon framed the issue more as a matter of competition than systemic risk: "At some point, it'll come down to speed—who gets the orders in first—and those are the guys who will prevail." In other words, even if multiple trading automatons independently arrive at the same strategies, the decisive factor will be latency; the fastest system will reap the rewards. That said, while latency hierarchies may ultimately marginalize slower systems, it remains possible that this convergence could still cause significant short-term market havoc.

The second reason Simon identified for ML systems producing similar actionable predictions stems from institutional factors. "I've worked in this industry for fifteen years," he said, and the basic ideas traders pursue are "all just recycled. People move from firm to firm and then bring a little from what the past firm had to the new firm, and then people end up doing largely the same things." While this recycling of ideas may pose a greater issue for first-generation systems, which are more directly shaped by their human creators, it could still manifest within the domain of second-generation systems. Gensler and Bailey touched on a related point, suggesting that over time the convergence of deep learning models could partly result from the dominance of certain ML paradigms:

Initially, in deep learning's complex and non-deterministic model environment, differences in initializing models and hyperparameters may lead to a greater diversity of outcomes. Further, finance being less transparent may make it less likely that model design converges rapidly. As the financial sector gains more experience, though, and deep learning becomes more fully adopted, there may emerge academic and industry consensus on hyperparameter selection, such as for the type of learning model, the size and shape of the network, and the loss function.... There may also be a human factor contributing to model design uniformity. There simply are not that many people trained to build and manage these models, and they tend to have fairly similar backgrounds. In addition, there are strong affinities among people who trained together: the so-called apprentice effect. For all of these reasons, the inductive bias of models may become more uniform over time. (2020, 22)

This argument circles back to observations made in earlier chapters regarding the dominant recruitment pathways in automated trading. The emergence of first-generation systems narrowed these pathways, prioritizing candidates with academic backgrounds for core systems design roles. With the advent of second-generation systems, the focus has tightened even further, as ML expertise has become indispensable. This increasing specialization among personnel raises the likelihood of a corresponding trend toward model homogeneity, as the convergence in human expertise may feed into a growing uniformity in the models themselves.

While the prospect of trading automatons moving in lockstep and wreaking systemic havoc is a legitimate concern, it is crucial to nuance this notion of systemic risk along two dimensions. First, the proliferation of alternative data significantly broadens the spectrum of potentially tradeable signals, fostering greater data and signal diversity rather than uniformity. Gensler and Bailey acknowledge the rise of alternative data but argue that its primary limitation lies in the brevity of its time horizons, stating that alternative data "simply do not have long enough time horizons to cover even a single, complete financial cycle. . . . Models built using these datasets may be fragile due to their reliance on limited time series datasets" (2020, 21). I touched on this issue of limited time horizons in chapter 3. However, just as Gensler and Bailey make predictions about longer-term trends, it is plausible that future alternative datasets will encompass significantly more data points, mitigating these fragility concerns.

Second, Gensler and Bailey's suggestion that the convergence of human expertise might translate into model homogeneity assumes that deep learning–based second-generation systems are more *semi*-independent than semi-*independent*. In their view, human design decisions play a disproportionately large role in shaping these systems, with human inputs heavily influencing the models' outputs. This contrasts with the perspective I advanced in chapter 3. As I argued there, although humans certainly frame the overall modus operandi of trading automatons, these systems remain operationally closed vis-à-vis their human designers. In Ian's words: "We're automating the process of creating financial models. . . . In the most extreme case, you could say [DEPS] develops a new financial model every day" because of its adaptive capabilities. Given this operational autonomy, some skepticism is warranted about how quickly model homogeneity might emerge across second-generation systems.

Whether the semi-independent nature of second-generation systems will ultimately lead to model convergence remains an open question. This could happen (a) if an increasing number of deep learning systems are acting and interacting within the same markets (as well as being trained on and responding to similar types of data); and/or (b) due to a convergence in human expertise. Gensler and Bailey's argument, for all its rigor, clearly ventures into speculative territory, relying on assumptions about future developments in both finance and ML. Nonetheless, the speculative nature of their claim is justified by the potential stakes. If deep learning model convergence were to occur, it would likely present markets with systemic risks far exceeding what classic HRO measures could manage. Indeed, it is difficult to envision how firm-level HRO practices could effectively prevent the rapid escalation of incidents if widespread homogeneity—or resonance (Beunza and Stark 2012)—were to evolve inadvertently among the strategies produced by diverse deep learning–based trading automatons.

Compounding this issue is a specific characteristic of deep learning systems: their opacity to human understanding. The pathway from input to output in deep neural nets is notoriously difficult to decipher, which complicates efforts to detect and prevent evolving model homogeneity. This challenge underscores the critical importance of explainability. As I elaborate in chapter 5, explainability not only is a central concern within computer science but also is regarded as a key priority by firms developing deep learning–based second-generation systems.

FIVE

Explaining Automatons' Action and Interaction

CENTRAL TO SOCIOLOGICAL THEORY IS the aspiration to explain action (Hedström 2005; Martin 2011; Parsons 1937). Why do actors behave the way they do? Are their actions molded by overarching social structures? Can specific mechanisms account for particular forms of action? These questions have not only fueled foundational debates in social theory but also shaped subfields such as economic sociology. Within this realm, when considering markets broadly—and financial markets more specifically—what drives the behavior of market participants? Is market activity governed by status hierarchies or network configurations (Massó and Ruiz-León 2017; Podolny 1993; Preda 2005; Wansleben 2015)? Does it require an understanding of how action is enabled by material infrastructures (MacKenzie 2021; Pardo-Guerra 2019)? Or must the explanation lie elsewhere?

Not surprisingly, most sociological attempts to explain action, whether in markets or beyond, center on *human* action, driven by an enduring curiosity about why people act as they do. Even scholars who highlight the importance of understanding how technologies and materiality contribute to shaping action remain fundamentally concerned with human action, albeit framed within its entanglement with human-nonhuman relationships (e.g., Cerulo 2009; Latour 2005).

In this chapter, I explore how to explain action when key market participants are no longer human beings but automated trading systems. I argue that the distinction between first- and second-generation systems proves consequential once again in this chapter. First-generation systems, explicitly crafted to implement the ideas of their human creators in markets, allow for a sociological explanation of action that focuses on the intentions and meanings embedded by their designers. This explanatory approach aligns seamlessly with how practitioners perceive these systems—as direct extensions of human-conceived ideas. Second-generation systems, however, present a much more complex challenge. Designed to generate strategies semi-independently, these trading automatons challenge traditional sociological frameworks that anchor explanations of action in human agency. Specifically, they are difficult to reconcile with classic Weberian ideas of social action. When these systems incorporate deep learning techniques, the problem of explainability becomes even more acute, as such techniques are marked by significant opacity. Yet for market participants the need to explain the actions of these systems remains crucial—both internally (Do these systems generate profits in ways that are comprehensible and not excessively risky?) and externally (to exchanges and regulators, especially when suspicions of misconduct arise). I demonstrate that, in their efforts to develop such explanations, the inventors of trading automatons sometimes conceptualize these systems as entities capable of engaging in (post)social relations, framing the explanation of their actions around the creation, maintenance, and evolution of these relationships.[1]

Explaining the action of automated systems in markets is one challenge; explaining how these systems *interact* with one another and how such interactions shape their action is another. I address this issue in the final section of the chapter, arguing that automated interaction introduces a distinct explainability problem for both market participants and sociologists. Unlike earlier market arrangements—where sociological frameworks could effectively account for the actions of human market participants and their interactions with one another (Baker 1984a,1984b; Granovetter 1985; Knorr Cetina and Bruegger 2002a, 2002b; Preda 2009a; Weber 2000b)—it is far less clear how human-centric notions can make sense of the unexpected interaction effects that define automated trading.

As this suggests, the chapter contends that explaining action and interaction in contemporary markets is inseparable from the question of who—or what—the market actors are (similarly, Suchman 2007). Resolving this foundational question is a prerequisite for arriving at sociological explanations of their action, and doing so may necessitate letting go of some long-standing theoretical conventions.

Action Beyond Weber

How can machine action in the market arrangement of automated trading be explained? To tackle this question, I begin with Weber's well-known definitions of action and social action: "We shall speak of 'action' insofar as the acting individual attaches a subjective meaning to his *[sic]* behavior—be it overt or covert, omission or acquiescence. Action is 'social' insofar as its subjective meaning takes account of the behavior of others and is thereby oriented in its course" (1978, 4). It might seem straightforward to argue that since automated trading systems are not human beings capable of attaching subjective meaning to their behavior, neither first- nor second-generation systems can qualify as engaging in action or social action under Weber's definition. On closer examination, however, first-generation systems can be understood as entities that embody human instrumentally rational action as described by Weber. This interpretation, advanced by Nicholas Gane (2012) in his study of first-generation automated trading, draws on Weber's (1978, 7) observation that "every artifact, such as for example a machine, can be understood only in terms of the meaning which its production and use have had or were intended to have." Since their rules are fully defined by humans, first-generation systems operate as tools—"an instrumentally rational design that seeks to secure an advantage in an ongoing struggle over price" in markets (Gane 2012, 70). Or, to borrow Weber's own words: "That which is intelligible or understandable about [the machine] is thus its relation to human action in the role either of means or of end; a relation of which the [human] actor or actors can be said to have been aware and to which their action has been oriented" (1978, 7). First-generation systems are often designed—paraphrasing Weber—to account for the behavior of other market participants, making it reasonable to view this form of automated trading as engaging in social action at a distance. In this sense, these systems represent human social action at a distance (as per chapter 2). As a result, the task of explanation appears relatively straightforward: the surrogate social action of a first-generation system can be understood by examining "the meaning which its production and use have had or were intended to have" for its human creators (Weber 1978, 7).

This aligns with research showing that traders who design and deploy first-generation systems often see them as extensions of themselves, even forming emotional bonds with their creations and likening them to their own children (Borch and Lange 2017). In other words, these traders embrace the idea that their automated trading systems faithfully and uniformly execute the human-defined rules encoded in them. Consequently, understanding why these systems act as they do can be achieved through their human designers—via methods such as interviews.

However, this Weberian framing of automated surrogate instrumentally rational action is complicated by two factors. First, bugs or errors may cause first-generation systems to deviate from their designers' intentions. Second, and more fundamentally, these systems often exhibit a budding evolution. As discussed in chapter 4, these systems tend to grow organically over time, with new layers of code continuously added on top of earlier ones, making them progressively harder to unravel. While first-generation systems may initially function as clear enactments of human instrumentally rational action, the accumulation of layers can result in complex interactions and tight coupling among components, where what holds true for a single rule may no longer apply when these rules are stacked and interwoven.

Like their first-generation predecessors, second-generation systems exhibit alter orientation: the actions of order-book-focused trading automatons take account of the behavior of other market participants and are thereby oriented in their course. However, because their trading rules or strategies are semi-independently generated, their modus operandi cannot be fully grasped through a Weberian lens of social action. While the entire spectrum of human meaning-based decision-making—such as designing the underlying machine learning architectures, selecting training data, and fine-tuning parameters—reflects a clear ambition to generate profits in markets, and thus aligns in part with Weber's notion of machines as imbued with the meaning of their production and use, the resulting machine action resists reduction to human action or subjective meaning.

The theoretical implications of this shift are profound. Weber (2000a, 2000b) pioneered the sociological study of financial markets, and while later sociologists have not always explicitly adopted his conception of social action, nor embraced it in its entirety, the focus on understanding markets through the rationalities pursued by human participants, the meanings they assign to their own and others' actions, and the ways these are shaped by social relations within and beyond markets has remained a cornerstone of sociological thought (e.g., Abolafia 1996, 2020; Baker 1984a, 1984b; Fligstein, Stuart Brundage, and Schultz 2017; Granovetter 1985, 2017; MacKenzie and Millo 2003; Neely 2022; Preda 2009b; Smith 1999). However, when trading automatons become active in markets, the relevance of such human-centered sociological notions becomes fundamentally unclear. To restate the theoretical challenge: How can sociological frameworks, which prioritize human action and subjective meaning, account for the market action of automatons—action that cannot be directly linked to human agency or intention-ality, and whose connections with human decision-making are, at best, indirect, ambiguous, and nondeterministic?

Defenders of Weber's conceptual apparatus might argue that while trading au-tomatons exhibit alter orientation, their lack of subjective meaning makes it inap-propriate to analyze them through the lens of social action. Instead, these systems might better fit Weber's category of "merely reactive behavior to which no subjec-tive meaning is attached" (1978, 4). This move could salvage the notion of social action by restricting it, as Weber did, to behavior rooted in meaning. While con-venient for sociological orthodoxy—allowing economic sociologists to carry on as though nothing fundamental had changed in markets—it sidesteps the core chal-lenge: trading automatons now play a pivotal role in market action and interaction. Their status, modus operandi, and consequences cannot be understood through meaning-based frameworks. Instead, a significant theoretical adjustment is needed: sociologists must recognize that technological systems, such as trading automatons, are capable of acting and interacting within markets. At the very least, this possibil-ity warrants serious consideration. As Lucy A. Suchman (2007, 228) aptly observes, "We need to include in our analysis the question of just what constitutes agency in any case, for humans or nonhumans."

Granting automatons the capacity to act necessitates a broader conception of action—one that breaks with the human-centered framework foundational to We-ber's work and echoed throughout much of sociological theory. Mustafa Emirbayer and Ann Mische's seminal essay "What Is Agency?" (1998), for instance, restricts its analysis entirely to human agency. Yet sociology provides conceptual tools for em-bracing a broader, more-than-human view of action. Massimo Airoldi (2022, 72), in his discussion of machine agency, draws on Anthony Giddens's definition of action from *The Constitution of Society*. Giddens writes: "Action depends on the capability of the individual to 'make a difference' to a pre-existing state of affairs or course of events. An agent ceases to be such if he or she loses the capability to 'make a differ-ence,' that is, to exercise some sort of power" (1984, 14). As Airoldi points out, Gid-dens's definition is still firmly anthropocentric, tying agency to individuals. Yet the underlying logic of "making a difference" opens the door for extension to nonhu-man entities—precisely the role trading automatons fulfill when they place orders and influence market conditions. Bruno Latour takes this idea further, defining an actor as "*any thing* that does modify a state of affairs by making a difference . . . in the course of some other agent's action" (2005, 71, original emphasis). Latour's framework radically expands the category of entities capable of action, granting agency to objects and systems as they intersect with human activity. Whether it is a speed bump slowing down a driver or an algorithm determining creditworthiness, the actions of nonhuman entities are inseparably intertwined with and co-constitutive of human action.

The idea that nonhuman entities can act and influence human action—that action is distributed across humans and nonhumans—has been explored in various forms, particularly by scholars working within or influenced by science and technology studies and posthumanist anthropology (Cerulo 2009; Kohn 2013; Tsing 2015; Woolgar 1985). Attributing action to nonhumans requires severing the ties between action, meaning, and consciousness—and this analytical shift therefore involves breaking the connection that Weber (1978) emphasized in his conception of action, where subjective meaning was central. Trading automatons act in markets in ways that exceed the intentions of their human designers, yet they are devoid of meaning or consciousness. As Airoldi (2022, 72) puts it, these systems make a difference without being "sentient subjects."

Other sociologists have moved in a similar direction, advocating for attributing agency to ML systems alongside humans. Ceyda Yolgörmez, for example, proposes a relational perspective, arguing that ML-based "machinic thinking [is] irreducible to humanist notions of thought" (2021, 149; similarly 2025). Likewise, Elena Esposito (2017, 2022a) builds on Luhmann's (1995) shift from action theory to communication theory, using it as a foundation to conceptualize ML systems as communication partners—entities whose communication is not rooted in human subjectivity. Both approaches offer significant theoretical insights. They envision a world no longer inhabited solely by humans, but one where humans interact with and are shaped by ML systems. Yet these approaches also present challenges (Borch 2023). Yolgörmez's (2021) framework, though relational, remains tethered to human subjectivity, drawing on a Mead-inspired lens that interprets ML systems through the "I/me" structure of the self. Similarly, Esposito's (2022a) effort to move beyond human-centric thinking is constrained by Luhmann's phenomenological conception of communication, which is rooted in the medium of meaning. It remains unresolved how ML systems, which operate without subjective intentionality, can be fully integrated into this theoretical framework.[2]

These concerns are arguably minor when set against the broader analytical shift at hand: attributing ML systems, like the trading automatons discussed in this book, with agentic capacity or treating them as entities capable of communicating with humans. Even so, I suggest that trading automatons can be theorized in a way that better acknowledges their semi-independent ability to make trading decisions—decisions that include learning from their action and interaction in markets—and that further decouples the analysis from human-centric frameworks. Specifically, I propose that a more nuanced sociological theorization of trading automatons might draw inspiration from cybernetics (Borch, Skar-Gislinge, and David 2025; Wiener 1961). As cybernetic approaches emphasize, machines fundamentally observe and respond to their environments. Trading automatons operate in a similar manner: they observe changes in the order book caused by other market participants' orders and respond by placing or modifying their own orders.[3] As discussed in chapter 4's notion of mutual enactments, this dynamic is pervasive in markets. Firms design their machines to observe and respond to order-book and market data, embedding relationality at the core of their operations.

Granting trading automatons the capacity to act—treating them analytically and theoretically as entities whose semi-independent strategies produce action that cannot be reduced to the decisions of their human designers—is only the first, albeit critical, step. The next challenge lies in unpacking what this perspective implies for the explanation of their action. How, in other words, can the action of ML-based systems in markets be explained?

Explainability and Machine Learning

Humans' capacity to explain the action of ML systems depends significantly on the type of technique involved. At one end of the spectrum lie simpler methods, such as decision trees, which lend themselves to straightforward explanation. At the opposite end are rather more complex techniques, like those examined in chapter 3—genetic programming and various forms of deep learning. But even within this group of complex techniques, important distinctions in explainability exist. For example, in one of my interviews with him, Babak contrasted "white-box" systems with "black-box" systems:

> There are two primary tracks around explainability in AI. One is if your system is inherently explainable already. We call these white-box systems. Here the substrate that is used in order to map context to actions, or map data to predictions, is itself explainable. You can look at, for example, decision trees as a very, very simple version of that. When you look at a decision tree, you can map that to an "if" statement, and it's relatively explainable. Unfortunately, when things get a little more

complicated and you move on to, for example, random forests, or you move on to neural networks and deep learning–based systems, they're inherently unexplainable. They're black box, very, very difficult to explain. In those cases, the substrate itself is a black box, and so what [people] do [when seeking explainability] is try to make the system explainable after the fact. So it's more of an interrogation and investigation, and some guesswork as to what is it that triggers the black-box substrate to actually trigger.... [However, this] is not giving you a generalized explanation of its behavior. So, while there's a lot of work being done on that sort of explainability, it's difficult and not completely satisfying, and sometimes doesn't really pass muster with, for example, regulators that might be asking for explainability in their systems.

Babak elaborated that Sentient Technologies' genetic programming techniques were "inherently explainable. . . . In evolutionary computation and genetic programming, we can make the substrate explainable quite easily and still have nonlinear relationships and create more sophisticated, complex behavior out of our machine learning system." In practice, this meant that staff at Sentient Technologies could identify not only which specific rule or rules were triggered during a particular trade but, with more effort, trace the complete evolutionary history of every candidate solution generated through the genetic simulations. For each candidate, they could map the precise genealogy of its selection, crossover, and mutation over millions of iterations. This ability to reconstruct a full ancestry revealed how individual rules evolved. Coupled with their capacity to determine which rules were activated in specific market contexts, this process provided a detailed account of the system's actions and their underlying rationale.

Portraying his firm's ML technique as inherently explainable might, at first glance, appear self-serving. Yet several of my informants, including those specializing in deep learning techniques, corroborated this claim. They agreed that systems based on genetic programming offer a level of explainability that deep learning systems struggle to achieve. For instance, the CEO of a firm that had transitioned from a hybrid of first- and second-generation systems to a fully deep learning–based system remarked that with genetic programming "you actually have a program where you can go in and analyze what the program does." By contrast, "A deep learning model can contain . . . maybe hundreds of millions of variables. . . . It's very difficult to understand what's actually going on."

This strikes at the core of the skepticism many market participants express toward deep learning. As discussed in chapter 3, the fundamentally nonintuitive nature of deep learning systems and the inability of humans to trace their decision-making processes is a major reason cited for not adopting this technology (similarly K. Hansen 2020, 2021b). The opacity of deep learning–based systems also mirrors—and amplifies—the concerns raised by Gensler and Bailey (2020), as explored in chapter 4. These issues resonate widely across the industry (e.g., Cambridge Centre for Alternative Finance and World Economic Forum 2020; World Economic Forum 2018).[4]

Similar concerns are prevalent among computer scientists, who frequently explore different forms of opacity and challenges related to explainability in deep learning systems. One illustrative case involves the so-called Clever Hans predictors (Lapuschkin et al. 2019; Samek and Müller 2019, 7). Hans was a horse that gained fame in the early twentieth century for his purported arithmetic skills. When presented with a math problem by his trainer, Hans would tap his hoof in response. However, it was later revealed that Hans's abilities had been misinterpreted, or, more precisely, were rooted in a different skill: He had learned to detect and respond to subtle, involuntary cues given by his trainer—who was apparently unaware of providing them.

In the context of ML, Clever Hans predictors refer to scenarios where algorithms learn to rely on spurious correlations within training and test data, predicting accurately but for the "wrong" reasons (Samek and Müller 2019, 7). Samek and Müller, for instance, described algorithms that appeared capable of correctly identifying images of boats and trains. However, instead of genuinely recognizing the objects, these algorithms were actually focusing on the contextual elements: "boats by the presence of water and trains by the presence of rails" (Samek and Müller 2019, 7). As a result, when presented with atypical scenarios—such as a boat on a trailer or a train without rails—these algorithms would likely fail. Without a comprehensive understanding of how ML algorithms function and reach their conclusions, detecting such Clever Hans predictors is challenging and often occurs only by chance (see also Ribeiro, Singh, and Guestrin 2016).

The rise of ML has spurred a rapidly expanding body of computer science research focused on improving the explainability and interpretability of deep learning systems, aiming to prevent Clever Hans predictors and related issues. Although discussions about interpretability in computer science date back more than half a century (L. Hansen and Rieger 2019), over twenty thousand publications addressing interpretability and explainability in AI have been published since the mid-2010s alone (Doshi-Velez and Kim 2018, 5). Today, Explainable AI (XAI) is recognized as a critical area of research within the field.

As the sheer volume of this literature suggests, debates about explainability and interpretability in deep learning systems have branched in numerous directions, without a clear consensus on how to define these terms. Some researchers use *interpretability* and *explainability* interchangeably (e.g., Miller 2019), while others distinguish between the two. *Interpretability* often refers to a human's ability to understand an ML system on a "global" level—how well "a person can contemplate the entire model at once" (Lipton 2018, 40). *Explainability,* on the other hand, typically addresses the "local" level, focusing on the reasoning behind specific predictions made by the system, often in the form of "post hoc" explanations for individual outputs (Escalante et al. 2018; Lipton 2018; National Institute of Standards and Technology 2020).

Achieving global interpretability for deep learning systems is widely considered challenging. Instead, researchers have developed tools to clarify the logic behind specific local predictions (Escalante et al. 2018; Ribeiro, Singh, and Guestrin 2016; Samek et al. 2019; Zhou and Chen 2018). One foundational idea in XAI posits that "explanation need not require knowing the flow of bits through a complex neural architecture—it may be much simpler, such as being able to identify to which input the model was most sensitive" (Doshi-Velez and Kim 2018, 6). A prominent example of this approach is the use of visual heat maps, or "saliency analysis." In deep learning applications such as self-driving cars, heat maps have been developed to highlight which parts of the vehicle's visual field the algorithm prioritizes (e.g., Kim and Canny 2018). These visual cues offer a window into the system's inner workings, illuminating the inputs that shape its outputs. By providing this glimpse into machine logic, they help narrow the gap between human understanding and the opaque processes of deep learning systems.

Other approaches seek to weave human expertise into the process. To avoid the pitfalls of spurious Clever Hans predictors, some deep driving models incorporate neural networks that learn what human drivers focus on while navigating—a technique known as human gaze prediction. For instance, the DR(eye)VE model combines two extensive data sets for deep learning–based training: (1) ego-centric views collected through eye-tracking devices worn by drivers, and (2) car-centric views captured by roof-mounted cameras (Palazzi et al. 2018). The goal is for the deep learning system to emulate human attentiveness and use this learned behav-

ior to steer clear of irrelevant inputs, thereby enhancing explainability (Kim and
Canny 2018, 189).

While these tools and approaches are promising, they come with significant
limitations (Kindermans et al. 2019). For example, current sensitivity heat-map
visualizations focus on individual input features but overlook the interactions
between them. Moreover, saliency analyses "only uncover regions with high contributions for the final prediction, while the reasoning process still remains behind
the scenes" (Atanasova et al. 2020, 7353). Similarly, integrating human input into
models remains an early-stage endeavor, with persistent challenges in developing
interfaces that systematically incorporate user expertise (Ras, van Gerven, and
Haselager 2018; Samek and Müller 2019, 16–17).

Explainability Through Human-Machine Interaction

Despite the (at best) partial successes of XAI initiatives, trading firms utilizing deep
learning–based systems obviously have a vested interest in understanding what
their systems do and why. A robust grasp of how these systems operate in specific
market contexts is essential to mitigate market abuse and prevent overly risky behaviors. In our fieldwork, we found that discussions surrounding explainability—
and strategies for achieving it—were especially prominent at Cormac. One internal
document articulated the challenge as follows:

> The difficulty of tracing how decisions have been made by ML applications often
> makes it very difficult to prevent in advance, or to correct afterwards, undesirable
> model outcomes. For example, the neural net may discover complex, non-linear
> "hidden" correlations that are difficult or impossible to anticipate or discover. Fur-
> ther, it is very difficult to predict how a model trained on known historical data but
> "making its own decisions" will react when it is live in the market with a much larger
> dataset and it encounters events that have not been seen before in the data that was
> used to train it. (internal document, August 2020, Cormac Trading Group)

More specifically, Ian described the issue of explainability as revolving around a
series of critical questions: "Why did [DEPS] do what it did? Between one version
and another version [referring to the daily updates of DEPS's weights], what are its
preference changes? How can I explain that? When it does something that I wish it
didn't do, what are the root causes? What was it paying attention to?"

To tackle these and related concerns, staff undertook several initiatives aimed at achieving some degree of explainability. These efforts can be categorized into three concurrent and partly overlapping strategies. First, the team developed a suite of "DEPS Explain Tools," including an "Inspector" tool designed for post hoc analysis of both individual market positions held by DEPS and the broader portfolios it trades. These tools may reveal key aspects of hedging, risk allocation, and trading behaviors, providing insights into what the system focused on and the patterns it responded to in specific scenarios. During our fieldwork, Min and I observed staff using these tools to interpret DEPS's actions. The process involved both human traders and ML experts, each contributing their specialized knowledge in a collaborative effort to decode the system's behavior. Additionally, similar to how Cormac employs its MAR software not only for analyzing actual orders and trades but also for back-testing and simulations, the Inspector tool was used beyond just post hoc evaluation. It was deployed as well during simulations to understand DEPS's behavior early in the production process. The aim of applying the Inspector tool at this stage was to identify how and why DEPS observed and responded to market dynamics, allowing staff to address potential issues and refine the system's responses before live deployment.

The DEPS Explain Tools, as local explanation mechanisms using saliency analysis, are functionally equivalent to the XAI visual sensitivity heat maps discussed earlier. However, Cormac staff did not view such tools as sufficient on their own. Many of their explainability efforts were centered on what Ian described as the ambition of "humanizing technology." This involved treating DEPS as if it were a sentient entity, capable of sensing and reasoning. Ian, for instance, spoke of "increasing his scale, [or] increas[ing] the scope of what he does by going to new markets and exchanges," while Edwin emphasized the need to better understand what "his intentions" were. This anthropomorphizing of the trading automaton served as a foundation for several explainability initiatives.

For example, Cormac's second major explainability effort explicitly treated DEPS as a sensing entity. Here explainability involved equipping DEPS with sensory capabilities that were intuitive and understandable to human staff. This approach was evident in Ian's observation that when staff treated DEPS "as having senses and [sought] to give it either new senses or reframe information coming into its senses," the goal was to expand its perception bandwidth, effectively granting it "other ways to touch the world." This meant that rather than simply inundating the system with vast amounts of data, staff actively worked to provide DEPS with new modalities for interpreting these data, broadening its epistemological repertoire and refining its understanding of the market. One example involved adding capabilities that enabled the system to perform more precise hedging. Ian likened this to the experience of seeing infrared light:

> [Say,] in the room right now, there's a pattern on the wall and you're like, "I don't see a pattern." And I go, "Well, I'm not giving you that information." If I can install an infrared eyeball on your head, then, of course, you can see this pattern that exists there. But if you don't have the sense, you can't see it. So therefore you can't become fit to it. So sometimes the humans become aware of some piece of information that we don't believe has been represented as a sense to DEPS. Therefore, we try to give it that sense so that it can then do more, right? So that it can then come up with a more nuanced behavior.

The relation to explainability is straightforward: providing DEPS with new senses means trying to make it see markets in ways that are akin to how humans conceive of them. If humans succeed in integrating their understanding of markets into the automaton, they also obtain a better idea of why it acts as it does. "So, from an Explainable AI perspective," Ian said, "it's about actually making up something that we can make DEPS see and then control, and then it's already been explained because it was understood before DEPS understood it, right? . . . If you've conceived of it and taught it to DEPS, you understand what it means." The central limitation to this endeavor is obviously DEPS's semi-independent nature. If DEPS were a first-generation system, adding new senses to it would amount to changing its market action directly. However, as DEPS is a trading automaton, its very design means that what it does with any new senses need not align with human staff's ambitions or correspond to how human staff would make use of those same senses.

This is where Cormac's third explainability effort comes in. Running through much of staff's interaction with DEPS is the notion that the system is, in Howard's words, "a living, breathing organism" with whom humans can entertain some form of relationship. Indeed, Howard said that "we have a relationship with [DEPS], and we try to coach it" and provide it with "social cues." Similarly, Edwin explained that

> [DEPS] takes what we have given it, and it amplifies it to learn over time. So if we don't stay in close and continuous association with DEPS, if we don't invest in that relationship, then, you know, it can outgrow us. We might then struggle to teach it new skills, because we try to give it some new signals and it just doesn't think of it that way. It doesn't pick up those inputs that we're trying to give it. So yes, we can think of it as a relationship that needs to be maintained.

Accordingly, adding new senses to DEPS and using the Inspector tool to determine post hoc what the system focused on in specific situations are processes in which human staff effectively put themselves in the trading automaton's place. Through these efforts, they aim to understand—and, when necessary, possibly alter—how and why DEPS perceives the market as it does. What emerges from this is a dynamic human-machine relationship, characterized by a kind of caring interaction in which staff adopt DEPS's role and work to uncover the reasoning behind its market interpretations.

These efforts are driven, on one level, by a strong commitment to explainability. Ian even asserted that, thanks to the tools deployed at Cormac, the firm had achieved a level of system explainability superior to that of many companies specializing in first-generation systems. "We've been generally better able to explain our system than many of those sorts of systems," he stated. While I cannot validate this claim, the broader discussions about the limitations of XAI make me skeptical of any assertion that the firm has achieved a full understanding or explanation of DEPS's actions. On another level, however, these explainability initiatives serve a more pragmatic, secondary purpose: enabling greater influence over the system when necessary. As Ian succinctly put it, "To influence DEPS, you have to know him." In other words, without a strong understanding and explanation of the system's action in markets, staff would have minimal ability to guide it toward desired outcomes.

Treating Automatons "As If" They Were Humans: Weber's Concession

It might be tempting to dismiss Cormac staff's interactions with DEPS as an example of people unduly assigning human characteristics to technological systems. However, rather than viewing this anthropomorphizing gesture as inherently misplaced (Salles, Evers, and Farisco 2020; Watson 2019), I suggest that the effort to forge and sustain a social relationship with the ML system deserves sociological scrutiny. As Angèle Christin (2020, 907) observes, sociological examinations of algorithmic systems often "bypass algorithmic opacity." Yet Cormac's practices reveal how ML experts actively strive to make an opaque algorithmic system explainable, even within the confines of XAI's current limitations. Building on this, I propose that the human-machine interactions at Cormac represent an extension of similar dynamics found in nonautomated market arrangements and align with recent sociological debates on how best to explain social action.

In addressing these debates, I draw on John Levi Martin's *The Explanation of Social Action* (2011). Martin argues that much of sociological explanation adopts a detached, third-person perspective that overlooks or sidelines the lived, first-person experiences of the people being studied. Émile Durkheim's (2013) approach serves as a classic example, framing action in terms of social facts that function independently of individuals' self-understandings.[5] Martin contends that such explanations, by excluding first-person perspectives, often distort the reality of action, producing accounts that either clash with people's lived experiences or outright contradict their own perceptions of what they are doing. He argues that this disregard leads to flawed interpretations. Instead, he advocates placing first-person perspectives at the center of sociological explanation—not because individuals offer perfect accounts of their actions (as these accounts may be biased or incomplete), but because these perspectives provide indispensable insight into social action.

For Martin, a successful explanation of social action must therefore meet three criteria. First, it should reside "in the same phenomenological world as the actions it intends to explain, such that the actors could, with dialogue, understand the referent of every term in our explanation" (2011, 336). This avoids the detachment from lived experience that characterizes, for example, Durkheim's work. Second, Martin calls for "a coherent compilation of the first-person perspectives associated with situations [in which the action takes place]," thereby capturing the larger context. This requires placing first-person experiences "in ecological perspective" to find "intersubjectively valid compilations" of these experiences (2011, 337–38). Finally, Martin emphasizes the "transmission of intuitive quality," a criterion meant to reduce the risk of "false positives" in analysis. This might involve testing an explanation's predictive power or engaging directly with the actors to refine the understanding (2011, 338–39).[6]

As this suggests, Martin's framework for explaining social action implicitly views first-person perspectives as rooted in human behavior. First-person accounts are crucial because *action originates in human individuals* who can reflect on their own activities. But what about the actions of nonhuman deep learning systems? As I have outlined, focusing solely on the first-person accounts of the individuals who design these systems is insufficient to explain the systems' actions, given the lack of a direct connection between human intentions and the behavior of these systems. This disconnect is precisely why Weber's concept of social action is inapplicable to understanding trading automatons. However, while Weber emphasized that subjective meaning is central to social action, he also acknowledged that "in the great majority of cases actual action goes on in a state of inarticulate half-consciousness or actual unconsciousness of its subjective meaning." This, he argued, does not preclude sociological analysis, as the sociologist "may reason *as if* action actually proceeded on the basis of clearly self-conscious meaning" (1978, 21–22, emphasis added).[7]

This conditional-counterfactual approach finds resonance in sociology of finance research, which highlights how market participants engage with nonhuman systems by treating them *as if* they possess their own forms of experience and meaning. A key example is Knorr Cetina and Bruegger's (2002b) analysis of electronic screen traders, who perceive the market as an independent entity requiring a specific kind of relational understanding. According to Knorr Cetina and Bruegger (2002b, 179), these traders seek to interpret the onscreen market by "experiencing, feeling, remembering and responding to the market by means of 'identifying' with it" (for a parallel argument in a nonfinance context, see Keller 1983). The distinctive "feeling for the market" that traders develop resembles Mead's (1934) concept of role taking. When screen traders place buy and sell orders, they do so partly to "start experiencing the world from the viewpoint of a market element" (Knorr Cetina and Bruegger 2002b, 179). In electronic markets, where competing traders globally engage in similar practices, this results in reciprocal role taking: traders attempt to put themselves in the position of both anonymized others *and* the market itself. Of course, this reciprocity is inherently asymmetrical. As Knorr Cetina and Bruegger (2002b, 181) observe, while traders can adopt the role of the market, the market—an electronically produced entity—cannot assume the role of the traders. Nevertheless, traders treat the market-on-screen as if it had the capacity to act and experience. Without this as-if assumption, their attempts to identify with the market and position themselves in its place would be futile.[8]

I argue that the human-machine interactions at Cormac can be better understood through the lens of Martin's and Knorr Cetina and Bruegger's analyses. Rather than dismissing staff's attribution of reasoning and experiential capacities to DEPS as an overly anthropomorphized view of the trading automaton, their approach is better understood as an expectable outcome of the automaton's semi-independent nature: because DEPS's actions in markets are not fully determined by its human inventors, they treat it as if it generates its own experiences and understanding of markets. Using tools to uncover what the system focused on in specific situations serves to elicit its "as if" first-person experiences. Adding new senses to DEPS allows staff to imagine themselves in its place, enhancing their understanding of how it "experiences" the market. When the firm's ML experts and human traders come together to discuss and interpret DEPS's "as if" first-person experiences, they effectively situate these interpretations in an ecological perspective. They compare their own views of how the market functions with their inferences about DEPS's experiences. Through simulations, they test these interpretations, evaluating whether their predictions of the system's behavior align with the test results. Crucially, this process of putting themselves in the system's place and eliciting its "as if" first-person experiences enables staff to develop explanations of DEPS's actions that are embedded in the same "phenomenological world" in which the system operates.[9]

As noted, Knorr Cetina and Bruegger (2000, 2002b) use the term *postsocial* relations to describe the growing prominence of human interactions with non-human objects in an increasingly technologized world. These postsocial relations differ from the human-to-human dynamics traditionally central to sociological understandings of the social. While Knorr Cetina and Bruegger focused on postsocial relations in the context of preautomated systems, my analysis of Cormac's explainability efforts highlights how such relations might manifest within the ML domain.

The purpose of extending the notion of postsociality to this domain is not to argue that ML systems, such as trading automatons, are akin to humans. Ontologically and sociologically, claiming that they possess the capacity to form genuine experiences or inhabit a "phenomenological world" of their own is, at best, a gross oversimplification (Fazi 2021). Nevertheless, reducing human-machine interactions, like those observed at Cormac, to an anthropomorphic exercise misses a critical dimension (Borch and Min 2022). To be sure, Cormac's staff do describe DEPS as a human-like entity capable of sensing the market and expressing experiences. Yet there is more at stake, as Janet Vertesi's (2012) analysis of a wholly different field illustrates. Vertesi examined how NASA scientists work to understand the way their Rover robots on Mars perceive the landscape. To this end, the scientists cultivate a "sensibility to what the [robot] might see, think, or feel, in relation to specific activities that must be planned" (2012, 400). Rather than treating the robot as a mere extension of its designers, these human-machine encounters involve what Vertesi calls a "technomorphic" shift, where "team members take on the robot's body and experiences as part of their practice and narrative of their work" (2012, 400).

Cormac's human-machine interactions reflect a blend of anthropomorphic and technomorphic elements. While DEPS is imbued with human-like capabilities to navigate markets, staff also strive to adopt its perspective to better understand its actions and decisions. When staff emphasize the importance of maintaining a close relationship with the trading automaton, they reveal that their explainability efforts do not hinge on viewing humans and the ML system as fundamentally incommensurable (Fazi 2021). Instead, these efforts rely on cultivating a *companionship* with the system (Darling 2021; Haraway 2003; van Oost and Reed 2011). Donna Haraway's (2003, 4) analysis of human-dog companionships, which she characterizes as specific forms of postsocial relationships or even a kind of "cross-species sociality," provides a useful parallel. The forms of human-machine interaction at Cormac can be understood in similar terms: while these interactions also foster interhuman engagement and dialogue—particularly among ML experts and the trading team—their primary focus lies in building and sustaining a profound postsocial relationship, or companionship, with the trading automaton. The ultimate aim is to derive a deeper understanding of the system's decision-making logic through this relationship.

Machine Interaction

So far in this chapter, I have developed two central arguments. First, trading automatons challenge Weber's human-centered conceptual framework: they are not systems grounded in subjective meaning, yet they play a significant role as market participants and must be recognized as possessing agential capacity. These systems place orders in markets based on semi-independently generated strategies, which creates a distinctive explainability challenge. If their actions in the market could simply be traced back to the decision-making processes of their human creators, the Weberian framework would remain intact. However, situating automatons' actions within the intentions of their inventors is not a viable approach. Furthermore, as explored in relation to XAI, trading automatons built using deep neural network architectures present profound explainability challenges of their own, as it remains exceedingly difficult to determine why these ML systems arrive at specific actionable predictions. Second, given the significant explainability challenge and despite automatons not being meaning-oriented systems, some practitioners approach them "as if" they possess meaning. This perspective underpins the extensive efforts at Cormac to explain DEPS's actions by probing how and why it observes and responds to market conditions.

While the discussion so far has concentrated on explaining the *actions* of trading automatons, it is equally important to examine the forms of *interaction* in which they are involved. Indeed, the dynamics of such interactions pose a distinct and equally formidable set of explainability challenges. Explaining interaction among fully automated trading systems is a problem confronting firms regardless of whether they specialize in first- or second-generation systems. Both types interact with other fully automated systems in the market, as well as with a diminishing number of nonautomated participants. As demonstrated in chapter 4, the highly interconnected nature of contemporary markets means that the actions of one system can rapidly trigger a complex cascade—or avalanche—of responses from others (Borch 2020). The struggles of the SEC and the CFTC in unraveling the causes of the 2010 Flash Crash exemplify the difficulty of explaining interaction dynamics in the context of automated trading. Despite the event lasting only about thirty minutes, regulators have issued various contested accounts over the years, reflecting the persistent challenges of pinpointing its causes and mechanics (Borch 2016).

Interaction in the interhuman market arrangement occurred among traders on exchange floors, engaging directly and face-to-face with one another. In the electronic screen market arrangement, interaction takes place between traders placing electronic orders anonymously through their computers. Automated trading introduces interaction among trading systems, where firms often do not know whether their systems are interacting with first- or second-generation systems. A key feature shared by electronic screen trading and automated trading is that in both market arrangements, interaction is not direct in the sense of market participants observing and responding *directly* to one another, as was the case in the interhuman market arrangement. Instead, interaction is mediated by specific technological and market infrastructures. Most importantly, in automated trading, interaction occurs via the electronic order book. However, as MacKenzie (2018b, 2019a, 2021) has emphasized, this does not make automated interaction any less interactional. Rather, it indicates that, much like human interactions mediated through phones or social media, the electronic order book serves as the platform through which the interactions of automated systems are enacted.

The primary reason interaction among automated trading systems warrants careful analysis is that it is *even less* reducible to the intentions of their human designers. Interaction may produce outcomes that were neither planned nor expected during testing. This unpredictability ties directly to the concept of mutual enactment risk discussed in chapter 4. Since the action of any individual system alters the market, it can trigger responses from other systems that, in turn, reshape the market environment. These changes may prompt further responses, creating a feedback loop that ultimately places the initiating system in an unforeseen situation requiring adaptive responses. Unanticipated interactions can manifest in numerous ways, beyond the cascades triggered by stop-loss orders discussed in chapter 4. One notable example, particularly relevant to liquidity providers, relates to a challenge mentioned in earlier chapters: the market impact of an order is exceedingly difficult to simulate. This is why firms carefully phase in new strategies, aiming to discern the footprints their strategies leave and the interactions they may elicit. Yet my informants shared additional examples of intricate interaction dynamics that emerge in markets.

For example, some informants mentioned the use of execution algorithms like "Volume Weighted Average Price" (VWAP) and "Percentage of Volume" (POV). These algorithms are designed by brokers to mitigate the market impact of large orders, such as a substantial sell order, by breaking the parent order into smaller slices and submitting them in proportion to the traded market volume. For instance, a VWAP algorithm schedules trades according to historical or real-time intraday trading volume patterns. If 5 percent of the day's market volume typically occurs during the first half hour, the algorithm may place orders for 5 percent of the parent order during that window to align with the volume distribution. Similarly, a POV algorithm—also known as a participation rate algorithm—dynamically aims to trade a set percentage of the market volume within a specified time interval, such as consistently representing 5 percent of trading activity during each period. "Now, suppose," said Jim, the algorithmic trader, "there are twenty-five companies doing this [at the same time]. What happens then? They can't all be 5 percent of the market, right?" In such situations, he explained, the market "would just move like frantic" because of the unexpected interactions among systems pursuing identical objectives. Another informant, John, supported this observation, noting, "If enough of VWAPs react to a sudden change in liquidity, you could actually get mini flash crashes. There's nothing wrong with each individual VWAP, but the way they interact" creates instability that is "hard for an individual trading firm to predict."

Adam, the head of compliance at a firm specializing in automated commodities trading, offered an additional example: consider a firm operating a suite of fully automated systems placing orders across multiple venues. Each system is designed to function independently, with "all your algorithms [having] their own economic rationale. They're not referencing each other in the sense that they understand the price parameters within which they're operating." However, the venues where these systems trade may host order books for assets that are interrelated. As a result, even though each system is following its own strategy, it may indirectly account for order-book dynamics on other exchanges without directly trading on them. This interconnectedness can generate unexpected feedback loops between the systems, with each reacting to changes triggered by others. Adam's firm experienced this firsthand: "We're starting to see feedback loops where there's actually five or six levels of interconnectedness across multiple exchanges. Exchange 1 only has a view of what they see on their order books. Exchange 2 only has a view of what they see on their order books, but they're connected. Our portfolio of algorithms is connected." Interaction, then, operates on two intertwined levels: the interplay between different firms' systems observing and responding to each other's moves in the market, and the internal dynamics of a single firm's systems responding to one another's actions.

Adam emphasized that the complexities of interactions among systems carry significant implications for suspicions of misconduct. Consider the scenario where, in response to fluctuations at Exchange 2, a system operating on Exchange 1 places orders that might *appear* to be spoofing but are, in reality, bona fide responses to changes in the order book for a related asset on Exchange 2. This echoes the phenomenon discussed in chapter 4, where Cormac's DEPS system occasionally exhibited behavior resembling quote stuffing, though postmortem analysis revealed it was merely shadowing the actions of other market participants. The example mentioned by Adam extends this issue to interactions across venues. However, precisely because of its cross-venue character, and because each venue can only surveil what happens in its own order books, Exchange 1 might raise an alert about potential misconduct and subject the firm to an inquiry, asking it to explain why its system acted as it did. And the explanation might then consist in detailing that the system on Exchange 1 merely responded to market changes elsewhere.

I have simplified certain aspects of Adam's example for clarity, and it is important to note that, despite making "these observations in respect of feedback loops, market interconnectedness, and unexpected outcomes," Adam stressed that "we do not consider that what we have observed has actually resulted in market manipulation or the creation of disorderly markets." Still, the core point remains: interactions among automated systems can lead to profoundly unexpected outcomes. This has important implications. First, explaining machine-machine interaction is a challenge that trading firms face regardless of whether they rely on first- or second-generation systems. While explaining the behavior of a single system is difficult in its own right, accounting for how and why a system acts *in response to interactions* introduces an entirely different, and significantly more complex, dimension. For firms deploying deep learning–based second-generation systems, this challenge becomes a dual explainability problem of substantial magnitude. These firms must contend not only with the opacity of their systems' internal decision-making processes—the transformation of input into actionable strategies—but also with the difficulty of explaining how interactions shape subsequent learning and actions.

Second, this challenge represents an interaction-explainability superstructure to the observation I made in chapter 4 regarding different forms of risk and strategies for mitigating them. Even when firms enclose their automated systems within tight regulatory compliance frameworks, such as those required by MAR, and adhere to best practices for risk management, this does not eliminate the potential for problems. Once interaction dynamics begin to unfold, behavior that may seem prudent at the level of individual systems can cascade into unforeseen collective outcomes. Considering that some firms operate hundreds or even thousands of algorithmic strategies, the complexity of these interaction dynamics becomes exponentially greater than the relatively straightforward example described above.

Adam also highlighted a practical challenge stemming from how exchanges and regulators approach potential MAR violations. In the past, regulators often focused on *intent*—for example, whether a firm deliberately programmed its systems to manipulate order books, as described in the CFTC's definition of spoofing in chapter 4. Increasingly, however, exchanges are focusing on *outcomes*. This shift means that even in the absence of malintent, actions that inadvertently create undesirable conditions in the order book—such as orders rapidly canceled for bona fide reasons—might be treated as problematic if they resemble the effects of spoofing.

This tilt in emphasis—from an effectively Kantian focus on intent to a more utilitarian concern with outcomes—warrants deeper examination, but delving into it here would overextend the scope of this discussion. For now, I merely want to underline how this shift amplifies the significance of the interaction-explainability challenge. As Adam pointed out, individual venues have only a localized perspective on the market, limited to what occurs within their own order books. This means that any cross-exchange dynamics are naturally hidden from their view. When an exchange initiates an inquiry into potential market abuse, the firm under scrutiny often needs to undertake an extensive internal investigation. This involves unraveling how its system's actions at the exchange in question were linked to interactions elsewhere—specifically, how an outcome that was neither intended nor foreseen might have arisen from the complex interplay of systems operating across multiple, tightly interconnected venues.

Let me briefly underscore a final implication of recognizing that interactions among automated systems can produce unexpected and difficult-to-explain outcomes: this highlights the need to reconsider the theoretical framework underpinning the sociology of contemporary financial markets. Since these interaction dynamics cannot be fully accounted for by referencing human action, and given that interactions among systems may exhibit genuinely emergent behaviors, a new sociological framework is required to understand this fundamental aspect of asset trading—one that moves beyond human-centered concepts. I outline some directions this approach could take in the concluding chapter.

SIX

Automatons Unbound

Implications for Sociology and Beyond

IN *MACHINE DREAMS* (2002), PHILIP MIROWSKI examines how post–World War II developments in cybernetics and the concept of the cyborg reshaped the discipline of economics. Central to this transformation was John von Neumann's (1966) theory of automata, which provided a framework for reimagining economic agents as computational entities. By the end of the twentieth century, Mirowski argues, economics had been fundamentally transformed into a science modeled on the architecture and logic of the computer. The investigation presented in this book supplements Mirowski's analysis, showing that beyond serving as a conceptual template or *Denkbild* for economics, automatons have become an integral part of financial markets. Indeed, with the transition from first- to second-generation automated trading systems, these machine dreams have become reality: an expanding population of trading automatons now inhabits contemporary markets.

I have situated this transition within the broader history of financial markets, analyzing it through the lens of various market arrangements—complex institutional-material settings defined by rules, mediating mechanisms among participants, and the technologies they employ. While automated trading, regardless of generation, differs fundamentally from interhuman and electronic screen trading, I have argued that the distinctions between first- and second-generation systems are significant enough to warrant categorizing them as two distinct market arrangements. It is important to note that both forms operate under similar rules and rely on analogous infrastructures, generally utilizing comparable types of data, such as order-book and market data. The key difference lies in the ML technologies embedded in second-generation systems. Although this might initially appear to be a minor technical upgrade, I have argued that it represents a transformative shift. ML fuels the ambition to create trading automatons capable of generating their own strategies, making them semi-independent market actors despite the human curation they still require.

This book has illustrated the processes and challenges involved in constructing both generations of automated systems, the expertise they demand, and the motivations driving their development. At one level, the push for these systems reflects the enduring quest to leverage technology for even the slightest market advantage. However, for all the promise these systems hold, I have also outlined the numerous obstacles firms face when attempting to gain a competitive edge through these technologies. Automated trading, for all its sophistication, is fraught with risks. Both first- and second-generation systems must contend with connectivity issues, inaccuracies in simulation environments, and the quality of data used for back-testing. On a broader scale, they grapple with risks related to models, infrastructure, and mutual enactment.

Infrastructural and mutual enactment risks highlight the deep entanglement of trading systems with their environments—be it connectivity or data provision systems—or with each other, as seen when systems observe and respond to the same order books. The actions of one system can immediately affect others. While first- and second-generation systems face similar infrastructural risks, which can be mitigated through comparable HRO procedures, mutual enactment risks—such as manipulative behaviors—pose unique challenges for trading automatons. Even systems designed with the best intentions may learn to engage in undesirable manipulative practices. This highlights the need to apply HRO thinking, particularly with regard to MAR, at the core of their training and testing processes, while closely monitoring whether they might adopt unwanted behaviors through their interactions in the market.

Relatedly, I have addressed the potential for trading automatons to inadvertently converge on similar strategies, creating systemic risks like machine crowding or herding. This convergence, particularly if it occurs suddenly (and that is a big if), could lead to systemic chaos. The central challenge is that trading firms may find it difficult to guard against this risk, even with HRO measures in the extended system-environment form I have proposed. Addressing such outcomes likely requires interventions at the trading venue level, such as circuit breakers designed to halt trading during extreme price movements. However, as MacKenzie (2021, 261n26) observes, the efficacy of circuit breakers in stabilizing markets remains debatable, suggesting that no single mechanism can fully mitigate this risk.

One especially pressing challenge concerns explaining the behavior of deep learning–based automatons. Although deep learning techniques may excel at detecting patterns in order-book or alternative data, the lack of explainability regarding the strategies they develop and execute in markets is a significant concern. This "trading beyond understanding" exacerbates nearly all the risks posed by second-generation systems. While firms may attempt to develop postsocial relationships with their deep learning systems to gain a better understanding of their market action, it remains uncertain whether such efforts are adequate.

Although this is not the place for an exhaustive discussion on addressing the risks outlined in this book, I agree with Gensler and Bailey (2020) that existing regulatory frameworks in Europe and the US have significant blind spots regarding the adoption of ML and deep neural networks. Designed for first-generation systems, these regulations leave firms considerable latitude and create uncertainty about their adequacy for managing the distinctive risks of second-generation systems. While regulation will always lag behind technological innovation, the current gap is widening at an unsustainable pace. Given that explainability problems magnify the risks of second-generation systems, regulators might consider emphasizing this dimension. Mandating the use of state-of-the-art tools for local model explainability could be one step forward. However, this approach faces challenges: rapid advancements in these tools make them a moving target, and their limitations risk fostering a false sense of security.

Finally, this book has argued that the rise of second-generation systems not only presents firms and markets with new challenges but also raises significant theoretical questions. On one hand, existing theories—from NAT to postsociality to Martin's analysis of social action—can be reinterpreted to analyze trading automatons, their associated risks, and the nature of human-machine interaction. On the other hand, current sociological frameworks struggle to account for the semiautonomous actions of these systems. Weber's conception of social action, for instance, does not accommodate the reality of trading automatons as genuine market participants. This limitation extends beyond Weber: any human-centric framework will fail to fully grasp the phenomenon of semi-independent machine action.

I want to conclude the book by further exploring this idea, examining trading automatons through the lens of what is perhaps the most central concept in economic sociology: embeddedness. Following this, I will outline three key areas that, in my view, warrant attention in future research: quantum computing, financial practices in the Global South, and ML applications extending beyond automated trading.

What Is the Role of Embeddedness in Today's Markets?

In the early 1980s, a group of US sociologists charted a new course for understanding markets and finance through a sociological lens. Granovetter, in his seminal 1985 article, argued that economic action is deeply "embedded" in social relations (Granovetter 1985). Market participants, he contended, do not act in isolation but operate within a web of connections that shape their decisions and strategies. Baker (1984a, 1984b) brought this idea to life with empirical work on pit traders, showing how their behavior in the interhuman market arrangement was profoundly influenced by their social ties.

It is easy to see why embeddedness became a cornerstone of economic sociology. The idea resonates with the intuitive notion that people behave differently toward those they know or trust than toward strangers. Economic action rooted in established social relationships naturally reflects those bonds. Yet as markets march toward automation, the analytical power of embeddedness begins to feel less certain. Granovetter's framework offers little help here; his social universe is almost entirely human—technology is conspicuously absent (Granovetter 1985, 2017). This raises two questions: To what extent do first- and second-generation trading systems exhibit embeddedness? And how might their market activity be shaped by the social relationships of their human creators?

These questions echo the discussion of Weber's notion of social action in chapter 5. First-generation systems, designed entirely by humans, might still carry the imprint of their creators' social ties. The evidence presented in chapter 2 supports this idea. A tightly integrated team of traders, quants, and developers with a history of collaboration might, for instance, be better equipped to resolve bugs quickly or navigate conflicts arising from their distinct epistemic regimes. Their ongoing social interactions could subtly shape the behavior of the system they jointly develop. Similarly, the interactions between trading firms and exchange staff—particularly around protocol updates or infrastructural connections—point to the continued relevance of embeddedness within this market arrangement.[1] These interactions are often reciprocal. Trading firms consult exchange staff about new functionalities, but the relationship can also tilt toward negotiation or even strategic leverage. Gregor offered an illuminating example of this dynamic: "Sometimes we say, 'Okay, we can start trading [at your venue] if you implement such and such a feature for us.' For example, right now [we are] not trading at NYSE. They need to implement certain features—a certain order [type]—and they kind of promised us but didn't do it, so we said, 'Until you do it, our traders do not want to trade [there].'"

Embeddedness, as seen in the ongoing relationships between exchange and trading firm staff, is not confined to first-generation systems. Firms deploying second-generation systems also cultivate such relationships. However, it is far less likely that these relationships directly shape the strategies generated by the automatons themselves. As I have emphasized throughout, trading automatons mark a fundamental departure from human decision-making. These systems are designed to generate their own trading rules, meaning Granovetterian embeddedness offers limited analytical value for understanding their behavior. The economic actions of trading automatons cannot be traced back to the social relationships of their creators. Instead, these actions emerge from thousands of iterations of reproduction, crossover, and mutation in genetic programming, or from the millions of parameters in a deep neural network. In this sense, second-generation automated trading signifies a profound shift where embeddedness is no longer central to understanding the key actions driving financial markets.

That said, as I have highlighted in this book, trading automatons are not wholly autonomous. The extensive human curation involved in their design and testing—a concept I described as semi-independence—complicates any neat dismissal of embeddedness. Indeed, this semi-independence invites nuance when evaluating the role of embeddedness in markets increasingly shaped by second-generation systems. For example, some informants suggested that beyond defining their objective function, certain human-originated ideas might subtly influence the behavior of these systems, revealing a level of semidependence rather than semi-independence. Phil, Cormac's head of the Delta Trading Team, offered a telling example when reflecting on what had most surprised him about DEPS's trading behavior. He noted that the system exhibited distinct "embedded biases," clinging to initial human-defined principles that it struggled to move beyond over time:

> Phil: You do see embedded biases. . . . It surprises me that it does hold on to certain
> things, which is probably mean reversion. It seems to be whoever was responsible

for building the recurrent neural network may have had quite a strong input with
that.... It's a tell, sort of.

Christian: So these biases can live on for a long time?

Phil: Yeah, they can. I mean, one thing I've noticed is that when I speak to the guys
who are sort of heavy machine learning chaps, they would say, "It will learn." So
I say, "Learn when?" And the answer is "Eventually."

In a later interview, Ian, the CTO, acknowledged the presence of such embedded
biases. However, he emphasized that the firm had taken deliberate steps to address
this by intentionally pushing DEPS beyond "our zone of comfort." His comments
suggested that the system's long-promised break from the ideas embedded in its
original design might finally be approaching. Yet even when embedded biases surface, it is essential to understand that they represent an *inclination* of the trading
automaton rather than a direct reproduction of human-conceived ideas. If DEPS
were merely executing a human-defined mean-reverting strategy, there would be no
need for the extensive efforts devoted to explainability.

The implications are clear: Granovetter's concept of embeddedness offers little
analytical traction for understanding the actions of trading automatons. These
systems typically operate in markets without their behavior reflecting, in any
straightforward way, the social ties their creators may have with others. As second-
generation systems gain prominence, the relevance of Granovetterian embeddedness continues to diminish. Even when human biases or ideas are present within an
ML architecture, these traces of embeddedness exist in a highly attenuated form.
Such biases do not dictate the automaton's actions. As semi-independent entities,
capable of generating their own strategies and learning from their interactions in
markets, these systems render human influence indirect and largely indeterminate.
The relevance of embeddedness diminishes even further when considering the defining characteristic of contemporary financial markets: they are no longer shaped
primarily by interhuman or human-machine interactions but by *machine-machine
interactions*. As explored in chapter 5, the actions of machines observing and responding to one another can trigger complex dynamics that cascade within and
across markets. These interaction patterns defy reduction to the human ideas embedded in individual systems.

If embeddedness is increasingly irrelevant for understanding today's market arrangements, what might replace it? Which sociological concepts are better suited to
the task? While a detailed answer lies beyond the scope of this book, I can sketch
two promising avenues for further exploration.

First, as discussed in chapter 5, it is essential to recognize the capacity of technological systems—like trading automatons—for action. Anchoring their market behavior too closely to the intentions of their human designers risks ignoring their semi-independent nature. A growing body of scholarship already conceptualizes machines as semi-independent entities (Airoldi 2022, 2025; Esposito 2017, 2022a, 2022b; Lipp and Mayer 2025; Yolgörmez 2021, 2025). The challenge, as I see it, is to ensure that these conceptualizations are not confined to human-centric notions. Future sociology should aim to develop a distinctly nonhuman framework for understanding machines like trading automatons—one that does not reduce them to mere extensions of human subjective meaning.

Second, sociology must deepen its theorization of machine-machine interaction. As I have argued elsewhere (Borch, Skar-Gislinge, and David 2025), taking seriously the reality that automated trading revolves around interactions among fully autonomous systems demands an "intermachine sociology." This involves a sociological perspective on how machines engage with one another and the consequences of their interactions. Here, too, existing scholarship offers valuable entry points (Borch 2022a; MacKenzie 2019a, 2021; Rahwan et al. 2019). Yet despite these contributions, we still lack a comprehensive analytical and theoretical framework—one that similarly avoids human-centric foundations. Developing such a framework remains an important challenge for the sociology of contemporary markets.

One final comment is warranted, returning to the question of how the risks posed by trading automatons might be mitigated for firms and markets. A defining feature of the automated trading market arrangement—shared with electronic screen trading—is its anonymity. When fully automated systems place orders, their identities (specifically, the identities of their parent firms) are invisible to other market actors. From a Granovetterian perspective, one might argue that while automated trading has delivered efficiencies, this anonymity also serves as a significant risk generator. The interhuman market arrangement, for all its limitations, possessed a key stabilizing feature: human traders formed social ties with one another and leveraged these relationships during periods of instability to calm the market (Mattli 2019).

Admittedly, this idea is speculative, but one could imagine a market arrangement where trading automatons operated with identifiable counterparts. For instance, if every algorithmic participant were assigned a distinct and constant ID, they might, over time, learn—both in training and through market interaction—to avoid participants exhibiting lower market integrity while favoring those with higher integrity. In this scenario, Granovetterian embeddedness could reemerge in a novel form, not among humans but among machine agents. I acknowledge that this idea may sound both futuristic and overly nostalgic for the social embeddedness of the interhuman market arrangement. Nevertheless, it is not without precedent. Certain dark pool trading venues already classify algorithmic participants on the basis of labels such as "opportunistic," "aggressive," or "predatory," allowing other participants to choose whether to engage with or avoid specific groups (MacKenzie 2015a). While I harbor no illusions about the likelihood of introducing identifiers to markets—the resistance would undoubtedly be immense—I propose this as a speculative avenue for addressing the risks of second-generation systems. Such an approach could repurpose Granovetterian ideas for an ML-driven market setting, offering a way to rethink the dynamics of embeddedness in the age of machine agents.

Other Frontiers

I discussed the rise of trading automatons through the lens of embeddedness to highlight some of the significant theoretical implications ML holds within a market setting. To conclude this book, I turn to three additional domains or advancements to contextualize the uptake of ML. The first concerns the geographical scope of my analysis. The fieldwork underlying this study was conducted in Europe and the United States, prompting the question of whether my findings are generalizable to other geographies. Second, this book's central argument underscores how financial markets have historically embraced new technologies at remarkable speed. While ML may be the latest instance, it is unlikely to be the last. I will offer brief reflections on what seems poised to become the next technological frontier: quantum computing. Finally, it is pertinent to consider whether the characteristics and impacts of second-generation trading systems detailed in this book extend beyond financial markets. In other words, what broader societal implications might this analysis carry?

GLOBALIZING THE SOCIOLOGY OF FINANCE

Automated trading is not confined to European and US markets. Edemilson Paraná (2018, 2024) has examined its use within Brazil's capital markets, while Petry (2020, 2021) has explored the globalization of exchanges, including how they expand their automated trading platforms worldwide. Even exchanges outside global conglomerates, such as Turkey's Borsa İstanbul or South Africa's Johannesburg Stock Exchange, accommodate automated trading through offerings like colocation services and the FIX protocol for order entry. This global diffusion of automated trading suggests that the trends analyzed in this book resonate beyond the regions studied. However, I am cautious about drawing sweeping conclusions. Economic sociology, including my own work, reflects a notable bias: it disproportionately focuses on Global North markets, particularly those in Europe and the United States. This focus may be justified by the historical dominance of these markets, but it comes with clear limitations. Without comparable studies in other regions, it is difficult to generalize findings. While some social science research addresses financial markets outside the Global North—whether rooted in sociology or adjacent disciplines (e.g., Hertz 1998; Langley and Leyshon 2022; Maurer 2005; Miyazaki 2013; Pitluck 2014; Preda 2023)—such studies are vastly outnumbered by those centered on US markets.

Given this imbalance, I argue for a significant broadening of economic sociology's understanding of financial markets through empirical research in less commonly studied Global North contexts and, importantly, Global South regions. Expanding this scope would deepen our understanding of financial markets' operations worldwide and reveal the connections between Global North and South economies. This aligns with recent calls in geography to transcend conventional territorial analyses of finance (Wójcik and Bratton 2024) and in international political economy to examine how colonial histories continue to shape global economic dynamics (Antunes de Oliveira and Kvangraven 2023; Bhambra 2020).

In this spirit, consider a pertinent example of the challenges in generalizing this book's findings to non-US/European geographies. In Ethiopia—Africa's second-most populous country, with approximately 125 million people—the first full-scale securities exchange, the Ethiopian Securities Exchange (ESX), was established in October 2023 and launched operations in January 2025. Positioned as a cornerstone of the country's economic infrastructure, the ESX features a fully electronic platform built around an electronic limit order book with price-time priority matching and enforcement mechanisms to deter misconduct—structures closely aligned with those examined in this book.

At first glance, this may suggest that automated trading—whether through first- or second-generation systems—has found fertile ground in Ethiopia. Yet much remains uncertain. It is not yet clear which trading firms will participate on the exchange or how comprehensive the infrastructure will be. Notably, the ESX does not currently offer colocation services, a factor that will inevitably shape both the types of firms it attracts and the strategies they employ. More importantly, the trading automatons described in this book are unlikely to appear on the ESX in the near term. Building such systems requires years of order-book data for training, and even first-generation models depend on extensive datasets for effective testing. Thus, while the ESX aspires to foster a market arrangement eventually suited to automated trading, it is likely to begin as a hybrid environment—one in which non-automated processes continue to play a critical role.

This underscores a simple yet important point: aspects of financial markets, including the dynamics of automated trading, identified in the Global North may not apply uniformly—or at all—elsewhere. While it is a commonplace observation that findings from one context should not be overgeneralized, it bears repeating in discussions of finance and the limitations of sociological research in this domain. Accordingly, while this book offers a depiction of the shift from first- to second-generation automated trading in US and European markets, these insights may not fully align with the realities of other regions. For this reason, the research presented here must be supplemented with a more globally oriented approach to the sociology of finance.

QUANTUM FINANCE

If the rise of trading automatons has brought certain machine dreams to fruition, the prospect of quantum computing has sparked even grander aspirations. Quantum computing represents an effort to develop computers that exploit the principles of quantum mechanics, performing calculations not with traditional binary bits but with qubits—quantum units of information that utilize the unusual properties of superposition and entanglement. This is not the place to explore the technical complexities of quantum mechanics or the primary research approaches, such as superconducting circuits, trapped ions, and photonics. Suffice it to say that quantum computing represents a profound departure from traditional computing paradigms.

The hurdles to creating quantum computers capable of practical applications remain both numerous and daunting, far exceeding the challenges faced by trading firms developing ML applications. Yet the dream persists that significant break-throughs could emerge from this technology in the foreseeable future. Unsurprisingly, given the financial stakes involved, the finance industry is frequently cited as a prime candidate for early adoption. Indeed, institutions like JP Morgan and Goldman Sachs have already established quantum computing research teams to explore its potential applications in finance. Some of their work focuses on cybersecurity concerns (Muru 2024), while other efforts directly address financial applications.

Notably, a growing body of research investigates how quantum computing could revolutionize asset management, suggesting that it might enable better optimization of complex asset portfolios, improve index tracking, or refine pricing models (Egger et al. 2020; Herman et al. 2023; Orús, Mugel, and Lizaso 2019; S. Palmer et al. 2022; Pistoia et al. 2021). In theory, quantum computing could also enhance ML-based techniques by accelerating the identification of patterns in large datasets—whether conventional or alternative—and speeding up their training processes (Orús, Mugel, and Lizaso 2019). Additionally, new forms of hedging strategies may be achievable through quantum methods (Cherrat et al. 2023).

These developments indicate that quantum computing is no longer merely a speculative concept; it has become a tangible field of research and investment. Quantum finance, as one of the most likely early application areas for operational quantum computers, warrants close study. However, while quantum computing may represent the next technological frontier, there is little to suggest that the trading automatons analyzed in this book will be displaced by quantum systems anytime soon.

ML IN SOCIETY: THE AUTOMATONS PROLIFERATE

While financial markets have rapidly embraced ML techniques, particularly in asset trading, ML is now a pervasive force across virtually every sector of society (for an overview, see Borch and Pardo-Guerra 2025). It is only natural, then, to ask what this book contributes to our understanding of ML's broader societal impact and whether automatons—and the risks they entail—are manifesting in other domains, albeit in distinct forms and serving different purposes.

To reflect on this, it is crucial to consider what makes asset trading unique in its use of ML. In this domain, ML is employed to generate automated strategies that are executed without direct human involvement. This stands in sharp contrast to most other ML applications. For instance, in credit scoring—a different corner of the financial world—ML systems may generate predictions, but a human typically makes the final decision. Similarly, in medicine, ML tools are often used to detect patterns in diagnostic imaging, but those insights serve to inform a doctor's judgment rather than replace it outright. The notion of semi-independent decision-making machines is therefore not inherent to ML applications as a whole. Instead, it reflects a specific configuration of ML technology enabled by decades of advancements in automation within financial markets.

That said, even with this key distinction, certain issues discussed in this book resonate across all ML deployments. One universal concern is data quality. As this book has shown, maintaining data hygiene is a critical priority for firms operating second-generation trading systems. However, in other domains, poor data quality may carry even graver consequences. For example, Wanheng Hu (2025) highlights how some Chinese medical companies, constrained by the costs of sourcing expert labor, have hired minimally trained workers to interpret and annotate medical images for ML systems. Such practices are alarming, given that these systems ultimately inform life-altering decisions about patient diagnoses and treatments. Yet there is a silver lining: in this case, human expertise still overlays the ML systems, combining to create decisions that are not fully automated.

In contrast, certain ML systems outside finance exhibit parallels with the trading automatons examined in this book, as they act and interact autonomously, without human intervention. Consider fully autonomous vehicles communicating with one another in traffic (Bissell et al. 2020; Ganesh 2025; Stilgoe 2018), automated bidding systems competing in millisecond-scale online ad auctions to secure advertising slots (Introna 2016; MacKenzie, Caliskan, and Rommerskirchen 2023), autonomous warfare drones interacting with rival systems in combat scenarios (Elliott 2019), or cyber defense systems detecting and responding to attacks from automated adversaries (Murphy 2022). These systems, I argue, can also be classified as automatons. The framework presented in this book—examining their design, agentic capabilities, human-system interactions, and machine-machine interactions—offers valuable tools for understanding them. Like trading automatons, these systems are vulnerable to model risk, infrastructure risk, and mutual enactment risk, though their specific manifestations differ depending on the context.

Ultimately, my hope is that this book not only deepens our understanding of trading automatons and their implications for markets but also inspires a broader inquiry into the automatons proliferating throughout society as ML advances. Why should this attract attention? Because, despite the rewards they may bring, automatons operating beyond our understanding also pose significant risks.

Acknowledgments

Rather than being a solo endeavor, the research that I have undertaken over the past decade—and that forms the foundation of this book—has been part of a genuinely collective effort. I am immensely grateful for years of stimulating discussions with Zachary David, Kristian Bondo Hansen, Pankaj Kumar, Ann-Christina Lange, Bo Hee Min, Nicholas Skar-Gislinge, and Daniel Souleles, all of whom were part of one or both of the two major research projects on which this book is based. Dialogues within this group have profoundly shaped my understanding of the automated trading industry and its ongoing transformations. These exchanges were not only intellectually rewarding but also filled with laughter—and, inevitably, by the frustrations that come with large-scale research projects.

The two research projects in question—"Crowd Dynamics in Financial Markets" (funded by the Independent Research Fund Denmark, grant no. 1327–00028B) and "Algorithmic Finance: Inquiring into the Reshaping of Financial Markets" (funded by the European Research Council under the European Union's Horizon 2020 research and innovation program, grant agreement no. 725706)—were based at Copenhagen Business School, where I was employed during their execution. I am grateful to my colleagues there for many productive discussions over the years. In 2022, I returned to the University of Copenhagen, where I have been fortunate to continue my research on automated trading in a fantastically inspiring environment. This work was supported by grants from the Villum Fonden (grant no. 40543) and the Carlsberg Foundation (grant no. CF22–0986), for which I am deeply thankful. Together, these four grants opened up remarkable opportunities not only for me but also for my team members.

Over the years, I have also had the privilege of discussing the ideas behind this book with many brilliant colleagues outside the Copenhagen environment, including Jakob Arnoldi, Nathan Coombs, Karin Knorr Cetina, Marc Lenglet, Donald MacKenzie, Emilio Marti, Yuval Millo, Alex Preda, Juan Pablo Pardo-Guerra, Robert Seyfert, and Ekaterina Svetlova. Each of them has made vital contributions to the sociological study of electronic and automated trading, enriching my own understanding in countless ways.

Kristian Bondo Hansen, Lasse Suonperä Liebst, and Bo Hee Min kindly read earlier (and sometimes extensive) drafts of this book. I am deeply grateful for their valuable feedback, which has added significant depth and precision to the analysis. At Stanford University Press, Caroline McKusick, Erica Wetter, and Marcela Cristina Maxfield deserve special thanks for their extraordinary support and patience with the project. My gratitude also extends to the editors of the *Currencies* book series, Stefan Eich and Martijn Konings, as well as to the anonymous reviewers, who helped me sharpen the arguments in this work. As a non-native speaker, I used AI to refine the language; in addition, Elisabeth Magnus carefully copyedited the manuscript.

The book is informed by extensive interviews conducted within the automated trading industry. I am profoundly thankful to the informants who allowed my colleagues and me rare glimpses into the inner workings of this world. Their generosity with their time has been exceptional. I am also grateful to a large group of student assistants who transcribed the interviews and supported the research in various ways: Tobias Brask, Licia Calcagno, Philip Dubow, Céline Eschenbrenner, Alice Games, Freddie Greehy, Jackie Lam, Thomas Lauronen, Maria Lucchi, Laura Mortensen, Noah Pryke, Alexander Schierbeck-Hansen, Benjamin Schwarz, Toni Teschke, Sophia van Bon, Caitlin Welch, and Arthur Woodhouse.

Portions of the book draw on and expand ideas and sections from previously published works, specifically Borch (2022a, 2022b), Borch and Min (2022, 2023), K. Hansen and Borch (2022), and Min and Borch (2022). I am grateful to my coauthors for their willingness to allow me to build on this material.

Finally, and most importantly, my deepest gratitude goes to my loved ones: Martha, Albert, and Susanne. Thank you for your unwavering support and encouragement—and to Susanne, for your strength in battling that cruel disease that appeared in the midst of this book's writing.

Appendix: Studying Financiers in the Era of Automation and Machine Learning

STUDYING AUTOMATED TRADING AND THE individuals who operate within its opaque corridors presents an array of challenges. Chief among these is the industry's deep-rooted secrecy; those who design these systems are typically reluctant to be scrutinized, let alone to disclose the mechanisms they use to generate profits in financial markets. Compounding this difficulty is the absence of a comprehensive overview of firms engaged in this kind of trading. As noted in chapter 1, a few major players are known from media and academic circles. Beyond this limited group, however, the landscape consists of a diverse array of smaller firms that often operate discreetly, with little to no online footprint. This lack of visibility complicates efforts to secure access, develop representative samples, and ensure the generalizability of findings.

This book's data stem from two research projects I had the privilege of leading: "Crowd Dynamics in Financial Markets" and "Algorithmic Finance: Inquiring into the Reshaping of Financial Markets" (AlgoFinance), both briefly introduced in chapter 1. Addressing the challenges of studying automated trading required a strategy that was simultaneously collective and pragmatic. The collective aspect was rooted in the decision to approach the field not as a solitary researcher but as part of a team. This collaborative effort involved multiple researchers working together to identify and interview informants who could illuminate the industry's inner workings. Key contributors to this data collection effort included Kristian Bondo Hansen, Ann-Christina Lange, Bo Hee Min, Daniel Souleles, and me, with Pankaj Kumar and Nicholas Skar-Gislinge participating in a smaller number of interviews. Guided by semistructured templates that evolved as the research progressed, we sought insights into the fundamental nature of automated trading, the specialized knowledge it demands, the mundane and systemic issues it surfaces, and its organizational and technological dimensions. Biographical details of informants were also a key part of our inquiries.

The pragmatic side of our approach was evident in our reliance on LinkedIn as a starting point for identifying potential informants. We searched for individuals in roles associated with algorithmic trading—traders, quantitative analysts, software developers—and reached out with interview requests. The response rate was low, but the few who responded enabled us to launch the research, and many of these initial interviews generated referrals, expanding our network. Over the decade spanning 2013 to 2025, our cumulative efforts resulted in 223 interviews with 218 individuals from 152 institutions.[1] Of these, I conducted 80 interviews, either independently or with colleagues. Most interviews were one-on-one, but 30 were group interviews, some of which arose from informants' preferences to involve colleagues. Some informants agreed to participate in follow-up interviews, providing opportunities to delve deeper into specific topics or trace changes over time. In total, we conducted 25 repeat interviews with 17 informants.

Despite its pragmatic starting point, the data collection was deliberately expansive, aiming to capture a wide spectrum of the automated trading industry. This breadth was an attempt to address Seyfert's (2016, 272) observation that "there is no meta-perspective on the market"—no single vantage point from which the market can be comprehensively understood. Each market participant tends to offer a distinct perspective, shaped by their epistemological position. These positions may be individually valid but do not necessarily coalesce into a coherent whole. For instance, the concerns regulators emphasize about automated markets may diverge from what traders mention. What traders consider crucial might not align with the preoccupations of developers. Similarly, the aspects of automation that hedge funds find important may not correspond to the opportunities seen by banks—and the list goes on. I agree with Seyfert's assertion: no meta-perspective exists. Yet by assembling a diverse array of views, concerns, and interests, my aim has been to craft an account that captures both key overlaps and crucial contrasts among these many perspectives.

Reflecting this, our informants represented diverse organizations, including hedge funds, proprietary trading firms, brokers, investment and asset management firms, banks, exchanges, regulatory bodies, and data and technology providers—see table A1 for an overview. Their roles ranged from traders, analysts, and developers to IT staff, executives (such as CEOs, CTOs, and CROs), compliance officers, and others. Among the trading firms and hedge funds, most interviews were conducted with individuals from midsized or smaller organizations, typically employing anywhere from a handful to one hundred people. However, we also interviewed individuals from significantly larger entities, including some of the world's largest banks and leading firms in the hedge fund and proprietary trading spaces. Most interviews were conducted with professionals working in New York, Chicago, San Francisco, London, Paris, and Amsterdam, though a smaller group of participants was identified in the Scandinavian context.

If our group of informants is representative of the industry, it underscores two notable characteristics. First, the industry is overwhelmingly male dominated, as evidenced by the fact that only fourteen of our informants—just 6 percent—were women. This observation aligns with findings from other studies, including those by MacKenzie (2021) and Neely (2022). Second, the rise of ML has brought a significant influx of PhD holders into automated asset trading. Of our informants, 42 had earned PhDs, most commonly in computer science (10), physics (10), and mathematics (6). Thus, nearly 19 percent—roughly one in five—of our informants held a PhD.[2] Several others had been admitted to PhD programs but left before completing them, and many without PhDs mentioned working alongside colleagues with doctoral degrees. While the high number of PhDs in our sample may reflect a self-selection bias—those with academic backgrounds might be more inclined to

Table A1: Overview of informants.

Institutional type	Total no. of interviews (no. of firms)
Trading firms (hedge funds and proprietary trading firms)	91 (50)
Banks	23 (15)
Brokerage firms	9 (4)
Investment/asset management firms	29 (28)
Exchanges and trading venues	23 (12)
Data, technology, and analytics providers	26 (24)
Regulators	9 (7)
Other	12 (12)
Total	223 (152)

Source: Author.

participate in a research project—it likely also mirrors the growing importance of ML within the industry. It was not uncommon for informants to describe how, when recruiting talent, they found themselves competing with major tech companies like Google, where experts with ML-relevant PhDs have access to vast datasets and lucrative opportunities.

Interviews typically lasted about an hour, though some extended significantly beyond that. Most were recorded and transcribed, but a few informants declined to be recorded. While some interviews took place at the organizations where the informants worked, the secrecy surrounding the industry often led participants to prefer meeting in neutral settings like cafés or restaurants. These locations offered privacy, ensuring that colleagues or superiors would be less likely to discover their participation in this research. Some interviews were conducted online, particularly in the wake of COVID-19.

I assign pseudonyms to informants who play significant roles in the narrative, as well as to the small group of firms discussed most extensively. A few informants, however, requested that I use their real names and those of their firms. In my effort to keep this book closely aligned with the practices and language of those engaged in automated trading, I frequently include direct quotes. For readability, I have lightly cleaned and edited these quotes—consistent with Annette Lareau's (2021) recommendations—while preserving the tone and intent of my informants.

While the interviews offered a comprehensive mapping of the industry, we also pursued deeper insights into the modus operandi of specific firms specializing in first- or second-generation automated trading. This was achieved through the repeat interviews mentioned earlier or by interviewing multiple individuals from the same firm. For instance, in some cases, I interviewed 30 to 50 percent of a firm's staff, encompassing all major roles and functions. We also gained access to conduct ethnographic observations at two firms. Souleles spent a total of four weeks at a Chicago-based proprietary trading firm that was not fully automated, while Min and I made three two-day visits to a London-based proprietary trading firm, Cormac Trading Group. During our visits to Cormac, we were issued access cards that allowed us to move freely within the firm. We engaged with staff across all departments, observed their day-to-day tasks, and participated in both formal meetings—including leadership sessions—and informal gatherings within the organization.[3]

In some of the firms where we conducted interviews or observations, we also obtained access to internal documents that provided further insights into their operations. At Cormac, for instance, Min and I were granted access to over three hundred pages of internal materials. These documents detailed various aspects of their automated trading efforts, including their control wrappers, operational workflows, and other critical dimensions of their work. Such materials serve to enrich what is otherwise an "interview-centric" analysis (Seaver 2017, 7).

To be sure, the shorter periods of observational work we conducted pale in comparison with the extended immersion that characterizes classic ethnographic research. Nevertheless, given the secrecy of the automated trading industry, there is cause to appreciate even limited access.[4] As Ulf Hannerz (2003, 213) aptly observes, "Ethnography is an art of the possible, and it may be better to have some of it than none at all." That said, the limited nature of our observations naturally raises questions about whether the practices we witnessed were fully representative of the industry. There is also the possibility that we were exposed to practices that painted an overly favorable picture of the firms we studied. However, given the depth and breadth of our interview material, I do not believe this was a significant concern. What we observed in the firms generally aligned with the accounts provided by our informants, with any discrepancies being more about the level of detail than the substance of the practices. In addition, across the board, the individuals we interviewed and observed were keen to emphasize the wide array of challenges and complexities involved in designing and deploying automated trading systems. These challenges and complexities are explored extensively throughout the book.

The question of potentially sugarcoated information looms particularly large when interviews involve executives. One might assume that their distance from the granular details of day-to-day operations could lead to overly optimistic portrayals of their firms. Yet as previously noted, our dataset is weighted toward smaller automated trading firms. In such firms, executives—whether CEOs or CTOs—are often deeply embedded in the hands-on work. Many of them play a direct role in setting up automated trading systems, with some even having conceived of their design. So these executives, far from being aloof figureheads, are immersed in the operational intricacies, making their insights invaluable for understanding both the functioning and the vulnerabilities of these systems.

That said, I remain mindful that some informants may have had vested interests when speaking with my colleagues and me. While these interests were never openly declared, there were moments when it seemed apparent that informants had particular agendas. Even so, when presenting their work in the most flattering light, these individuals still acknowledged the challenges and risks inherent in automated trading. Moreover, I made it a point to triangulate their accounts with other data sources to evaluate their reliability. This process underscored an important finding: even when their narrative veered toward the promotional, the fundamental issues and complexities they described were strikingly consistent with those discussed by others.

Studying Up and Sideways

What is it like to study individuals specializing in automated trading, particularly those working with ML-powered systems? The informants featured in this book operate at the heart of financial markets, trading complex financial products through intricate systems. Examining their work might best be described as "studying up" (Nader 1972; Neely 2022)—a term acknowledging the need to scrutinize those segments of society where power and wealth are concentrated and reproduced. The concept of studying up implies a hierarchy, where the researcher seeks to unravel the roles, thought processes, and broader societal implications of their informants' work. There are, undeniably, ways in which those involved in automated trading wield more power than an average sociologist—in this case, me. They influence the allocation of capital on scales that can ripple through individuals, corporations, communities, and entire nations. And while the subject rarely surfaced in conversation—a CEO's quip about fresh PhDs demanding £500,000 per year being a notable exception (see chapter 3)—I have little doubt that my informants' compensation packages far exceed those of a sociology professor at a public university.

Yet my experience suggests that these hierarchies are more ambiguous than they first appear, particularly when viewed through the lens of expertise. On one level, studying individuals in automated trading and ML is undoubtedly an act of studying up. The field requires mastery of highly technical domains: on the financial side, instruments such as options can be bafflingly intricate, while on the automation side, the development of sophisticated software and hardware systems demands a distinct form of engineering and computer science acumen. Many of my interviews featured moments where I struggled to grasp the substance of what my informants were saying, often understanding their points only later, sometimes much later. Developing "interactional expertise" in this field therefore required sustained effort. As Harry Collins and Robert Evans define it, interactional expertise is "expertise in the *language* of a specialism [here, automated trading] in the absence of expertise in its *practice* [here, actually setting up and deploying automated trading systems]"

(2007, 28, original emphasis). While I believe I eventually gained that interactional expertise, during much of the data collection process I felt anything but powerful.

This imbalance, however, is not the full story. The expertise hierarchy between researcher and informant in automated trading often cuts both ways. There were moments when I sensed that informants sought my recognition, complicating the dynamic of who held the upper hand. One particularly memorable instance involved a highly articulate informant in a senior position at his firm. While he frequently challenged me during the interview—posing questions as much as answering mine—he also seemed eager to demonstrate his intellectual credentials. He made it clear he was familiar with thinkers like Émile Durkheim and Friedrich Nietzsche, and he and a colleague later sent me an article by Karin Knorr Cetina (2003), hoping I would find it thought-provoking. As it happened, I was already familiar with the paper; it appeared in a special issue I had coedited.

Such instances were not entirely unusual. While references to sociological literature were rare, as one might expect, many informants drew on forms of expertise that resonated with broader social science discourses. At times, I felt less like I was studying up and more as though I were in a university seminar—studying sideways, as it were (Hannerz 1998; Plesner 2011). For instance, one informant, Dr. Paul Bilokon, when asked about the role of intuition in ML-based trading, offered a conceptual history of the term *intuition*, tracing its roots from Hebrew scripture through Isaac Newton, to Friedrich Engels, and finally to the French mathematician Jacques Hadamard. This was an extreme case, but it exemplified the intellectual depth of many informants. Since a significant number held PhDs, they were not only highly erudite but also accustomed to academic environments. Studying financiers of this type—those deeply entrenched in automated trading and ML—thus involves more than examining their financial decision-making. It also requires engaging with individuals who, despite their roles in shaping markets of immense societal consequence, often move through the world with an intellectual posture that is recognizable to sociologists.

Notes

Chapter 1

1. It follows that the book sits at the intersection of—and draws from—different sociological literatures, including studies of (a) financial markets and their technologies and transformations (Knorr Cetina and Preda 2007; MacKenzie 2018b, 2021; Pardo-Guerra 2010, 2012, 2019; Preda 2006, 2017); (b) automation and the role of data and algorithmic systems (Brayne 2017; Burrell and Fourcade 2021; Christin 2020); and (c) more specifically, the adoption of ML and its implications (Airoldi 2022; Borch and Pardo-Guerra 2025; Esposito 2022a).

2. This characterization is idealized in the sense that it encapsulates the motivation often given by market participants for investing in second-generation automated trading. As already indicated, creating successful trading automatons is far from easy, and later chapters will spell out some of the complexities involved.

3. In a somewhat similar vein, Karin Knorr Cetina refers to "semi-autonomous" algorithms in contemporary markets (Knorr Cetina 2021, 196).

4. See Citadel Securities, "What We Do: Equities," accessed May 28, 2024, https://www.citadelsecurities.com/what-we-do/equities/, and PitchBook, "Citadel Securities," accessed May 28, 2024, https://pitchbook.com/profiles/company/51054-76.

5. See Optiver, "About Us," accessed December 22, 2023, https://optiver.com/about-us/.

6. One of my informants, a bank employee, admitted that proprietary trading firms were ahead of them. "It's a lot easier for them to be nimble and agile because there's less regulatory pressure on them to provide the documentation and the testing that [are required of] banks—rightfully so, I guess, given the credit crunch."

7. To be sure, Abolafia did refer to certain technological aspects, such as the phones traders used to communicate with each other and the material design of exchange trading

floors. However, he did not consider the extent to which these and other technological dimensions were intrinsically intertwined with market arrangements.

8. I discuss the architectural design of the Chicago trading pits in more detail in Borch (2020).

9. Runners served as communication channels between brokerage firms and floor traders, bringing orders from the former to the latter and returning trade slips, or trade cards, confirming any executions.

10. It is easy to imagine how a veritable arms race could evolve, with traders adding higher and higher heels to their shoes. This is indeed what happened. Eventually, exchanges intervened and regulated the height of the heels traders were allowed to wear. Alongside detailing what jackets, shirts, pants, and so on are permitted in the trading pits, the 2004 *CME Rulebook* contains the following specifications concerning shoes: "Shoes must be clean, safe and not torn or frayed. The following footwear is specifically prohibited: all shoes without backs, canvas slippers, moccasins, rubber boots, rubber overshoes, clogs, bedroom slippers, and shoes with platforms over 2 inches. All shoes must be tied with laces or appropriately fastened" (CME Group 2004, ch. 5, 49).

11. I give priority here to professional traders, that is, traders working in established financial institutions. However, the rise of electronic trading also enabled individual investors—day traders and retail traders—to participate electronically in markets, for example, through social trading platforms. This form of trading has been extensively analyzed by Alex Preda (Preda 2009a, 2013, 2017; Tong and Preda 2024).

12. Though this is the conventional understanding of the interhuman market arrangement (as reflected in the work of, e.g., Abolafia 1996), I add "largely" to indicate that materiality and technology are not absent from it; as mentioned earlier, they co-constitute the interhuman relations that exist within it.

13. For an overview, see Carlson (2007). For an analysis that contests claims about program trading playing a critical role in the 1987 crash, see Furbush (1989).

Chapter 2

1. Zaloom (2006, ch. 1) offers an extensive, and fascinating, discussion of the building's history.

2. Since market makers are valuable to an exchange because they facilitate the buying and selling of financial assets for other participants, many exchanges have introduced "rebates" to incentivize market makers to provide liquidity. These rebates are small compensations offered whenever bids to buy or offers to sell are accepted by counterparties, who are then charged a minor fee. As MacKenzie (2021, 201) notes, this rebate-fee system "has become predominant in US share trading." This seemingly small change in what financial economists refer to as the "market microstructure"—that is, the rules and mechanisms affecting how asset prices are eventually formed (e.g., Lehalle and Laruelle 2014; O'Hara 1995, 2015)—significantly affects which market behaviors are likely to occur. Specifically, as one of my informants, Alex, explained, the rebate system led to the transformation of certain auto-

mated strategies, such as market making. It allowed for "algorithms that wouldn't make or lose any money on the trade, they would just make money on the rebate."

3. Not all exchanges have equally long trading hours. For example, the NYSE operates Monday through Friday from 9:30 a.m. to 4:00 p.m. ET. However, NYSE management is currently considering expanding these hours to twenty-four-hour trading on weekdays. A similar recalibration appears to be under way at Nasdaq (Hughes 2024, 2025).

4. However, MacKenzie (2021) also points out that the significance of latency varies by market. For instance, FX markets are structured in a way that makes low-latency strategies less advantageous.

5. There is a substantial body of literature on the role of emotions in financial markets, with key contributions from Hassoun (2005), Pixley (2004), and Preda (2009c).

6. As the discussion of ECNs in chapter 1 highlights, asset trading is not limited to formal exchanges. For this reason, I use the more general term *trading venues*. These venues include dark pools—typically operated by banks or brokers—where participants can trade without revealing their intentions publicly through order books. Dark pools were originally designed for institutional investors needing to execute large block trades while avoiding adverse price movements. Over time, low-latency automated trading systems became prominent players within these dark pools (MacKenzie 2015a, 2019b).

7. See CME Group, "Develop to CME Globex," accessed January 5, 2023, https://www.cmegroup.com/globex/develop-to-cme-globex.html.

8. Financial exchanges maintain extensive price lists, often several pages long, that outline the fees for different types of data access: e.g., New York Stock Exchange, "NYSE Proprietary Market Data Fees," accessed August 9, 2024, https://www.nyse.com/publicdocs/nyse/data/NYSE_Market_Data_Fee_Schedule.pdf. As Johannes Petry (2021) has demonstrated, selling market data has become a significant revenue stream for financial exchanges.

9. Further underscoring the boundaries between roles, Adnan, a quantitative analyst, noted that traders "manage the portfolio. . . . They turn on the algos. They look at the [trading] book. I don't do that. I'm not involved in the management of the book."

10. Regardless of the specific type of signal that informs a strategy, many automated trading strategies are designed to end the day "flat," meaning that any positions accumulated over the trading day are exited before the exchange closes. The primary reason for this is regulatory: much of the trading is done using leverage, and if positions are carried overnight, additional margin is required (in other words, more money must be placed as security with a broker or clearinghouse).

11. For example, Elliott, a former hedge fund trader, remarked that "some of [our] most complex trades that required a lot of specialist knowledge would be profitable for years," likely because "we had some sense that maybe only a few other people in the world are doing this."

12. As I discuss in chapter 3, this process of learning is one of the key objectives that second-generation systems aim to achieve autonomously.

13. For discussions of this consolidation among financial exchanges and the transformations they are undergoing, see Petry (2021).

14. Reflecting this, some "how to" books instruct prospective algorithmic traders about how to set limits to their losses so as to not let unprofitable strategies run for too long (e.g., Davey 2014).

15. The individuals studied by Neely (2022) occupy a wider range of roles than those discussed here, which explains some of the broader track diversity she identifies.

16. Souleles's (2024) investigation of a US trading firm offers a scene more reminiscent of a *Wolf of Wall Street*–like environment, where swearing is common. However, that firm is also less quant driven.

17. In a fascinating twist to her analysis, Lange (2016, 244–45) recounts that at the end of her fieldwork the CEO called her in for a debriefing. The meeting, however, was not to discuss her research findings but to subtly prompt her to reveal what the traders had confided in her during her visits. This episode highlights just how deeply ingrained the secrecy and compartmentalization were—so much so that the traders withheld their strategies even from the CEO.

18. However, this secrecy around the underlying infrastructure and its compartmentalized setup can also create vulnerabilities and bottlenecks—an issue some informants raised. Eric, a developer, explained that he actively sought to address this by thoroughly documenting his code and bringing more people into the code base.

19. A significant part of this inquiry involves the risks that automated trading presents. Since I address risk in detail in chapter 4, here I focus on other dimensions of these consequences.

20. By criticizing how automated market making is entangled with latency issues and the race for ever-faster speeds, Jack's argument aligns with broader discussions on the negative impact that high-speed technologies can have on markets. One notable proposal for addressing the latency race in financial markets is the "batch auction" system, suggested by Chicago economist Eric Budish and colleagues Peter Cramton and John Shim (Budish, Cramton, and Shim 2015). They propose replacing continuous order matching with a discrete-time auction system to reduce the incentives for speed-based competition. In this system, orders submitted within a specified time window—such as a second or even a millisecond—are grouped together into a single batch. At the end of each interval, the exchange matches orders on the basis of aggregate supply and demand at that moment, establishing a single clearing price. Orders that are unmatched remain in the order book for the next auction. The key idea behind this design is that the exact time an order arrives within the interval does not affect its priority, significantly reducing the need for costly low-latency systems and shifting competition from speed to price. However, Jack was not impressed by this proposal. "Oh man, only an academic can invent that," he said. "That's like using an atom bomb to kill an ant." Instead, he suggested that "the solution might actually be as simple as imposing some limits on the latency and saying, 'No, an order has to be a bona fide order, and a bona fide order has to be capable of being executed—being accepted by a counterparty—and that requires the order to be there for X amount of time.'"

21. Elliott explained that the importance of such announcements "would depend on the strategy. For some strategies, a large price movement could be risky. For others, a large price movement was exactly what you wanted."

Chapter 3

1. Some informants added that regulatory pressures have also contributed to rising costs. An ML expert at a large proprietary trading firm remarked, "The way markets operate causes the exchanges to put more accountability, responsibility, and compliance needs on the firms that trade there." As a result, he explained, to avoid "get[ting] our asses sued, we have to invest more in lawyers or people just looking at the [message] traffic."

2. Margin trading involves the use of borrowed funds—typically provided by a broker or clearing firm—allowing trading firms to take leveraged positions.

3. On the topic of machine semi-independence, Ian elaborated on two extreme approaches to using ML in automated trading. At one end of the spectrum, the ML system is trained directly on raw data from a trading venue without any human organization or preprocessing. In such cases, Ian noted, "it's extremely unlikely that it would learn anything." At the other end, the ML system is provided with "highly transformed data" and human-designed models, with the system's role limited to assembling opinions based on these preconceived inputs. In this scenario, Ian argued, the actual ML contribution would be "very small." Positioning their firm's approach within these extremes, Ian remarked, "Certainly we're closer to the first one. But we do have people; we endeavor to model financial aspects and feed it to the machine. . . . What's appropriate still is to model the intelligence of the domain experts into a kit of parts that the computer can understand," enabling the system to generate its own models from these inputs.

4. Elaborating on the importance of refraining from intervening in the machine's decisions, another informant shared an anecdote about an early learning algorithm: "There were times where we would look at positions [the machine] had taken, and we by nature were contrarian, meaning if something went up a lot, we'd be inclined to sell it. It was not a rare occurrence that there would be news about something—maybe a merger or whatever—that was moving [the market] either up or down with the result that it was never going to revert. You could look at that and go, 'Well, we know that there's been a merger announced and that stock's not coming back' so we experimented with trying to override our machine—look at certain positions and say, 'We think that's a mistake.' The result of that was that we lost money relative to the machine. Our net changes were losers. They weren't dramatic losers, but the problem was that while we could identify some losers with great certainty, there were other things that we identified as losers that turned out not to be, and so the machine was smarter than we were. We then worked with a friend of mine who was a trader—pretty successful trader on her own—and allowed her to cherry-pick. She would look at what the machine was doing and say, 'I like that idea. I don't like that idea,' and she ended up zero. She did that for three months. She did better than we did! We stank! But she was a good trader and her net result was nothing, so we figured, 'Okay, we just leave the machine on.'"

5. Illustratively, an informant from a bank leading an ML-driven portfolio management team emphasized the importance of integrating "domain expertise, data engineering, and data science into one team. If we didn't have that, we would have done less than 10 percent of what we've done now."

6. I discuss market integrity issues in chapter 4.

7. Babak described a similar process for evaluating genetically evolved rule sets: "We take the candidates that have run on a similar number of stock days, and we compare them to one another. This is multiobjective, so we might be comparing them on P&L as well as risk and a whole bunch of other things. Once that comparison is done, we retain the best, kill off the rest, and we take bits and pieces of the rule sets of those best guys."

8. Given that the firm trades in US markets, monitoring requires long hours. As one of the infrastructure staff explained: "My general hours are from 6:30 [a.m.] anywhere to 10:30 at night, depending on which shift. . . . We provide 24/5 cover. We finish up at ten o'clock on a Friday evening, when the markets shut. And then we have someone in overnight on a Sunday evening, for the US opening."

9. Another informant emphasized the broader implications of nonstationarity, framing it as a fundamental obstacle to the use of ML in trading. "In finance we deal with nonstationary time series, and . . . there's no one model that can catch things all the time the correct way." Once a pattern is detected, "maybe markets are already evolving to something else." Because of this constant evolution, this informant expressed skepticism about trading automatons' ability to make longer-term predictions. "You can only predict for a few seconds or a few hours, but beyond one day or one week, it's impossible."

10. Even some ML experts echoed this skepticism. Reflecting on his experience at a former firm, one informant recounted how a second-generation trading system he had helped design persistently responded to the same core signals year after year. Despite the system's supposed adaptability, no ongoing learning seemed to alter this behavior. As he observed, "Some of us had strong suspicions that you could do away with all that machine learning stuff and get quite similar results."

11. Phil's remarks underscore the order-book-centric focus of Cormac's ML design. As I explore below, other firms have developed ML systems capable of analyzing news.

12. Social media data, in particular, can elicit lightning-fast market reactions. The "Hack Crash" of April 23, 2013, is a striking case in point (Karppi and Crawford 2016). On that day, a hacked Associated Press Twitter account posted the false claim, "@AP: Breaking: Two Explosions in the White House and Barack Obama is injured." Within seconds, US financial markets plummeted, with the Standard & Poor's 500 Index shedding over $130 billion in value. Although markets rebounded within minutes after the tweet was debunked, the speed of the initial reaction highlights how automated trading systems were already integrating and responding to social media feeds. The role of speed in market reactions to news is further illustrated by Gregor's anecdote: "Years ago we did research at [name of major investment bank] looking at Eurodollar futures, news, and how the market reacted. What we couldn't understand was how come very, very significant news from Reuters or Dow Jones was coming after the market already reacted—like two hundred milliseconds later than the

market. Then in our research we found a small firm which was doing the news much faster. Some people were getting information earlier than others. It's probably less noticeable right now, but it's still a game, so people are trying to get news as fast as possible."

13. The acquisition of these vendors by financial exchange groups underscores a broader trend discussed in chapter 2: leading exchanges are evolving into global financial infrastructure giants, with data emerging as a significant revenue source (Petry 2021).

14. None of the individuals I interviewed reported using satellite imagery as input for their automated trading strategies. This may be because many of them operated in the low-latency domain, where the primary focus is on order-book data. For a discussion of how satellite imagery can be harnessed for investment purposes, see Denev and Amen (2020, chs. 13 and 14).

15. Note that the early-stage models David described were designed to produce a two-state sentiment outcome, while more recent NLP approaches yield more granular results.

16. The 2021 GameStop event offers a striking example of how social media sentiment might factor into the range of data considered by hedge funds (K. Hansen 2022). Media reports suggest that some hedge funds, caught off guard by the mobilization of retail investors on the subreddit WallStreetBets, began deploying NLP algorithms to identify early shifts in subreddit sentiment that could signal future market movements (Darbyshire et al. 2021). In alignment with this, one informant, William, noted that his firm—a major hedge fund—utilized data from platforms like StockTwits, where retail investors post stock commentary. These platforms sell their datasets, including postings, to hedge funds, which can develop strategies around them. In William's case, his firm employed a contrarian strategy: "The idea is that [retail investors are] not smart. It doesn't matter whether they say the stock is going up or down, but what matters is how many people pay attention to a certain stock. And if a lot of people pay attention, then you bet against them. And that actually works."

Chapter 4

1. According to the SEC (2013, 5), "Throughout 2011 and 2012, Knight's aggregate trading (both for itself and for its customers) generally represented approximately ten percent of all trading in listed U.S. equity securities. SMARS generally represented approximately one percent or more of all trading in listed U.S. equity securities."

2. For more detailed discussions of the Quant Meltdown, see K. Hansen (2021a) and Min and Hansen (2024).

3. This means that I will set aside whether manipulative practices such as "spoofing" (discussed below) were involved in the event, as later suggested in the indictment and sentencing of British trader Navinder Singh Sarao (Vaughan 2020).

4. Subsequent HRO scholarship expanded its focus to include organizations that may not be as technologically sophisticated but nonetheless operate in hazardous environments, such as firefighting units (see Colquitt et al. 2011). It also examined organizations—including virtual and digital organizations (Grabowski and Roberts 1999; Salovaara, Lyytinen, and Penttinen 2019)—that are technologically advanced but where failures, while significant, do not necessarily result in catastrophic outcomes.

5. An exception within HRO literature is Min and Borch (2022), on which this chapter draws. Classic HRO research includes only one study of a financial institution committed to HRO principles: a bank that implemented risk-mitigation procedures for its lending operations (Roberts and Libuser 1993).

6. While Perrow's discussion of financial systems was brief, others have since applied NAT more systematically to financial markets, particularly in analyzing the 2008 financial crisis. Scholars have argued that the securitization of mortgages created complex interactions and tight coupling among market participants in the US financial system, contributing to the crisis (Curran 2020; Guillén and Suárez 2010; D. Palmer and Maher 2010; Schneiberg and Bartley 2010). However, Perrow (2010) himself expressed skepticism about whether the 2008 crisis was truly the result of a systemic failure. While financial markets in 2008 undeniably exhibited complex interactions and tight coupling—partly driven by the widespread use of sophisticated financial models (MacKenzie and Spears 2014a, 2014b)—Perrow viewed the crisis as equally attributable to the misconduct of human actors who exploited systemic vulnerabilities for personal gain.

7. Spoofing has not always been classified as illegal market manipulation. In her study of electronic screen trading, Zaloom (2006, 158) describes how, during the 1990s, the screen traders she observed took pride in "calling [a spoofer's] bluff." This meant identifying when anonymous market participants entered orders with the intent to manipulate the market and then outmaneuvering them. Interestingly, the traders did not consider exposing a spoofer praiseworthy because it symbolically restored legality—at the time, "there was nothing illegal about a spoofer's maneuver." Instead, the achievement was in reestablishing the "verisimilitude of the bid/ask representation" that the spoofer's actions had disrupted (2006, 158). With the rise of automation, the order book acquired a moral status it previously lacked, becoming a symbol of fair market representation—something that market participants were increasingly expected not to distort (MacKenzie 2022; Pardo-Guerra 2019). This emerging moral dimension was reinforced by a regulatory one. As Arnoldi (2016) notes, some early first-generation automated trading systems were vulnerable to deception by human spoofers, creating a need for regulatory protections. Consequently, efforts to clamp down on spoofing are closely tied to the advent of automated trading. These regulatory measures aim to safeguard automated trading systems by ensuring that the orders in the order book reflect genuine intentions, free from manipulation.

8. In many respects, the Electronic Trading Risk Principles overlapped with earlier regulatory measures. Moreover, numerous exchanges had already adopted comparable guidelines. For instance, the CME Rulebook (ch. 5, Rule 575) explicitly prohibits "disruptive practices" related to mutual enactment risks, such as quote stuffing and spoofing (accessed April 26, 2024; https://www.cmegroup.com/content/dam/cmegroup/rulebook/CME/I/5/5.pdf).

9. For example, one specific concern shared by regulators in the US and Europe has been the risks associated with broker-dealers granting clients market access. Known as "direct," "sponsored," or "naked" access—depending on the degree of oversight—these practices expose markets to varying levels of risk. In direct access, client orders are subject to pretrade

controls by the broker-dealer. Sponsored access routes orders through the broker-dealer's systems with fewer preset controls. Naked access, in contrast, involves orders being routed through the broker-dealer's infrastructure without any risk controls. Given the potential for incidents at individual firms to escalate into systemic risks in tightly coupled, high-speed markets, the SEC adopted the Exchange Act Rule 15c3–5 in 2011. This rule emphasizes pretrade risk controls and explicitly prohibits naked access (SEC 2010). MiFID II echoes these requirements (European Parliament and EUC 2014b, Article 17(5)). Additional regulatory measures in the automated trading space include FINRA's (2015) best practices for automated trading firms and Rule 5210, which prohibits "fraudulent, deceptive or manipulative" quotations; FINRA, "Rules and Guidance," Rule 5210, Publication of Transactions and Quotations, accessed April 24, 2024, https://www.finra.org/rules-guidance/rulebooks/finra-rules/5210.

10. This regulatory approach might reflect a strategy of achieving compliance indirectly. Nathan Coombs (2016, 2021) demonstrates how earlier German regulatory measures targeting the automated trading industry inadvertently empowered compliance officers within trading firms, despite this not being an explicit aim. Coombs argues that even when regulations lack specificity, they can still produce material effects, steering the behavior of regulated entities closer to the broader goals of oversight.

11. It is worth noting, however, that the Tylenol poisonings occurred in the Chicago area rather than in California.

12. Gary Gensler, "AI, Finance, Movies, and the Law: Prepared Remarks before the Yale Law School," February 13, 2024, SEC, https://www.sec.gov/news/speech/gensler-ai-021324.

Chapter 5

1. Throughout this chapter, the discussion builds on and extends the analyses in Borch (2022a, 2022b) and Borch and Min (2022, 2023).

2. For a broader discussion on the interplay between meaning and machines in the context of ML, see Stuhler, Stoltz, and Martin (2025).

3. MacKenzie (2019a) offers a similar observation, though his analysis is rooted in a human-centered framework, specifically that of Goffman.

4. The opacity of deep learning models presents challenges even to their proponents. If the designers themselves cannot explain how these models function internally, management may choose to shelve them, regardless of their strong performance. While this may pose less of a problem for proprietary trading firms, it represents a significant concern for hedge funds and asset managers handling clients' money (K. Hansen and Borch 2021; Kilburn 2018). One informant explained: "We did have, at some point, one model which was actually doing fantastically well, but we couldn't get it past senior management for exactly that reason. Senior management said, 'It's too much of a black box model. You cannot explain to us where the predictions are coming from, and so we're not gonna trade on it, even if it's done well in back-tests for ten years.' And it's quite a reasonable approach, because . . . I could design a strategy that looks great for ten years, and is consistently making money every month for ten years, but unless you understand what tail risk you're taking, you shouldn't

necessarily be trading on it, because the loss that you make in this one in a hundred or one in a thousand event may be much larger than all the small little gains you've made over the years.... In some sense, it was a shame. It was the best we'd ever done. But without being able to explain where the money's coming from, we can't trade it."

5. A similar example is Freudian psychoanalysis, where the patient's first-person account is subordinated to the analyst's interpretive framework (Martin 2011, 88).

6. Martin's proposal is echoed by other sociologists who recommend taking first-person perspectives seriously and grounding sociological explanations in "participants' own actual conduct and understandings thereof" (Maynard 2019, 26), be it in examinations of medical diagnosis (Maynard and Turowetz 2019), religion (Ammerman 2020), or scientific practice (Lynch 1994).

7. A comparable argument is offered in Hans Vaihinger's *Philosophy of "As If"* (2021).

8. Mead (1934, 1938, 2002) delved extensively into the role of nonhuman objects, but a full exploration of his treatment lies beyond the scope of this discussion. For further insights, see instead Joas (1997) and Leys (1993).

9. This analysis resonates with Esposito's (2022b) perspective on addressing the challenge of explaining opaque ML systems: "The goal of explanation is not to give full access to the operations, criteria and elements by which the machine operates, which can remain obscure. The goal is *understandability*. . . . It is sufficient that the human observer understands what the algorithm does well enough to be able to elaborate, control and possibly contest its results" (2022b, 20, original emphasis). For such understanding to emerge, users—in this case, Cormac's staff—must engage in communication with the ML system, treating it as a communication partner alongside others.

Chapter 6

1. Reflecting this, one informant observed: "It's just a much smaller industry than I thought, from the outside.... It's a very first-name terms kind of industry, that's my impression and that somewhat surprises me."

Appendix

1. Before data collection became a more collaborative effort, Lange conducted several interviews as part of the "Crowd Dynamics in Financial Markets" research project. These interviews are not included in the tally presented here; I have counted only those conducted jointly with her. It is also worth noting that I continued my fieldwork beyond the formal conclusion of the "AlgoFinance" project in 2021.

2. For context, in 2021, less than 2 percent of the US population held a PhD degree (see "World Population Review, "PhD Percentage per Country 2025," accessed November 28, 2024, https://worldpopulationreview.com/country-rankings/phd-percentage-by-country?utm_source=chatgpt.com.

3. Drawing on our interviews at Cormac, Souleles (2024, 37) asserts that management "set up" the interviews Min and I conducted, thereby shaping our data collection. This claim is inaccurate. While it is true that for our initial visit, management prepared a program that

allowed us to interview representatives from various parts of the organization, the circumstances of subsequent visits were markedly different. During those later visits, Min and I (a) specifically requested to speak with certain individuals from the firm, (b) conducted unplanned observations at employees' desks, and (c) asked for access to various internal documents to supplement our research. Each of these requests was granted.

4. Lange's six-week ethnography, conducted as part of the "Crowd Dynamics in Financial Markets" project, remains the most thorough study in this area to date (e.g., Lange 2016). Sociological investigations of automated trading typically rely on far shorter visits—half a day or, at best, a full day (MacKenzie 2021; Seyfert 2016).

References

Abolafia, Mitchel Y. 1996. *Making Markets: Opportunism and Restraint on Wall Street.* Cambridge, MA: Harvard University Press.

Abolafia, Mitchel Y. 2020. *Stewards of the Market: How the Federal Reserve Made Sense of the Financial Crisis.* Cambridge, MA: Harvard University Press.

Aggarwal, Charu C. 2018. *Neural Networks and Deep Learning: A Textbook.* Cham: Springer.

Airoldi, Massimo. 2022. *Machine Habitus: Toward a Sociology of Algorithms.* Cambridge: Polity Press.

Airoldi, Massimo. 2025. "Computational Authority in Platform Society: Dimensions of Power in Machine Learning." Pp. 697–714 in *The Oxford Handbook of the Sociology of Machine Learning,* edited by C. Borch and J. P. Pardo-Guerra. New York: Oxford University Press.

Aldrich, Eric Mark, Joseph A. Grundfest, and Gregory Laughlin. 2017. "The Flash Crash: A New Deconstruction." SSRN, March 26. https://ssrn.com/abstract=2721922.

Alegria, Sharla. 2025. "Race and Intersecting Inequalities in Machine Learning." Pp. 311–25 in *The Oxford Handbook of the Sociology of Machine Learning,* edited by C. Borch and J. P. Pardo-Guerra. New York: Oxford University Press.

Alonso, Miquel N., Gilberto Batres-Estrada, and Americ Moulin. 2019. "Deep Learning in Finance: Prediction of Stock Returns with Long Short-Term Memory Networks." Pp. 250–77 in *Big Data and Machine Learning in Quantitative Investment,* edited by T. Guida. Chichester: Wiley.

Alpaydin, Ethem. 2016. *Machine Learning: The New AI.* Cambridge, MA: MIT Press.

Ammerman, Nancy T. 2020. "Rethinking Religion: Toward a Practice Approach." *American Journal of Sociology* 126 (1): 6–51.

Antunes de Oliveira, Felipe, and Ingrid Harvold Kvangraven. 2023. "Back to Dakar: Decolonizing International Political Economy Through Dependency Theory." *Review of International Political Economy* 30 (5): 1676–700.

Aquilina, Matteo, Eric Budish, and Peter O'Neill. 2021. "Quantifying the High-Frequency Trading 'Arms Race.' " *Quarterly Journal of Economics* 137 (1): 493–564.

Arjaliès, Diane-Laure, Philip Grant, Iain Hardie, Donald MacKenzie, and Ekaterina Svetlova. 2017. *Chains of Finance: How Investment Management Is Shaped*. Oxford: Oxford University Press.

Arnoldi, Jakob. 2016. "Computer Algorithms, Market Manipulation and the Institutionalization of High Frequency Trading." *Theory, Culture & Society* 33 (1): 29–52.

Asgari, Nikou. 2024. "Citadel Securities Moves Data and Algorithm Testing to Google Cloud." *Financial Times,* April 10, 2024.

Assefa, Samuel, Danial Dervovic, Mahmoud Mahfouz, Tucker Balch, Prashant Reddy, and Manuela Veloso. 2020. "Generating Synthetic Data in Finance: Opportunities, Challenges and Pitfalls." SSRN, June 23. https://ssrn.com/abstract=3634235.

Atanasova, Pepa, Jakob Grue Simonsen, Christina Lioma, and Isabelle Augenstein. 2020. "Generating Fact Checking Explanations." Pp. 7352–64 in *Proceedings of the 58th Annual Meeting of the Association for Computational Linguistics*, edited by Dan Jurafsky, Joyce Chai, Natalie Schluter, and Joel Tetreault. Stroudsburg, PA: Association for Computational Linguistics.

Baker, Wayne E. 1984a. "Floor Trading and Crowd Dynamics." Pp. 107–28 in *The Social Dynamics of Financial Markets,* edited by P. A. Adler and P. Adler. Greenwich, CT: JAI Press.

Baker, Wayne E. 1984b. "The Social Structure of a National Securities Market." *American Journal of Sociology* 89 (4): 775–811.

Bank of England and Financial Conduct Authority. 2019. *Machine Learning in UK Financial Services*. London: Bank of England and Financial Conduct Authority.

Belfort, Jordan. 2007. *The Wolf of Wall Street*. New York: Bantam Books.

Beunza, Daniel, Iain Hardie, and Donald MacKenzie. 2006. "A Price Is a Social Thing: Towards a Material Sociology of Arbitrage." *Organization Studies* 27 (5): 721–45.

Beunza, Daniel, and David Stark. 2004. "Tools of the Trade: The Socio-Technology of Arbitrage in a Wall Street Trading Room." *Industrial and Corporate Change* 13 (2): 369–400.

Beunza, Daniel, and David Stark. 2012. "From Dissonance to Resonance: Cognitive Interdependence in Quantitative Finance." *Economy and Society* 41 (3): 383–417.

Bhambra, Gurminder K. 2020. "Colonial Global Economy: Towards a Theoretical Reorientation of Political Economy." *Review of International Political Economy* 28 (2): 307–22.

Biais, Bruno, and Thierry Foucault. 2014. "HFT and Market Quality." *Bankers, Markets & Investors* 128:5–19.

Bierly, Paul E., and J.-C. Spender. 1995. "Culture and High Reliability Organizations: The Case of the Nuclear Submarine." *Journal of Management* 21 (4): 639–56.

Bigley, Gregory A., and Karlene H. Roberts. 2001. "The Incident Command System: High-

Reliability Organizing for Complex and Volatile Task Environments." *Academy of Management Journal* 44 (6): 1281–99.

Bissell, David, Thomas Birtchnell, Anthony Elliott, and Eric L. Hsu. 2020. "Autonomous Automobilities: The Social Impacts of Driverless Vehicles." *Current Sociology* 68 (1): 116–34.

Black, Fischer. 1971a. "Toward a Fully Automated Stock Exchange (Part I)." *Financial Analysts Journal* 27 (4): 28–35, 44.

Black, Fischer. 1971b. "Toward a Fully Automated Stock Exchange (Part II)." *Financial Analysts Journal* 27 (6): 24–28, 86–88.

Bloomberg News. 2024. "Shanghai Exchange Races to Fix Glitch That Rocked Hedge Funds." September 29, 2024. https://www.bloomberg.com/news/articles/2024-09-29/shanghai-exchange-races-to-fix-glitch-that-rocked-hedge-funds.

Boehmer, Ekkehart, Dan Li, and Gideon Saar. 2018. "The Competitive Landscape of High-Frequency Trading Firms." *Review of Financial Studies* 31 (6): 2227–76.

Borch, Christian. 2007. "Crowds and Economic Life: Bringing an Old Figure Back In." *Economy and Society* 36 (4): 549–73.

Borch, Christian. 2016. "High-Frequency Trading, Algorithmic Finance and the Flash Crash: Reflections on Eventalization." *Economy and Society* 45 (3–4): 350–78.

Borch, Christian. 2020. *Social Avalanche: Crowds, Cities and Financial Markets*. Cambridge: Cambridge University Press.

Borch, Christian. 2022a. "Machine Learning and Social Theory: Collective Machine Behaviour in Algorithmic Trading." *European Journal of Social Theory* 25 (4): 503–20.

Borch, Christian. 2022b. "Machine Learning, Knowledge Risk, and Principal-Agent Problems in Automated Trading." *Technology in Society* 68:101852.

Borch, Christian. 2023. "Machine Learning and Postcolonial Critique: Homologous Challenges to Sociological Notions of Human Agency." *Sociology* 57 (6): 1450–66.

Borch, Christian. 2025. "Colonialities of Machine Learning." Pp. 753–68 in *The Oxford Handbook of the Sociology of Machine Learning*, edited by C. Borch and J. P. Pardo-Guerra. New York: Oxford University Press.

Borch, Christian, and Ann-Christina Lange. 2017. "High-Frequency Trader Subjectivity: Emotional Attachment and Discipline in an Era of Algorithms." *Socio-Economic Review* 15 (2): 283–306.

Borch, Christian, and Bo Hee Min. 2022. "Toward a Sociology of Machine Learning Explainability: Human-Machine Interaction in Deep Neural Network-Based Automated Trading." *Big Data & Society* 9 (2): 20539517221111361.

Borch, Christian, and Bo Hee Min. 2023. "Machine Learning and Social Action in Markets: From First- to Second-Generation Automated Trading." *Economy and Society* 25 (1): 37–61.

Borch, Christian, and Juan Pablo Pardo-Guerra, eds. 2025. *The Oxford Handbook of the Sociology of Machine Learning*. New York: Oxford University Press.

Borch, Christian, Nicholas Skar-Gislinge, and Zachary David. 2025. "Beyond Embeddedness: Machine-Machine Interaction in Financial Markets." Unpublished paper, University of Copenhagen.

Brayne, Sarah. 2017. "Big Data Surveillance: The Case of Policing." *American Sociological Review* 82 (5): 977–1008.

Brogaard, Jonathan, Allen Carrion, Thibaut Moyaert, Ryan Riordan, Andriy Shkilko, and Konstantin Sokolov. 2018. "High Frequency Trading and Extreme Price Movements." *Journal of Financial Economics* 128 (2): 253–65.

Buck, James E. 1992. *The New York Stock Exchange: The First 200 Years*. Essex, CT: Greenwich.

Budish, Eric, Peter Cramton, and John Shim. 2015. "The High-Frequency Trading Arms Race: Frequent Batch Auctions as a Market Design Response." *Quarterly Journal of Economics* 130 (4): 1547–621.

Buolamwini, Joy, and Timnit Gebru. 2018. "Gender Shades: Intersectional Accuracy Disparities in Commercial Gender Classification." Paper presented at the Proceedings of the 1st Conference on Fairness, Accountability and Transparency, Proceedings of Machine Learning Research, vol. 81. http://proceedings.mlr.press.

Burrell, Jenna, and Marion Fourcade. 2021. "The Society of Algorithms." *Annual Review of Sociology* 47 (1): 213–37.

Bush, Nathaniel I., Peter F. Martelli, and Karlene H. Roberts. 2012. "Failures of High Reliability in Finance." Pp. 167–87 in *Learning from the Global Financial Crisis: Creatively, Reliably, and Sustainably*, edited by P. Shrivastava and M. Statler. Stanford, CA: Stanford Business Press.

Callon, Michel, and Fabian Muniesa. 2005. "Peripheral Vision: Economic Markets as Calculative Collective Devices." *Organization Studies* 26 (8): 1229–50.

Cambridge Centre for Alternative Finance and World Economic Forum. 2020. *Transforming Paradigms: A Global AI in Financial Services Survey*. Cambridge: Cambridge Centre for Alternative Finance and World Economic Forum.

Cameron, Angus, Geoff Lightfoot, Simon Lilley, and Steven D. Brown. 2010. "Placing the 'Post-social' Market: Identity and Spatiality in the Xeno-Economy." *Marketing Theory* 10 (3): 299–312.

Carlson, Mark. 2007. *A Brief History of the 1987 Stock Market Crash with a Discussion of the Federal Reserve Response*. Finance and Economics Discussion Series. Washington, DC: Divisions of Research and Statistics and Monetary Affairs, Federal Reserve Board.

Castelle, Michael, Yuval Millo, Daniel Beunza, and David C. Lubin. 2016. "Where Do Electronic Markets Come From? Regulation and the Transformation of Financial Exchanges." *Economy and Society* 45 (2): 166–200.

Cerulo, Karen A. 2009. "Nonhumans in Social Interaction." *Annual Review of Sociology* 35:531–52.

CFTC (Commodity Futures Trading Commission). 2013. *Interpretive Guidance and Policy Statement on Disruptive Practices*. Washington, DC: Commodity Futures Trading Commission.

CFTC (Commodity Futures Trading Commission). 2015. *Fact Sheet—Notice of Proposed*

Rulemaking on Regulation Automated Trading (Regulation AT). Washington, DC: Commodity Futures Trading Commission.

CFTC (Commodity Futures Trading Commission). 2021. "Electronic Trading Risk Principles (17 CFR Part 38; Rin 3038–Af04)." *Federal Register* 86 (6): 2048–77.

CFTC and SEC (Commodity Futures Trading Commission and Securities and Exchange Commission). 2010. *Findings Regarding the Market Events of May 6, 2010: Report of the Staffs of the CFTC and SEC to the Joint Advisory Committee on Emerging Regulatory Issues*. Washington, DC: CFTC and SEC.

Cherrat, El Amine, Snehal Raj, Iordanis Kerenidis, et al. 2023. "Quantum Deep Hedging." *Quantum* 7 (1191). https://doi.org/10.22331/q-2023-11-29-1191.

Christin, Angèle. 2020. "The Ethnographer and the Algorithm: Beyond the Black Box." *Theory and Society* 49:897–918.

CME Group. 2004. *CME Rulebook*. https://www.cmegroup.com/rulebook/CME/.

Cohen, Samuel N., Derek Snow, and Lukasz Szpruch. 2021. "Black-Box Model Risk in Finance." SSRN, February 9. https://ssrn.com/abstract=3782412.

Collins, Harry, and Robert Evans. 2007. *Rethinking Expertise*. Chicago: University of Chicago Press.

Colquitt, Jason A., Jeffery A. LePine, Cindy P. Zapata, and R. Eric Wild. 2011. "Trust in Typical and High-Reliability Contexts: Building and Reacting to Trust Among Firefighters." *Academy of Management Journal* 54 (5): 999–1015.

Coombs, Nathan. 2016. "What Is an Algorithm? Financial Regulation in the Era of High-Frequency Trading." *Economy and Society* 45 (2): 278–302.

Coombs, Nathan. 2021. "Financial Regulation." Pp. 137–53 in *The Routledge Handbook of Critical Finance Studies*, edited by C. Borch and R. Wosnitzer. New York: Routledge.

Cronon, William. 1991. *Nature's Metropolis: Chicago and the Great West*. New York: W. W. Norton.

Curran, Dean. 2020. "Connecting Risk: Systemic Risk from Finance to the Digital." *Economy and Society* 49 (2): 239–64.

Darbyshire, Madison, Laurence Fletcher, Colby Smith, and Michael Mackenzie. 2021. "Hedge Funds Rush to Get to Grips with Retail Message Boards." *Financial Times,* January 29.

Darling, Kate. 2021. *The New Breed: What Our History with Animals Reveals About Our Future with Robots*. New York: Henry Holt.

Davey, Kevin J. 2014. *Building Winning Algorithmic Trading Systems: A Trader's Journey from Data Mining to Monte Carlo Simulation to Live Trading*. Hoboken, NJ: Wiley.

Davidson, Thomas R. 2025. "Hate Speech Detection and Bias in Supervised Text Classification." Pp. 121–39 in *The Oxford Handbook of the Sociology of Machine Learning*, edited by C. Borch and J. P. Pardo-Guerra. New York: Oxford University Press.

de Goede, Marieke. 2005. *Virtue, Fortune, and Faith: A Genealogy of Finance*. Minneapolis: University of Minnesota Press.

Degryse, Hans, Rudy De Winne, Carole Gresse, and Richard Payne. 2020. "Cross-venue Liquidity Provision: High Frequency Trading and Ghost Liquidity." ESMA Working

Paper No. 4. European Securities and Markets Authority. https://www.esma.europa.eu /sites/default/files/library/esma_wp_4_2020_hft_and_ghost_liquidity.pdf.

Denev, Alexander, and Saeed Amen. 2020. *The Book of Alternative Data: A Guide for Investors, Traders, and Risk Managers*. Hoboken, NJ: Wiley.

Denton, Emily, Alex Hanna, Razvan Amironesei, Andrew Smart, and Hilary Nicole. 2021. "On the Genealogy of Machine Learning Datasets: A Critical History of Imagenet." *Big Data & Society* 8 (2): 20539517211035955.

Derman, Emanuel. 2004. *My Life as a Quant: Reflections in Physics and Finance*. Hoboken, NJ: John Wiley and Sons.

Dixon, Matthew F., Igor Halperin, and Paul Bilokon. 2020. *Machine Learning in Finance: From Theory to Practice*. Cham: Springer.

Doshi-Velez, Finale, and Been Kim. 2018. "Considerations for Evaluation and Generalization in Interpretable Machine Learning." Pp. 3–17 in *Explainable and Interpretable Models in Computer Vision and Machine Learning*, edited by H. J. Escalante, S. Escalera, I. Guyon, et al. Cham: Springer.

Durkheim, Émile. 2013. *The Rules of Sociological Method*. Translated by W. D. Halls. Basingstoke: Palgrave Macmillan.

Egger, D. J., C. Gambella, J. Marecek, et al. 2020. "Quantum Computing for Finance: State-of-the-Art and Future Prospects." *IEEE Transactions on Quantum Engineering* 1:1–24.

Egginton, Jared F., Bonnie F. Van Ness, and Robert A. Van Ness. 2016. "Quote Stuffing." *Financial Management* 45 (3): 583–608.

Elliott, Anthony. 2019. "Automated Mobilities: From Weaponized Drones to Killer Bots." *Journal of Sociology* 55 (1): 20–36.

Emirbayer, Mustafa, and Ann Mische. 1998. "What Is Agency?" *American Journal of Sociology* 103 (4): 962–1023.

Escalante, Hugo Jair, Sergio Escalera, Isabelle Guyon, et al., eds. 2018. *Explainable and Interpretable Models in Computer Vision and Machine Learning*. Cham: Springer.

Esposito, Elena. 2017. "Artificial Communication? The Production of Contingency by Algorithms." *Zeitschrift für Soziologie* 46 (4): 249–65.

Esposito, Elena. 2022a. *Artificial Communication: How Algorithms Produce Social Intelligence*. Cambridge, MA: MIT Press.

Esposito, Elena. 2022b. "Does Explainability Require Transparency?" *Sociologica* 16 (3): 17–27.

European Commission. 2017. *Commission Delegated Regulation (EU) 2017/589 of 19 July 2016 Supplementing Directive 2014/65/EU of the European Parliament and of the Council with Regard to Regulatory Technical Standards Specifying the Organisational Requirements of Investment Firms Engaged in Algorithmic Trading*. Brussels: Official Journal of the European Union, L 87/417.

European Parliament and EUC (Council of the European Union). 2014a. *Regulation (EU) No 596/2014 of the European Parliament and of the Council of 16 April 2014 on Market Abuse (Market Abuse Regulation) and Repealing Directive 2003/6/EC of the European*

Parliament and of the Council and Commission Directives 2003/124/EC, 2003/125/EC and 2004/72/EC.

European Parliament and EUC (Council of the European Union). 2014b. *Directive 2014/65/ EU of the European Parliament and of the Council of 15 May 2014 on Markets in Financial Instruments and Amending Directive 2002/92/EC and Directive 2011/61/EU Text with EEA Relevance.*

Fazi, M. Beatrice. 2021. "Beyond Human: Deep Learning, Explainability and Representation." *Theory, Culture & Society* 38 (7–8): 55–77.

Ferrari, Fabian, and Fenwick McKelvey. 2023. "Hyperproduction: A Social Theory of Deep Generative Models." *Distinktion: Journal of Social Theory* 24 (2): 338–60.

FINRA (Financial Industry Regulatory Authority). 2015. *Regulatory Notice 15–09: Equity Trading Initiatives: Supervision and Control Practices for Algorithmic Trading Strategies.* Washington, DC: FINRA.

Fisher, Melissa S. 2012. *Wall Street Women.* Durham, NC: Duke University Press.

Fligstein, Neil, Jonah Stuart Brundage, and Michael Schultz. 2017. "Seeing Like the Fed: Culture, Cognition, and Framing in the Failure to Anticipate the Financial Crisis of 2008." *American Sociological Review* 82 (5): 879–909.

Foucault, Thierry, and Sofie Moinas. 2018. "Is Trading Fast Dangerous?" Working Paper No. 18-881. Toulouse School of Economics. https://www.tse-fr.eu/sites/default/files/ TSE/documents/doc/wp/2018/wp_tse_881.pdf.

Fourcade, Marion, and Kieran Healy. 2024. *The Ordinal Society.* Cambridge, MA: Harvard University Press.

Fraher, Amy L., Layla Jane Branicki, and Keith Grint. 2017. "Mindfulness in Action: Discovering How U.S. Navy SEALs Build Capacity for Mindfulness in High-Reliability Organizations (HROs)." *Academy of Management Discoveries* 3 (3): 239–61.

Furbush, Dean. 1989. "Program Trading and Price Movement: Evidence from the October 1987 Market Crash." *Financial Management* 18 (3): 68–83.

Furbush, Dean. 1993. "Program Trading." Pp. 597–601 in *The Fortune Encyclopedia of Economics,* edited by D. R. Henderson. New York: Warner Books.

Gane, Nicholas. 2012. *Max Weber and Contemporary Capitalism.* Basingstoke: Palgrave Macmillan.

Ganesh, Maya Indira. 2025. "Epistemic Infrastructures of Moral Decision-Making in the Ethics of Autonomous Driving." Pp. 461–82 in *The Oxford Handbook of the Sociology of Machine Learning,* edited by C. Borch and J. P. Pardo-Guerra. New York: Oxford University Press.

Gensler, Gary. 2021. "Testimony Before the House Financial Services Committee." May 6. https://www.sec.gov/newsroom/speeches-statements/gensler-testimony-20210505.

Gensler, Gary, and Lily Bailey. 2020. "Deep Learning and Financial Stability." SSRN, November 1. https://ssrn.com/abstract=3723132.

Giddens, Anthony. 1984. *The Constitution of Society: Outline of the Theory of Structuration.* Cambridge: Polity Press.

Godechot, Olivier. 2012. "Is Finance Responsible for the Rise in Wage Inequality in France?" *Socio-Economic Review* 10 (3): 447–70.

Goffman, Erving. 1959. *The Presentation of Self in Everyday Life.* London: Penguin.

Gorham, Michael, and Nidhi Singh. 2009. *Electronic Exchanges: The Global Transformation from Pits to Bits.* Burlington, MA: Elsevier.

Grabowski, Martha, and Karlene H. Roberts. 1999. "Risk Mitigation in Virtual Organizations." *Organization Science* 10 (6): 704–21.

Granovetter, Mark. 1985. "Economic Action and Social Structure: The Problem of Embeddedness." *American Journal of Sociology* 91 (3): 481–510.

Granovetter, Mark. 2017. *Economy and Society: Framework and Principles.* Cambridge, MA: Belknap Press of Harvard University Press.

Guillén, Mauro F., and Sandra L. Suárez. 2010. "The Global Crisis of 2007–2009: Markets, Politics, and Organizations." Pp. 257–79 in *Markets on Trial: The Economic Sociology of the U.S. Financial Crisis,* Research in the Sociology of Organizations, Vol. 30, Part A, edited by M. Lounsbury and P. M. Hirsch. Bingley: Emerald.

Hagströmer, Björn, and Lars Nordén. 2013. "The Diversity of High-Frequency Traders." *Journal of Financial Markets* 16 (4): 741–70.

Handel, John. 2022. "The Material Politics of Finance: The Ticker Tape and the London Stock Exchange, 1860s–1890s." *Enterprise & Society* 23 (3): 857–87.

Hannerz, Ulf. 1998. "Other Transnationals: Perspectives Gained from Studying Sideways." *Paideuma* 44: 109–23.

Hannerz, Ulf. 2003. "Being There . . . and There . . . and There! Reflections on Multi-site Ethnography." *Ethnography* 4 (2): 201–16.

Hansen, Kristian Bondo. 2015. "Contrarian Investment Philosophy in the American Stock Market: On Investment Advice and the Crowd Conundrum." *Economy and Society* 44 (4): 616–38.

Hansen, Kristian Bondo. 2020. "The Virtue of Simplicity: On Machine Learning Models in Algorithmic Trading." *Big Data & Society* 7 (1): 2053951720926558. https://doi.org/10.1177/2053951720926558.

Hansen, Kristian Bondo. 2021a. "Financial Contagion: Problems of Proximity and Connectivity in Financial Markets." *Journal of Cultural Economy* 14 (4): 388–402.

Hansen, Kristian Bondo. 2021b. "Model Talk: Calculative Cultures in Quantitative Finance." *Science, Technology, & Human Values* 46 (3): 600–627.

Hansen, Kristian Bondo. 2022. "The Market and the Masses: From Chaotic Corners to Social Media (Re)Tail Events." *Finance and Society* 8 (1): 67–77.

Hansen, Kristian Bondo. 2024. "The Stack Inversion: On Algo-Centrism and the Complex Architecture of Automated Financial Securities Trading Systems." *Science, Technology, & Human Values* 0 (0): 01622439241269983.

Hansen, Kristian Bondo, and Christian Borch. 2021. "The Absorption and Multiplication of Uncertainty in Machine-Learning-Driven Finance." *British Journal of Sociology* 72 (4): 1015–29.

Hansen, Kristian Bondo, and Christian Borch. 2022. "Alternative Data and Sentiment Analysis: Prospecting Non-standard Data in Machine Learning-Driven Finance." *Big Data & Society* 9 (1): 20539517211070701.

Hansen, Kristian Bondo, and Daniel Souleles. 2023. "Expectations, Competencies and Domain Knowledge in Data- and Machine-Driven Finance." *Economy and Society* 52 (3): 421–48.

Hansen, Kristian Bondo, and Nanna Thylstrup. 2024. "Stack Bricolage and Infrastructural Impermanence in Financial Machine-Learning Modelling." *Journal of Cultural Economy* 17 (1): 20–38.

Hansen, Lars Kai, and Laura Rieger. 2019. "Interpretability in Intelligent Systems—a New Concept?" Pp. 41–49 in *Explainable AI: Interpreting, Explaining and Visualizing Deep Learning,* edited by W. Samek, G. Montavon, A. Vedaldi, L. K. Hansen, and K.-R. Müller. Cham: Springer.

Haraway, Donna J. 2003. *The Companion Species Manifesto: Dogs, People, and Significant Otherness.* Chicago: Prickly Paradigm Press.

Hassoun, Jean-Pierre. 2005. "Emotions on the Trading Floor: Social and Symbolic Expressions." Pp. 102–20 in *The Sociology of Financial Markets,* edited by K. Knorr Cetina and A. Preda. Oxford: Oxford University Press.

Hedström, Peter. 2005. *Dissecting the Social: On the Principles of Analytical Sociology.* Cambridge: Cambridge University Press.

Hendershott, Terrence, Charles M. Jones, and Albert J. Menkveld. 2011. "Does Algorithmic Trading Improve Liquidity?" *Journal of Finance* 66 (1): 1–33.

Herman, Dylan, Cody Googin, Xiaoyuan Liu, et al. 2023. "Quantum Computing for Finance." *Nature Reviews Physics* 5 (8): 450–65.

Hertz, Ellen. 1998. *The Trading Crowd: An Ethnography of the Shanghai Stock Market.* Cambridge: Cambridge University Press.

Ho, Karen. 2009. *Liquidated: An Ethnography of Wall Street.* Durham, NC: Durham University Press.

Hochfelder, David. 2006. "'Where the Common People Could Speculate': The Ticker, Bucket Shops, and the Origins of Popular Participation in Financial Markets, 1880–1920." *Journal of American History* 93 (2): 335–58.

Holzer, Boris, and Yuval Millo. 2005. "From Risks to Second-Order Dangers in Financial Markets: Unintended Consequences of Risk Management Systems." *New Political Economy* 10 (2): 223–45.

Hu, Wanheng. 2025. "Machine Learning in Medical Systems: Toward a Sociological Agenda." Pp. 483–508 in *The Oxford Handbook of the Sociology of Machine Learning,* edited by C. Borch and J. P. Pardo-Guerra. New York: Oxford University Press.

Hughes, Jennifer. 2024. "NY Exchange Seeks Views on Trading Stocks 24 Hours a Day." *Financial Times,* April 23.

Hughes, Jennifer. 2025. "Nasdaq Joins Race to Offer 24-Hour US Stock Trades." *Financial Times,* March 8–9, 12.

Introna, Lucas D. 2016. "The Algorithmic Choreography of the Impressionable Subject." Pp. 26–51 in *Algorithmic Cultures: Essays on Meaning, Performance and New Technologies*, edited by R. Seyfert and J. Roberge. London: Routledge.

Jacobsen, Benjamin N. 2023. "Machine Learning and the Politics of Synthetic Data." *Big Data & Society* 10 (1): 20539517221145372.

Jacobsen, Benjamin N. 2024. "The Logic of the Synthetic Supplement in Algorithmic Societies." *Theory, Culture & Society* 41 (4): 41–56.

Jarrow, Robert A., and Philip Protter. 2012. "A Dysfunctional Role of High Frequency Trading in Electronic Markets." *International Journal of Theoretical and Applied Finance* 15 (3): 1–15.

Joas, Hans. 1997. *G. H. Mead: A Contemporary Re-examination of His Thought*. Translated by R. Meyer. Cambridge, MA: MIT Press.

Kang, Minsoo. 2011. *Sublime Dreams of Living Machines: The Automaton in the European Imagination*. Cambridge, MA: Harvard University Press.

Karppi, Tero, and Kate Crawford. 2016. "Social Media, Financial Algorithms and the Hack Crash." *Theory, Culture & Society* 33 (1): 73–92.

Katzenbach, Nicholas deB. 1987. *An Overview of Program Trading and Its Impact on Current Market Practices*. New York: New York Stock Exchange.

Keller, Evelyn Fox. 1983. *A Feeling for the Organism: The Life and Work of Barbara McClintock*. New York: W. H. Freeman.

Kennedy, Devin. 2017. "The Machine in the Market: Computers and the Infrastructure of Price at the New York Stock Exchange, 1965–1975." *Social Studies of Science* 47 (6): 888–917.

Kilburn, Faye. 2018. "Blackrock Shelves Unexplainable AI Liquidity Models." *Risk.net,* November 12. https://www.risk.net/asset-management/6119616/blackrock-shelves-unexplainable-ai-liquidity-models.

Kim, Jinkyu, and John Canny. 2018. "Explainable Deep Driving by Visualizing Causal Attention." Pp. 173–93 in *Explainable and Interpretable Models in Computer Vision and Machine Learning*, edited by H. J. Escalante, S. Escalera, I. Guyon, et al. Cham: Springer.

Kindermans, Pieter-Jan, Sara Hooker, Julius Adebayo, et al. 2019. "The (Un)Reliability of Saliency Methods." Pp. 267–80 in *Explainable AI: Interpreting, Explaining and Visualizing Deep Learning,* edited by W. Samek, G. Montavon, A. Vedaldi, L. K. Hansen, and K.-R. Müller. Cham: Springer.

Kirilenko, Andrei, and Andrew Lo. 2013. "Moore's Law Versus Murphy's Law: Algorithmic Trading and Its Discontents." *Journal of Economic Perspectives* 27 (2): 51–72.

Knorr Cetina, Karin. 2003. "From Pipes to Scopes: The Flow Architecture of Financial Markets." *Distinktion: Scandinavian Journal of Social Theory* (4): 7–23.

Knorr Cetina, Karin. 2021. "Karin Knorr Cetina: An Interview with Alex Preda." *Sociologica* 15 (3): 189–98.

Knorr Cetina, Karin, and Urs Bruegger. 2000. "The Market as an Object of Attachment: Exploring Postsocial Relations in Financial Markets." *Canadian Journal of Sociology* 25 (2): 141–68.

Knorr Cetina, Karin, and Urs Bruegger. 2002a. "Global Microstructures: The Virtual Societies of Financial Markets." *American Journal of Sociology* 107 (4): 905–50.

Knorr Cetina, Karin, and Urs Bruegger. 2002b. "Traders' Engagement with Markets: A Postsocial Relationship." *Theory, Culture & Society* 19 (5/6): 161–85.

Knorr Cetina, Karin, and Alex Preda. 2007. "The Temporalization of Financial Markets: From Network to Flow." *Theory, Culture & Society* 24 (7–8): 116–38.

Kohn, Eduardo. 2013. *How Forests Think: Toward an Anthropology beyond the Human.* Berkeley: University of California Press.

Komporozos-Athanasiou, Aris. 2022. *Speculative Communities: Living with Uncertainty in a Financialized World.* Chicago: University of Chicago Press.

Konings, Martijn. 2018. *Capital and Time: For a New Critique of Neoliberal Reason.* Stanford, CA: Stanford University Press.

Konings, Martijn. 2021. "Speculation." Pp. 73–95 in *The Routledge Handbook of Critical Finance Studies,* edited by C. Borch and R. Wosnitzer. New York: Routledge.

Koza, John R., and Riccardo Poli. 2014. "Genetic Programming." Pp. 143–85 in *Search Methodologies: Introductory Tutorials in Optimization and Decision Support Techniques,* edited by E. K. Burke and G. Kendall. Cham: Springer.

Krause, Monika. 2021. *Model Cases: On Canonical Research Objects and Sites.* Chicago: University of Chicago Press.

La Porte, Todd R. 1996. "High Reliability Organizations: Unlikely, Demanding and at Risk." *Journal of Contingencies and Crisis Management* 4 (2): 60–71.

La Porte, Todd R., and Paula M. Consolini. 1991. "Working in Practice but Not in Theory: Theoretical Challenges of 'High-Reliability Organizations.'" *Journal of Public Administration Research and Theory: J-PART* 1 (1): 19–48.

Lange, Ann-Christina. 2016. "Organizational Ignorance: An Ethnographic Study of High-Frequency Trading." *Economy and Society* 45 (2): 230–50.

Lange, Ann-Christina. 2020. "High-Frequency Trading " Pp. 244–57 in *The Routledge Handbook of Critical Finance Studies,* edited by C. Borch and R. Wosnitzer. London: Routledge.

Lange, Ann-Christina, Marc Lenglet, and Robert Seyfert. 2024. "High-Frequency Trading, Spoofing and Conflicting Epistemic Regimes: Accounting for Market Abuse in the Age of Algorithms." *Economy and Society* 53 (4): 603–26.

Langley, Paul, and Andrew Leyshon. 2022. "Neo-colonial Credit: Fintech Platforms in Africa." *Journal of Cultural Economy* 15 (4): 401–15.

Lapuschkin, Sebastian, Stephan Wäldchen, Alexander Binder, et al. 2019. "Unmasking Clever Hans Predictors and Assessing What Machines Really Learn." *Nature Communications* 10 (1): 1096.

Lareau, Annette. 2021. *Listening to People: A Practical Guide to Interviewing, Participant Observation, Data Analysis, and Writing It All Up.* Chicago: University of Chicago Press.

Latour, Bruno. 2005. *Reassembling the Social: An Introduction to Actor-Network-Theory.* Oxford: Oxford University Press.

LeCun, Yann, Yoshua Bengio, and Geoffrey Hinton. 2015. "Deep Learning." *Nature* 521 (7553): 436–44.

Lehalle, Charles-Albert, and Sophie Laruelle, eds. 2014. *Market Microstructure in Practice.* Singapore: World Scientific Publishing.

Lépinay, Vincent Antonin. 2011. *Codes of Finance: Engineering Derivatives in a Global Bank.* Princeton, NJ: Princeton University Press.

Lewis, Michael. 2014. *Flash Boys: Cracking the Money Code.* London: Allen Lane.

Leys, Ruth. 1993. "Mead's Voices: Imitation as Foundation, or, the Struggle Against Mimesis." *Critical Inquiry* 19 (2): 277–307.

Lipp, Benjamin, and Henning Mayer. 2025. "Theoretical Challenges of Human-Machine Interaction: Toward a Sociology of Interfaces." Pp. 737–52 in *The Oxford Handbook of the Sociology of Machine Learning*, edited by C. Borch and J. P. Pardo-Guerra. New York: Oxford University Press.

Lipton, Zachary C. 2018. "The Mythos of Model Interpretability." *Communications of the ACM* 61 (10): 36–43.

López de Prado, Marcos. 2018. *Advances in Financial Machine Learning.* Hoboken, NJ: Wiley.

López de Prado, Marcos. 2020. *Machine Learning for Asset Managers.* Cambridge: Cambridge University Press.

Luhmann, Niklas. 1995. *Social Systems.* Translated by John Bednarz Jr. with Dirk Baecker. Stanford, CA: Stanford University Press.

Luhmann, Niklas. 2012. *Theory of Society.* Vol. 1. Translated by Rhodes Barrett. Stanford, CA: Stanford University Press.

Luhmann, Niklas. 2013. *Introduction to Systems Theory.* Translated by Peter Gilgen. Cambridge: Polity Press.

Lynch, Michael. 1994. *Scientific Practice and Ordinary Action: Ethnomethodology and Social Studies of Science.* Cambridge: Cambridge University Press.

MacKenzie, Donald. 2009. *Material Markets: How Economic Agents Are Constructed.* Oxford: Oxford University Press.

MacKenzie, Donald. 2015a. "Dark Markets." *London Review of Books* 37 (11): 29–32.

MacKenzie, Donald. 2015b. "Mechanizing the Merc: The Chicago Mercantile Exchange and the Rise of High-Frequency Trading." *Technology and Culture* 56 (3): 646–75.

MacKenzie, Donald. 2017. "A Material Political Economy: Automated Trading Desk and Price Prediction in High-Frequency Trading." *Social Studies of Science* 47 (2): 172–94.

MacKenzie, Donald. 2018a. "'Making,' 'Taking' and the Material Political Economy of Algorithmic Trading." *Economy and Society* 47 (4): 501–23.

MacKenzie, Donald. 2018b. "Material Signals: A Historical Sociology of High-Frequency Trading." *American Journal of Sociology* 123 (6): 1635–83.

MacKenzie, Donald. 2019a. "How Algorithms Interact: Goffman's 'Interaction Order' in Automated Trading." *Theory, Culture & Society* 36 (2): 39–59.

MacKenzie, Donald. 2019b. "Market Devices and Structural Dependency: The Origins and Development of 'Dark Pools.'" *Finance and Society* 5 (1): 1–19.

MacKenzie, Donald. 2021. *Trading at the Speed of Light: How Ultrafast Algorithms Are Transforming Financial Markets*. Princeton, NJ: Princeton University Press.

MacKenzie, Donald. 2022. "Spoofing: Law, Materiality and Boundary Work in Futures Trading." *Economy and Society* 51 (1): 1–22.

MacKenzie, Donald, Koray Caliskan, and Charlotte Rommerskirchen. 2023. "The Longest Second: Header Bidding and the Material Politics of Online Advertising." *Economy and Society* 52 (3): 554–78.

MacKenzie, Donald, and Yuval Millo. 2003. "Constructing a Market, Performing Theory: The Historical Sociology of a Financial Derivatives Exchange." *American Journal of Sociology* 109 (1): 107–45.

MacKenzie, Donald, and Taylor Spears. 2014a. "'A Device for Being Able to Book P&L': The Organizational Embedding of the Gaussian Copula." *Social Studies of Science* 44 (3): 418–40.

MacKenzie, Donald, and Taylor Spears. 2014b. "'The Formula That Killed Wall Street': The Gaussian Copula and Modelling Practices in Investment Banking." *Social Studies of Science* 44 (3): 393–417.

Malinova, Katya, Andreas Park, and Ryan Riordan. 2018. "Do Retail Traders Suffer from High Frequency Traders?" SSRN, January 11. http://ssrn.com/abstract=2183806.

Martin, John Levi. 2011. *The Explanation of Social Action*. Oxford: Oxford University Press.

Marx, Karl. 1993. *Grundrisse: Foundation of the Critique of Political Economy*. Translated by M. Nicolaus. London: Penguin Books.

Massó, Matilde, and Alejandro Arnulfo Ruiz-León. 2017. "The Configuration of a Status Based Model of Economic Actors: The Case of Spanish Government Debt Market." *Social Networks* 48: 23–35.

Mattli, Walter. 2019. *Darkness by Design: The Hidden Power in Global Capital Markets*. Princeton, NJ: Princeton University Press.

Maurer, Bill. 2005. *Mutual Life, Limited: Islamic Banking, Alternative Currencies, Lateral Reason*. Princeton, NJ: Princeton University Press.

Maynard, Douglas W. 2019. "Why Social Psychology Needs Autism and Why Autism Needs Social Psychology: Forensic and Clinical Considerations." *Social Psychology Quarterly* 82 (1): 5–30.

Maynard, Douglas W., and Jason Turowetz. 2019. "Doing Abstraction: Autism, Diagnosis, and Social Theory." *Sociological Theory* 37 (1): 89–116.

Mayor, Adrienne. 2018. *Gods and Robots: Myths, Machines, and Ancient Dreams of Technology*. Princeton, NJ: Princeton University Press.

McCulloch, Warren S., and Walter Pitts. 1943. "A Logical Calculus of the Ideas Immanent in Nervous Activity." *Bulletin of Mathematical Biophysics* 5 (4): 115–33.

Mead, George Herbert. 1934. *Mind, Self, and Society: From the Standpoint of a Social Behaviorist*. Chicago: University of Chicago Press.

Mead, George Herbert. 1938. *The Philosophy of the Act*. Chicago: University of Chicago Press.

Mead, George Herbert. 2002. *The Philosophy of the Present*. Amherst, NY: Prometheus Books.

Miller, Tim. 2019. "Explanation in Artificial Intelligence: Insights from the Social Sciences." *Artificial Intelligence* 267: 1–38.

Min, Bo Hee. 2020. "Snap Interactions and Programmed Panic: Normal Accidents in Complex Financial Markets." Unpublished paper, Copenhagen Business School.

Min, Bo Hee, and Christian Borch. 2022. "Systemic Failures and Organizational Risk Management in Algorithmic Trading: Normal Accidents and High Reliability in Financial Markets." *Social Studies of Science* 52 (2): 277–302.

Min, Bo Hee, and Kristian Bondo Hansen. 2024. "The Confidence-Trust Chain in Sustaining Algorithmic Practices: The Transitive Properties of Confidence in Algorithmic Finance." Unpublished manuscript, Copenhagen Business School.

Mirowski, Philip. 2002. *Machine Dreams: Economics Becomes a Cyborg Science*. Cambridge: Cambridge University Press.

Miyazaki, Hirokazu. 2013. *Arbitraging Japan: Dreams of Capitalism at the End of Finance*. Berkeley: University of California Press.

Murphy, Hannah. 2022. "Machine-on-Machine Cyber Defence Edges Closer." *Financial Times,* November 9.

Murphy, Hannah, and Philip Stafford. 2021. "How Social Media Accounts Fuel Surges in Penny Stocks." *Financial Times,* May 19, 17.

Muru, Suneet. 2024. "Will Banks Be Ready for Post-quantum Chaos If They're Too Focused on a Pre-quantum World?" *Retail Banker International,* July 9. https://www.re tailbankerinternational.com/analyst-comment/will-banks-be-ready-for-post-quantum -chaos/?utm_source=substack&utm_medium=email&cf-view.

Nader, Laura. 1972. *Up the Anthropologist: Perspectives Gained from Studying Up*. Washington, DC: US Department of Health Education and Welfare, Office of Education.

National Institute of Standards and Technology. 2020. "Four Principles of Explainable Artificial Intelligence." Draft NISTIR 8312. National Institute of Standards and Technology. https://nvlpubs.nist.gov/nistpubs/ir/2021/NIST.IR.8312.pdf.

Neely, Megan Tobias. 2022. *Hedged Out: Inequality and Insecurity on Wall Street*. Oakland: California University Press.

Noble, Safiya Umoja. 2018. *Algorithms of Oppression: How Search Engines Reinforce Racism*. New York: New York University Press.

NYSE (New York Stock Exchange). 2020. "Market-Wide Circuit Breakers FAQ." https:/ /www.nyse.com/publicdocs/nyse/NYSE_MWCB_FAQ.pdf#:~:text=URL%3A%20 https%3A%2F%2Fwww.nyse.com%2Fpublicdocs%2Fnyse%2FNYSE_MWCB_FAQ .pdf%0AVisible%3A%200%25%20.

O'Hara, Maureen. 1995. *Market Microstructure Theory*. Oxford: Blackwell.

O'Hara, Maureen. 2015. "High Frequency Market Microstructure." *Journal of Financial Economics* 116 (2): 257–70.

Orús, Román, Samuel Mugel, and Enrique Lizaso. 2019. "Quantum Computing for Finance: Overview and Prospects." *Reviews in Physics* 4: 100028.

Palazzi, Andrea, Davide Abati, Simone Calderara, Francesco Solera, and Rita Cucchiara.

2018. "Predicting the Driver's Focus of Attention: The Dr(Eye)Ve Project." Preprint, arXiv, June 6. https://arxiv.org/pdf/1705.03854v3.

Palma, Stefania, and Patrick Jenkins. 2023. "Gary Gensler Urges Regulators to Tame AI Risks to Financial Stability." *Financial Times,* October 15.

Palmer, Donald, and Michael Maher. 2010. "A Normal Accident Analysis of the Mortgage Meltdown." Pp. 219–56 in *Markets on Trial: The Economic Sociology of the U.S. Financial Crisis,* Research in the Sociology of Organizations, Vol. 30, Part A, edited by M. Lounsbury and P. M. Hirsch. Bingley: Emerald.

Palmer, Samuel, Konstantinos Karagiannis, Adam Florence, et al. 2022. "Financial Index Tracking via Quantum Computing with Cardinality Constraints." Preprint, arXiv, August 24. arXiv:2208.11380.

Paraná, Edemilson. 2018. *Digitalized Finance: Financial Capitalism and Informational Revolution.* Leiden: Brill.

Paraná, Edemilson. 2024. "Artificial Intelligence and the Digitalization of Finance in Latin America: Evidence from Brazil." *Globalizations,* October 31, 1–20. https://doi.org/10.1080/14747731.2024.2415257.

Pardo-Guerra, Juan Pablo. 2010. "Creating Flows of Interpersonal Bits: The Automation of the London Stock Exchange, c. 1955–90." *Economy and Society* 39 (1): 84–109.

Pardo-Guerra, Juan Pablo. 2012. "Financial Automation, Past, Present, and Future." Pp. 567–86 in *The Oxford Handbook of the Sociology of Finance,* edited by K. Knorr Cetina and A. Preda. Oxford: Oxford University Press.

Pardo-Guerra, Juan Pablo. 2019. *Automating Finance: Infrastructures, Engineers, and the Making of Electronic Markets.* Cambridge: Cambridge University Press.

Parsons, Talcott. 1937. *The Structure of Social Action: A Study in Social Theory with Special Reference to a Group of Recent European Writers.* New York: McGraw-Hill.

Patterson, Scott. 2010. *The Quants: The Math Geniuses Who Brought Down Wall Street.* London: Random House.

Patterson, Scott. 2012. *Dark Pools: The Rise of A.I. Trading Machines and the Looming Threat to Wall Street.* New York: Random House Business Books.

Perrow, Charles. 1999. *Normal Accidents: Living with High-Risk Technologies.* Rev. ed. Princeton, NJ: Princeton University Press.

Perrow, Charles. 2010. "The Meltdown Was Not an Accident." Pp. 309–30 in *Markets on Trial: The Economic Sociology of the U.S. Financial Crisis,* Research in the Sociology of Organizations, Vol. 30, Part A, edited by M. Lounsbury and P. M. Hirsch. Bingley: Emerald.

Petry, Johannes. 2020. "Securities Exchanges: Subjects and Agents of Financialization." Pp. 253–64 in *The Routledge International Handbook of Financialization,* edited by P. Mader, D. Mertens, and N. van der Zwan. London: Routledge.

Petry, Johannes. 2021. "From National Marketplaces to Global Providers of Financial Infrastructures: Exchanges, Infrastructures and Structural Power in Global Finance." *New Political Economy* 26 (4): 574–97.

Pinzur, David. 2021a. "Infrastructural Power: Discretion and the Dynamics of Infrastructure in Action." *Journal of Cultural Economy* 14 (6): 644–61.

Pinzur, David. 2021b. "Infrastructure, Ontology and Meaning: The Endogenous Development of Economic Ideas." *Social Studies of Science* 51 (6): 914–37.

Pistoia, M., S. F. Ahmad, A. Ajagekar, et al. 2021. "Quantum Machine Learning for Finance ICCAD Special Session Paper." Pp. 1–9 in *2021 IEEE/ACM International Conference on Computer Aided Design (ICCAD)*. Piscataway, NJ: Institute of Electrical and Electronics Engineers.

Pitluck, Aaron Z. 2014. "Watching Foreigners: How Counterparties Enable Herds, Crowds, and Generate Liquidity in Financial Markets." *Socio-Economic Review* 12 (1): 5–31.

Pixley, Jocelyn. 2004. *Emotions in Finance: Distrust and Uncertainty in Global Markets.* Cambridge: Cambridge University Press.

Plesner, Ursula. 2011. "Studying Sideways: Displacing the Problem of Power in Research Interviews with Sociologists and Journalists." *Qualitative Inquiry* 17 (6): 471–82.

Podolny, Joel M. 1993. "A Status-Based Model of Market Competition." *American Journal of Sociology* 98 (4): 829–72.

Polanyi, Karl. 2001. *The Great Transformation: The Political and Economic Origins of Our Time.* Boston: Beacon Press.

Preda, Alex. 2005. "Legitimacy and Status Groups in Financial Markets." *British Journal of Sociology* 56 (3): 451–71.

Preda, Alex. 2006. "Socio-Technical Agency in Financial Markets: The Case of the Stock Ticker." *Social Studies of Science* 36 (5): 753–82.

Preda, Alex. 2009a. "Brief Encounters: Calculation and the Interaction Order of Anonymous Electronic Markets." *Accounting, Organizations and Society* 34 (5): 675–93.

Preda, Alex. 2009b. *Framing Finance: The Boundaries of Markets and Modern Capitalism.* Chicago: University of Chicago Press.

Preda, Alex. 2009c. *Information, Knowledge, and Economic Life: An Introduction to the Sociology of Markets.* Oxford: Oxford University Press.

Preda, Alex. 2013. "Tags, Transaction Types and Communication in Online Anonymous Markets." *Socio-Economic Review* 11 (1): 31–56.

Preda, Alex. 2017. *Noise: Living and Trading in Electronic Finance.* Chicago: University of Chicago Press.

Preda, Alex. 2020. "Financial Noise." Pp. 96–114 in *The Routledge Handbook of Critical Finance Studies*, edited by C. Borch and R. Wosnitzer. New York: Routledge.

Preda, Alex. 2023. *The Spectacle of Expertise: Why Financial Analysts Perform in the Media.* New York: Columbia University Press.

Preda, Alex. 2025. "Coding and Expertise." Pp. 549–66 in *The Oxford Handbook of the Sociology of Machine Learning*, edited by C. Borch and J. P. Pardo-Guerra. New York: Oxford University Press.

Presidential Task Force on Market Mechanisms. 1988. *Report of the Presidential Task Force on Market Mechanisms: Submitted to the President of the United States, the Secretary of the Treasury and the Chairman of the Federal Reserve Board.* Washington, DC: US Government Printing Office.

Rahwan, Iyad, Manuel Cebrian, Nick Obradovich, et al. 2019. "Machine Behaviour." *Nature* 568: 477–86.

Ras, Gabriëlle, Marcel van Gerven, and Pim Haselager. 2018. "Explanation Methods in Deep Learning: Users, Values, Concerns and Challenges." Pp. 19–36 in *Explainable and Interpretable Models in Computer Vision and Machine Learning,* edited by H. J. Escalante, S. Escalera, I. Guyon, et al. Cham: Springer.

Rella, Ludovico, Kristian Bondo Hansen, Nanna Bonde Thylsturp, et al. 2024. "Hybrid Materialities, Power, and Expertise in the Era of General Purpose Technologies." *Distinktion: Journal of Social Theory* 26 (1): 138–57.

Ribeiro, Marco Tulio, Sameer Singh, and Carlos Guestrin. 2016. "'Why Should I Trust You?': Explaining the Predictions of Any Classifier." Preprint, arXiv, August 9. arXiv :1602.04938v3.

Roberts, Karlene H. 1990. "Some Characteristics of One Type of High Reliability Organization." *Organization Science* 1 (2): 160–76.

Roberts, Karlene H., and Carolyn Libuser. 1993. "From Bhopal to Banking: Organizational Design Can Mitigate Risk." *Organizational Dynamics* 21 (4): 15–26.

Roberts, Karlene H., Suzanne K. Stout, and Jennifer J. Halpern. 1994. "Decision Dynamics in Two High Reliability Military Organizations." *Management Science* 40 (5): 614–24.

Robertson, Harry, and Alun John. 2024. "Swiss Stock Exchange Suffers Hours-Long Outage After Data Glitch." Reuters, July 31. https://www.reuters.com/markets/europe/ swiss-six-exchange-says-trading-halted-due-technical-issues-2024-07-31/.

Roe, Emery, and Paul Schulman. 2018. *Reliability and Risk: The Challenge of Managing Interconnected Infrastructures.* Stanford, CA: Stanford University Press.

Rosenblatt, Frank. 1958. "The Perceptron: A Probabilistic Model for Information Storage and Organization in the Brain." *Psychological Review* 65 (6): 386–408.

Salles, Arleen, Kathinka Evers, and Michele Farisco. 2020. "Anthropomorphism in AI." *AJOB Neuroscience* 11 (2): 88–95.

Salovaara, Antti, Kalle Lyytinen, and Esko Penttinen. 2019. "High Reliability in Digital Organizing: Mindlessness, the Frame Problem, and Digital Operations." *MIS Quarterly* 43 (2): 555–78.

Samek, Wojciech, Grégoire Montavon, Andrea Vedaldi, Lars Kai Hansen, and Klaus-Robert Müller, eds. 2019. *Explainable AI: Interpreting, Explaining and Visualizing Deep Learning.* Cham: Springer.

Samek, Wojciech, and Klaus-Robert Müller. 2019. "Towards Explainable Artificial Intelligence." Pp. 5–22 in *Explainable AI: Interpreting, Explaining and Visualizing Deep Learning,* edited by W. Samek, G. Montavon, A. Vedaldi, L. K. Hansen, and K.-R. Müller. Cham: Springer.

Schneiberg, Marc, and Tim Bartley. 2010. "Regulating or Redesigning Finance? Market Architectures, Normal Accidents, and Dilemmas of Regulatory Reform." Pp. 281–307 in *Markets on Trial: The Economic Sociology of the U.S. Financial Crisis,* edited by M. Lounsbury and P. M. Hirsch, Research in the Sociology of Organizations, Vol. 30, Part A. Bingley: Emerald.

Schulman, Paul R., and Emery Roe. 2018. "Extending Reliability Analysis Across Organizations, Time, and Scope." Pp. 194–214 in *Organizing for Reliability: A Guide for Research and Practice*, edited by R. Ramanujam and K. H. Roberts. Stanford, CA: Stanford University Press.

Seaver, Nick. 2017. "Algorithms as Culture: Some Tactics for the Ethnography of Algorithmic Systems." *Big Data & Society* 4 (2): https://doi.org/10.1177/2053951717738104.

SEC (Securities and Exchange Commission). 1998. *Regulation of Exchanges and Alternative Trading Systems*. Washington, DC: Securities and Exchange Commission. https://www.sechistorical.org/collection/papers/1990/1998_1208_SECATS.pdf.

SEC (Securities and Exchange Commission). 2005. *Regulation NMS*. Washington, DC: Securities and Exchange Commission. https://www.sec.gov/files/rules/final/34-51808.pdf.

SEC (Securities and Exchange Commission). 2010.

SEC (Securities and Exchange Commission). 2013. "In the Matter of Knight Capital Americas LLC." https://www.sec.gov/files/litigation/admin/2013/34-70694.pdf.

SEC (Securities and Exchange Commission). 2014. "Regulation Systems Compliance and Integrity (17 CFR Parts 240, 242, and 249)." *Federal Register* 79 (234): 72252–447.

Seyfert, Robert. 2016. "Bugs, Predations or Manipulations? Incompatible Epistemic Regimes of High-Frequency Trading." *Economy and Society* 45 (2): 251–77.

Shin, Eun Kyong. 2025. "Fitting Paradox: Machine Learning Algorithms Versus Statistical Modeling." Pp. 211–26 in *The Oxford Handbook of the Sociology of Machine Learning*, edited by C. Borch and J. P. Pardo-Guerra. New York: Oxford University Press.

Shumailov, Ilia, Zakhar Shumaylov, Yiren Zhao, Nicolas Papernot, Ross Anderson, and Yarin Gal. 2024. "AI Models Collapse When Trained on Recursively Generated Data." *Nature* 631 (8022): 755–59.

Smith, Charles W. 1999. *Success and Survival on Wall Street: Understanding the Mind of the Market*. Oxford: Rowman and Littlefield.

Souleles, Daniel. 2024. *Whoosh Goes the Market: Algorithms, Automation, and Alienation*. Chicago: University of Chicago Press.

Spears, Taylor, and Kristian Bondo Hansen. 2025. "The Use and Promises of Machine Learning in Financial Markets: From Mundane Practices to Complex Automated Systems." Pp. 421–39 in *The Oxford Handbook of the Sociology of Machine Learning*, edited by C. Borch and J. P. Pardo-Guerra. Oxford: Oxford University Press.

Stäheli, Urs. 2013. *Spectacular Speculation: Thrills, the Economy, and Popular Discourse*. Translated by E. Savoth. Stanford, CA: Stanford University Press.

Stilgoe, Jack. 2018. "Machine Learning, Social Learning and the Governance of Self-Driving Cars." *Social Studies of Science* 48 (1): 25–56.

Stuhler, Oscar, Dustin S. Stoltz, and John Levi Martin. 2025. "Meaning and Machines." Pp. 635–48 in *The Oxford Handbook of the Sociology of Machine Learning*, edited by C. Borch and J. P. Pardo-Guerra. New York: Oxford University Press.

Suchman, Lucy. 2007. *Human-Machine Reconfigurations: Plans and Situated Actions*. Cambridge: Cambridge University Press.

Sutcliffe, Kathleen M. 2011. "High Reliability Organizations (HROs)." *Best Practice & Research Clinical Anaesthesiology* 25 (2): 133–44.

Svetlova, Ekaterina. 2012. "On the Performative Power of Financial Models." *Economy and Society* 41 (3): 418–34.

Svetlova, Ekaterina. 2018. *Financial Models and Society: Villains or Scapegoats?* Northampton, MA: Edward Elgar.

Tong, Xiaochuan, and Alex Preda. 2024. "Does Social Communication Make Investors Stay in the Market?" *Socio-Economic Review* 22 (4): 1865–90.

Tsing, Anna Lowenhaupt. 2015. *The Mushroom at the End of the World: On the Possibility of Life in Capitalist Ruins*. Princeton, NJ: Princeton University Press.

Vaananen, Jay. 2015. *Dark Pools and High-Frequency Trading for Dummies*. Chichester: John Wiley.

Vaihinger, Hans. 2021. *The Philosophy of "as If."* 2nd ed. London: Routledge.

van Oost, Ellen, and Darren Reed. 2011. "Towards a Sociological Understanding of Robots as Companions." Pp. 11–18 in *Human-Robot Personal Relationships*, edited by M. H. Lamers and F. J. Verbeek. Berlin: Springer Berlin Heidelberg.

Vaughan, Liam. 2020. *Flash Crash: A Trading Savant, a Global Manhunt and the Most Mysterious Market Crash in History*. London: William Collins.

Vertesi, Janet. 2012. "Seeing Like a Rover: Visualization, Embodiment, and Interaction on the Mars Exploration Rover Mission." *Social Studies of Science* 42 (3): 393–414.

Virtu Financial. 2022. *2022 Annual Report*. New York: Virtu Financial.

von Neumann, John. 1966. *Theory of Self-Reproducing Automata*. Urbana: University of Illinois Press.

Wansleben, Leon. 2015. *Cultures of Expertise in Global Currency Markets*. London: Routledge.

Watson, David. 2019. "The Rhetoric and Reality of Anthropomorphism in Artificial Intelligence." *Minds and Machines* 29 (3): 417–40.

Weber, Max. 1978. *Economy and Society: An Outline of Interpretive Sociology*. Edited by Guenther Roth and Claus Wittich. Berkeley: University of California Press.

Weber, Max. 2000a. "Commerce on the Stock and Commodity Exchanges ['Die Börsenverkehr']." *Theory and Society* 29 (3): 339–71.

Weber, Max. 2000b. "Stock and Commodity Exchanges ['Die Börse' (1894)]." *Theory and Society* 29 (3): 305–38.

Weick, Karl E. 1977. "Enactment Processes in Organizations." Pp. 267–300 in *New Directions in Organizational Behavior*, edited by B. N. Staw and G. R. Salancik. Chicago: St. Clair Press.

Weick, Karl E., and Karlene H. Roberts. 1993. "Collective Mind in Organizations: Heedful Interrelating on Flight Decks." *Administrative Science Quarterly* 38 (3): 357–81.

Weick, Karl E., and Kathleen M. Sutcliffe. 2001. *Managing the Unexpected: Assuring High Performance in an Age of Complexity*. San Francisco: Jossey-Bass.

Weick, Karl E., and Kathleen M. Sutcliffe. 2007. *Managing the Unexpected: Resilient Performance in an Age of Uncertainty*. Hoboken, NJ: Wiley.

Weick, Karl E., and Kathleen M. Sutcliffe. 2015. *Managing the Unexpected: Sustained Performance in a Complex World*. 3rd ed. Hoboken, NJ: Wiley.

Wiener, Norbert. 1961. *Cybernetics: Or Control and Communication in the Animal and the Machine*. 2nd ed. Cambridge, MA: MIT Press.

Wójcik, Dariusz, and William Bratton. 2024. "Theory, Explanation, and Economics in Financial Geographies." *Dialogues in Human Geography* 0 (0): 20438206241280659.

Woolgar, Steve. 1985. "Why Not a Sociology of Machines? The Case of Sociology and Artificial Intelligence." *Sociology* 19 (4): 557–72.

World Economic Forum. 2018. *The New Physics of Financial Services: Understanding How Artificial Intelligence Is Transforming the Financial Ecosystem*. Geneva: World Economic Forum.

Wright, Lance. 2017. *People, Risk, and Security: How to Prevent Your Greatest Asset from Becoming Your Greatest Liability*. London: Palgrave Macmillan.

Yadav, Yesha. 2018. "Algorithmic Trading and Market Regulation." Pp. 232–59 in *Global Algorithmic Capital Markets: High Frequency Trading, Dark Pools, and Regulatory Challenges*, edited by W. Mattli. Oxford: Oxford University Press.

Yolgörmez, Ceyda. 2021. "Machinic Encounters: A Relational Approach to the Sociology of AI." Pp. 143–66 in *The Cultural Life of Machine Learning: An Incursion into Critical AI Studies*, edited by J. Roberge and M. Castelle. Cham: Springer.

Yolgörmez, Ceyda. 2025. "Machine Agencies: Large Language Models as a Case for a Sociology of Machines." Pp. 613–31 in *The Oxford Handbook of the Sociology of Machine Learning*, edited by C. Borch and J. P. Pardo-Guerra. New York: Oxford University Press.

Young, Brendon. 2011/12. "Leadership and High-Reliability Organizations: Why Banks Fail." *Journal of Operational Risk* 6 (4): 67–87.

Zaloom, Caitlin. 2003. "Ambiguous Numbers: Trading Technologies and Interpretation in Financial Markets." *American Ethnologist* 30 (2): 258–72.

Zaloom, Caitlin. 2006. *Out of the Pits: Traders and Technology from Chicago to London*. Chicago: University of Chicago Press.

Zhou, Jianlong, and Fang Chen, eds. 2018. *Human and Machine Learning: Visible, Explainable, Trustworthy and Transparent*. Cham: Springer.

Zimmerman, David A. 2006. *Panic! Markets, Crises, and Crowds in American Fiction*. Chapel Hill: University of North Carolina Press.

Zuckerman, Ezra W. 2004. "Structural Incoherence and Stock Market Activity." *American Sociological Review* 69 (3): 405–32.

Zuckerman, Gregory. 2019. *The Man Who Solved the Market: How Jim Simons Launched the Quant Revolution*. London: Penguin.

Index

CURRENCIES

New Thinking for Financial Times
STEFAN EICH AND MARTIJN KONINGS, EDITORS

Lars Cornelissen, *Neoliberalism and Race*

Michael Lazarus, *Absolute Ethical Life: Aristotle, Hegel and Marx*

Noam Yuran, *The Sexual Economy of Capitalism*

Joscha Wullweber, *Central Bank Capitalism:
Monetary Policy in Times of Crisis*

Eli Jelly-Schapiro, *Moments of Capital:
World Theory, World Literature*

Jakob Feinig, *Moral Economies of Money:
Politics and the Monetary Constitution of Society*

Charly Coleman, *The Spirit of French Capitalism:
Economic Theology in the Age of Enlightenment*

Amin Samman, *History in Financial Times*

Thomas Biebricher, *The Political Theory of Neoliberalism*

Lisa Adkins, *The Time of Money*

Martijn Konings, *Capital and Time:
For a New Critique of Neoliberal Reason*

The authorized representative in the EU for product safety and compliance is:
Mare Nostrum Group
B.V Doelen 72
4831 GR Breda
The Netherlands

www.ingramcontent.com/pod-product-compliance
Lightning Source LLC
Chambersburg PA
CBHW030320270326
41926CB00010B/1439